Estate Planning
for the
Blended Family

Estate Planning
for the
Blended Family

L. Paul Hood, Jr.
and Emily Bouchard

Self-Counsel Press acknowledges the financial support of the Government of Canada through the Canada Book Fund (CBF) for our publishing activities.

Printed in Canada.

First edition: 2012

Library and Archives Canada Cataloguing in Publication

Hood, L. Paul, 1960–

    Estate planning for the blended family / L. Paul Hood.

ISBN 978-1-77040-103-7

    1. Estate planning. 2. Stepfamilies. 3. Wills. I. Title.

K4568.H66 2012   346.05'2   C2011-907043-X

Self-Counsel Press Inc.
(a subsidiary of)
International Self-Counsel Press Ltd.

Bellingham, WA   North Vancouver, BC
USA   Canada

Contents

Preface   xi

Introduction   xiii

Part 1: The Basics   1

1. The Human Side of Estate Planning   3

  1. Key Elements of a Successful Estate
    Plan   3

  2. Common Fears Associated with Estate
    Planning   4

    2.1   What do these fears of estate
      planning cause?   9

  3. You Are the Sum of Your Life
    Experiences   10

  4. What Constitutes Being *Wealthy* to You?   11

  5. Your Union   12

  6. Health Issues   14

  7. Finances   14

  8. What Will Your Family Look Like
    at Your Death?   15

  9. Your Views on Life   16

  10. Past Experiences with Estates or Trusts   17

  11. Action Steps   18

2. Communication Strategies   19

  1. Money Types   20

    1.1   Awareness of Money Types   20

  2. General Communication Strategies
    and Approaches   23

    2.1   Defining conversations   23

    2.2   Setting the stage   24

    2.3   Gratitude and acknowledgment   25

  3. Communication Strategies for When
    Emotions Flare   27

    3.1   Slow down   27

    3.2   Breathe   28

    3.3   Seek to understand   28

    3.4   Recognize when you are full   30

    3.5   Strive for alignment   32

  4. Communicating about Prenuptial
    and Property Agreements   32

  5. Communicating about Commingling
    Property   33

  6. Withholding Information   33

  7. Communication about Funeral
    Planning   34

  8. Putting Children and Stepchildren
    in Key Roles   35

  9. Taking Care of Your Spouse after
    You Pass May Take Away from the
    Children's Inheritance   35

  10. Discussion about Separate
    Representation When Creating
    Your Estate Plan   36

3. Basic Estate Planning Considerations   37

  1. Your Estate-Planning Goals   38

    1.1   Retain control over assets
      and business decisions   38

    1.2   Provide support for children
      and the surviving partner   38

    1.3   Protect loved ones from
      predators and themselves   39

    1.4   Keep certain property
      in the family   39

    1.5   Protect your assets from creditors,
      lawsuits, and undue influence 39

    1.6   Avoid probate   40

    1.7   Maintain flexibility   40

    1.8   Retain access to capital   40

    1.9   Make lifetime gifts   40

    1.10 Transfer future appreciation   41

    1.11 Transfer an opportunity   41

1.12   Move property to grandchildren or more remote descendants   41

1.13   Defer estate or income tax   41

1.14   Avoid estate tax   41

1.15   Avoid gift tax   42

1.16   Maximize usage of US estate tax exclusions   42

1.17   Donate to favorite charities   42

1.18   Achieve tax predictability or finality   42

1.19   Provide tax-deferred diversification   43

1.20   Provide guidance and management for your children   43

1.21   Encourage or discourage certain behaviors   43

1.22   Level the playing field   43

1.23   Provide a mechanism for resolution of disputes   44

1.24   Keep certain assets away from certain people   44

2. Your Estate-Planning Concerns   44

2.1   Choosing between a partner and the children   44

2.2   Plan for the payment and apportionment of estate taxes   45

2.3   Dealing with problem children   45

2.4   Protecting young or disabled children   45

2.5   Caring for elderly parents   46

3. Prioritize and Communicate   46

4. Action Step   46

4. Property Ownership: Means and Issues   48

1. Marriage Contracts and Property Agreements   48

1.1   Agreement issues   49

1.2   Postnuptial agreements   50

2. Co-ownership Issues   50

3. Community Property   50

4. Separate Property and the Perils of Commingling Property   51

5. Contracts to Make a Will and Joint Will   53

6. Prior Relationship Obligations and Benefits   53

5. Types of Property   55

1. Family Home   56

2. Living Arrangements and Support   57

3. Family Business Issues   58

3.1   To sell or not to sell   59

3.2   Buy-sell agreements   59

3.3   Less than all of the children working in the business   60

4. Retirement Plans   61

4.1   US Individual Retirement Account (IRA)   61

5. Tangible Personal Property   61

6. Bank Accounts   62

7. Action Steps   62

6. Estate-Planning Documents   63

1. Wills   63

1.1   Wills and minor children   64

1.2   Wills and probate   65

2. Trusts   65

2.1   Revocable living trusts   65

2.2   Irrevocable trusts   66

2.3   Beneficiary designations   66

3. Powers of Attorney for Property   66

4. Powers of Attorney for Health Care and Living Wills   68

5. Ethical Wills   70

6. Letters of Instruction   71

7. Burial or Cremation Instructions   72

7.1   Appoint someone to be in charge of your funeral arrangements   73

7.2   Write your own obituary   73

		7.3	Delineate mode of interment or inurnment	74
		7.4	Delineate who is to be invited to the memorial service or funeral	74
	8.	Action Steps		75

7. The Estate-Planning Players 76

1.	Characteristics of Blended Family Partners		77
2.	Estate Planners		77
3.	Children		80
	3.1	Stepchildren	81
	3.2	Partners of your children	81
4.	Your Parents and Possibly Your Stepparents		81
5.	Grandchildren and Step-Grandchildren	82
6.	Other Players		82
7.	Action Steps		83

Part 2: Planning Issues 85

8. Reasons Estate Plans Fail 87

1.	Failure to Complete and Implement the Estate Plan		87
	1.1	Actions for success	88
2.	Failure to Provide Complete and Accurate Information to Estate Planners		88
	2.1	Actions for success	89
3.	Failure to Coordinate		90
	3.1	Actions for success	90
4.	Failure to Communicate about Your Estate Plan		90
	4.1	Actions for success	91
5.	Incomplete or Incorrect Beneficiary Designations		92
	5.1	Actions for success	92
6.	Failure to Keep Estate Plan Current	93
	6.1	Actions for success	93

7.	Choosing the Wrong Trustee or Executor		93
	7.1	Actions for success	95
8.	Bad Estate-Planning Advice		95
	8.1	Actions for success	96
9.	Elections against a Will		96
	9.1	Actions for success	96
10.	Post-Death Will and Trust Challenges	96
	10.1	Actions for success	97
11.	Too Much Joint-Tenancy Property	97
	11.1	Action for success	97
12.	Failure to Properly Plan for Disability	98
	12.1	Actions for success	98
13.	Overfunding of the US Marital Deduction Portion		98
	13.1	Action for success	98
14.	Relying on a Beneficiary to Do the "Right Thing"		98
	14.1	Action for success	99

9. Lifetime Estate Planning 100

1.	Irrevocable Lifetime Estate Planning	101
2.	Techniques Applicable to All Wealth Categories		101
	2.1	Severing joint-tenancy arrangements	101
	2.2	Life insurance	103
	2.3	Annuities	105
	2.4	Opportunity shifts	105
	2.5	Charitable gift annuities	106
	2.6	Below-market loans	106
3.	Strategies for People Who Have Wealth of More Than $1,000,000		106
	3.1	Life insurance trusts	106
	3.2	Annual exclusion gifts	108
	3.3	Unlimited direct payments to qualified educational institutions and qualified health-care providers	109

3.4	Charitable remainder trusts	109
3.5	Gift splitting	110
3.6	Private unitrusts	111

4. Strategies for Those Who Are Worth More Than $5,000,000 — 111

4.1	Private annuities	111
4.2	Qualified Personal Residence Trust (QPRT)	112
4.3	Family limited entities	112

5. Strategies for Those Who Are Worth More Than $15,000,000 — 113

5.1	Large gifts, including defined value gifts	113
5.2	Equalization of estates	114
5.3	Lifetime Qualified Terminable Interest Property (QTIP)	115
5.4	Grantor Retained Annuity Trust (GRAT)	115
5.5	Charitable lead trusts	116
5.6	Sale to an Intentionally Defective Grantor Trust (IDGT)	116
5.7	Guarantees	117

6. Action Steps — 117

10. Testamentary Estate Planning — 119

1. *In Terrorem* Clauses — 119
2. Disinheriting Family — 120
3. Equalization of Estates — 121
4. Powers of Appointment — 121
5. Marital Deduction Transfers — 122

5.1	Qualified Terminable Interest Property (QTIP)	123
5.2	Marital deductions and QTIP options	125

6. Unitrust Option — 125
7. Life Estates — 126
8. Charitable Lead Trusts — 126
9. Who Should Serve as Executor and Successor Trustee of a Living Trust? — 126

10.	Why the Surviving Partner May Have Conflicts of Interest	128
11.	Why the Children of the Deceased Partner May Have Conflicts of Interest	128
12.	Estate-Tax Apportionment Issues	129
13.	Disclaimers	130
14.	Elections against a Will	131

Part 3: Observations and Suggestions — 133

11. Working with Estate Planners — 135

1. Who Does Estate Planning? — 135
2. Where Do You Find Estate Planners? — 136
3. Who Should Be on Your Estate-Planning Team? — 137
4. How Do Estate Planners Charge for Their Services? — 137
5. How Do Estate-Planning Attorneys Do Their Work? — 137
6. The Initial Interview — 138

6.1	Showing up to the initial interview prepared	142

7. Action Steps — 145

12. Putting It All Together — 147

1. Yours, Mine, and Ours — 147
2. Empty Nesters — 152
3. Eat, Drink, and Remarry — 152
4. Brady Bunch — 154
5. May-December Relationship — 155
6. Nontraditional Blended Family — 156

13. Last Words of Advice — 158

1. First, Involve Your Family — 158
2. Shouldn't Privacy Take Precedence? — 159
3. Different Tools and Techniques Have Different Effects — 159
4. Understanding Taxes — 159
5. Be Careful about Buying into Panaceas — 160

6. Take Control, Get Involved, and Stay
   in Control   160

7. Avoid Planning Paralysis   161

Illustrations

1 Why Is a Good Estate-Planning Result
  So Hard to Achieve?   4

2 Key Elements of a Successful Estate
  Plan   5

Checklists

1 Identifying Your Goals and Concerns   47

2 Information the Estate Planner
  Will Need   143

Worksheets

1 Our Key Characteristics   78

2 Characteristics of a Potential Advisor   84

Charts

1 Questions a Client May Secretly Have
  during an Initial Interview with
  an Estate Planner   139

2 What the Estate Planner Is Wondering
  about the Client during the Initial
  Interview   141

Notice to Readers

Laws are constantly changing. Every effort is made to keep this publication as current as possible. However, the authors, the publisher, and the vendor of this book make no representations or warranties regarding the outcome or the use to which the information in this book is put and are not assuming any liability for any claims, losses, or damages arising out of the use of this book. The reader should not rely on the authors or the publisher of this book for any professional advice. Please be sure that you have the most recent edition.

Preface

Congratulations! We want to acknowledge you right from the start, as your choice to open this book puts you in a very unique group of people who are proactively considering their particular blended family's future needs and well-being after the time of their deaths.

Even though it is well-known that there is a potential cost of not creating a formalized estate plan, the percentage of people who have their planning documents in good working order remains dramatically low. Only 45 percent of all adult Americans have a will according to a research study conducted from 2004 to 2007 by Harris Interactive® for Martindale-Hubbell®. Awareness of the issue brings you 80 percent closer to success; the remaining 20 percent comes from taking the necessary, informed actions towards accomplishing your goals.

We, the authors, are strong proponents of starting with the end in mind, and we meet our clients exactly where they are. With more than 50 years of combined experience working with blended and step-family dynamics and estate planning, we've discovered some key distinctions and practices that allow you to develop your strategy and plan in conjunction with your advisors in a way that will address your particular, unique family needs and goals. Our purpose is to address the complexities that blended families face in estate planning, and to allow you to be informed in a way that promotes decisions that truly work for all the members of your family, further strengthening your bonds and connections during your life and long after your passing.

This book is not an introduction to estate planning (although we've certainly explained some of the basics). There are plenty of books that explain estate planning at varying levels of complexity — our favorites can be found in the Resources section on the CD. However, very little has been written to date on estate planning for "blended" families — also known as "step-families." In this book, we'll refer to them as blended families, as we consider these terms interchangeable.

The purpose of this book is to address in detail the nuances of estate planning for blended families and to help them meet their goals, address their concerns, and address their particular issues with their estate planner. Communication is the key to good estate planning.

Benjamin Disraeli once said: "There are three kinds of lies: lies, damned lies, and statistics." With Disraeli's quote in mind, we also feel it is important to give a nod to the United States Census Bureau's data that contains some interesting statistics concerning blended families. Approximately 1,300 blended families are formed every day in the US. It is estimated that more than 50 percent of all families in the US contain partners that are either remarried or recoupled. The 1990 census estimated that there would be more blended families than regular families by the year 2000, meaning that there are likely now more blended families than any other type of family.

It is estimated that approximately 30 percent of marriages in the US are remarriages for one or both partners. The marriage statistics for blended family couples are grim: 60 percent of second marriages and 73 percent of third marriages end in divorce, which exceeds the 50 percent divorce rate for single-marriage couples. While we all want to enter into our first, second, or third (or more) marriages and partnerships believing we can beat the odds, these very real statistics must be taken into consideration in your estate planning.

While *irrevocable* estate planning can be a useful tool, it is generally not recommended for blended couples because of the larger possibility of splitting up. The regret and high cost in legal fees to attempt to reverse irrevocable decisions can have a dramatic impact on the future well-being of the estate for those you want to benefit from it the most. See Chapter 9 for more information about irrevocable estate planning.

This book will discuss many topics that relate to estate planning for blended families. We intend that the book be used as a reference guide for attorneys and regular folks alike. It can be read sequentially, or you can choose chapters and topics that are most relevant to you at the time. The materials on the CD are intended as supplemental resources. Estate planning for the blended family is hard enough. We wanted to do our part to make it a bit easier to navigate.

Part I focuses on the basics of estate planning for the blended family. In Part II, we tackle planning issues that impact blended families. Part III offers observations and suggestions based on years of experience working with blended family estate-planning issues. In particular, Chapter 12 discusses possible estate plans for a number of blended family scenarios.

Introduction

This introduction will define terms that you will need to know as you work through your estate planning. We will also give you some examples of blended families, which you'll see again in Chapter 12. We'll conclude this chapter with an attempt to frighten you about the perils of intestacy for the blended family, which will hopefully move you to action on your estate planning! Never underestimate the importance of estate planning — especially for the blended family.

1. Definition of Estate Planning

Estate planning is a process that does not end completely until death. Estate planning is every bit as much of a process as life itself.

You can do estate planning without even realizing it. For example, when you buy real estate, you are doing estate planning by how you title the property. When you buy life insurance or get a new job and fill out the beneficiary designations for your employee benefits, you're doing estate planning. Sometimes, when you open a bank or brokerage account, you are doing estate planning as well.

Don't get distressed about the never-ending nature of the estate-planning process. By the fact that you've chosen to read this book, you're showing you know how important it is to accomplish all that you can today in your estate planning. We also know, without a doubt, that you'll feel better when you take action and complete and sign your important documents. You're giving yourself and your family peace of mind and assurances that would not otherwise be there. It would be unfortunate, costly, and unnecessarily painful for those you leave behind if you were to die unexpectedly without an estate plan or with unsigned drafts of estate-planning documents.

Our purpose is to bring to light all the various sections of estate planning you will want to consider and the ramifications of your choices. We will also show you that your documents and decisions will likely need to be updated and changed over time as your family grows and evolves so that you can have your assets and your values be fully expressed and utilized during and after your lifetime.

> **Unsigned documents don't count!**

Estate planning involves more than preparing a will. Your estate plan communicates your thoughts and desires about financial management, health care, and property distributions through the drafting and execution of legal documents and beneficiary designations.

Your estate plan involves periodic review and revision to reflect the changes that you will experience throughout your lifetime, such as a new child, divorce, remarriage, loss of a loved one, or other life-altering event. An estate plan should also be reviewed upon a major change in the law. We advise you to review your estate-planning documents every year to see if your plan still outlines what you want to have happen at the time of your death.

There is no reason to hire a professional to review the documents annually unless a major change has happened in your life. However, we advise that a professional review your estate plan about every five years to make sure you are taking full advantage of any legal changes.

2. Definition of Blended Family

A blended family is one in which two people are partners and at least one of the partners has one or more children who are not birth children of the other partner.

Note that we'll be referring to the couple as "partners" and not as "spouses" throughout this book. The simple fact is that many people are opting, for a variety of reasons, to not get legally married nowadays; yet, they are together as a couple. Some can't legally marry, and some choose not to, yet they are together as a couple and may even have children from that relationship or other relationships. In our opinion, it would have been an oversight to leave out any type of blended family of this book.

We also believe it is important to consider two adults who are looking at mindfully approaching their last wishes and legacy planning as partners, and treat our clients in this manner. We have seen a lot of damage done to relationships by lawyers and other advisors working with individuals by not taking into consideration the concerns of the multifaceted partnership they comprise.

2.1 Examples of blended families

The focus of this book is on the issues that arise with estate planning for blended families. Other books cover general estate planning and sophisticated methods and techniques of estate planning. They're useful to read in conjunction with this book. Throughout this book we'll discuss various estate-planning techniques and how those techniques work with blended family dynamics. Let's get started by exploring various blended family scenarios.

Blended families come in all shapes, sizes, and configurations. Perhaps the best known blended family is the make-believe *The Brady Bunch* of television fame. However, blended families can look quite different from *The Brady Bunch*. Consider the following six different examples, all of which are blended families (Chapter 12 goes into more detail about each of these types of blended families):

1. **Yours, Mine, and Ours:** Harry, age 62 and divorced, marries Marge, age 48 and divorced. Each has adult children from their prior marriages. Harry and Marge also have a minor son together. They have been married for 15 years and Marge stays at home to raise the child, while Harry works to support the family.

2. **Empty Nesters:** Bill, age 72, is a widower with grown children, a pension, and he is the benefactor of his wife's life insurance. Bill marries Marlene, age 72, who is a widow. The couple survives on Social Security, rental income from Bill's condo, and Bill's IRA.

3. **Eat, Drink, and Remarry:** John, age 63, marries Judith, age 35, as his fourth wife. John has some expensive alimony obligations to his first wife. He also has a son, age 37. Judith, who has been divorced twice, has two sons, ages 11 and 8, each with a different father, with whom she splits custody. Judith has substantially more wealth than John, while John has far greater income-earning potential as a professional. John and Judith have a separate property prenuptial agreement.

4. **The Brady Bunch:** Mike, age 40, a widower, has three sons. Mike marries Carol, age 38, a widow who has three daughters. They have no joint children. The children are all minors who live together. Mike owns his own business, and Carol has a substantial separate estate that she inherited from her late first husband.

5. **May-December Relationship:** Franklin, age 80, a wealthy widower with three grown children in their 50s, marries Bambi, age 26, an impecunious dance instructor who has a daughter, age 7. Franklin and Bambi would like to have a child of their own. Franklin has done a substantial amount of lifetime estate planning and he has given significant wealth to his children and grandchildren.

6. **Nontraditional Blended Family:** Marie, age 46, and Angela, age 37, are a couple. As a single parent, Marie adopted a child, who is now 18. Angela, who has been divorced once, has a child, age 10, whom she is raising alone with only meager, sporadic child support. Marie stands to inherit money from her parents, but that may be in doubt due to her recent lifestyle choices. Angela has the greater income, and she owns the home that they live in, although both are contributing to the payment of the mortgage.

These are all examples of what blended families can look like. These examples are not intended to be exhaustive. There are many other examples of blended families, all of which have valid, vital concerns when it comes to making sure the needs of loved ones are addressed in life and after death. Even a quick consideration of each example demonstrates the diversity of blended families. In some of the examples, the couples have minor children living with them. Others do not. One couple has joint minor children. One couple wants to have a child together. In a few of the examples, the couple has children of a prior union living part time in their home, while other couples do not have to deal with part-time resident children. In two of the examples, the new partner is younger than the children of the other partner.

Advisors with a narrow focus of what defines family and how to protect assets may miss the various ways individuals in blended families consider all the people in their lives to be part of their family. These concerns need to be taken into account in the estate-planning process.

Each of these examples presents very different estate-planning issues. In some of the examples, one partner has substantially more wealth than the other partner. If that partner dies first, should his or her entire estate be held for the surviving partner? This becomes even more complicated when taking into consideration the disparate ages of adult children from a prior marriage and minor children from the current marriage, all of whom are concerned about how the estate will pan out for them — whether they say so or not.

In other examples, one partner has substantially greater earning capacity than the other. Should that earning capacity be cut off because of death and how will the other partner be sustained financially? In one of the examples, one of the partners has very little financial experience. Who should manage her assets if she is the surviving partner? One of the couples has a prenuptial agreement. Is it consistent with the couple's other estate-planning documents? In one of the examples, one partner has significant obligations to former spouses. How will the obligations be affected should that partner die first? Simply put, there is no "one size fits all" estate plan for the blended family. Every estate plan for a blended family is different, and the concerns and goals of the families are undoubtedly different also.

3. The Perils of Intestacy

You have an estate plan even if you don't deliberately and proactively create one.

What happens if you don't do any estate planning? If the next few pages don't scare you into doing some formalized estate planning, then perhaps nothing will.

If you don't do anything, it's called *intestacy* (literally, being without or dying without a legally valid will). You are probably unaware of it and its particular ramifications in blended family situations. Under current law, intestacy tends to choose the surviving spouse as the recipient of the bulk of the property and usually puts the surviving spouse in control of the estate, which can be very challenging and potentially lead to hard feelings and possible litigation from any children of a prior union. You may have wanted your children to be considered and you may even have made promises to them verbally. In the past, the law strongly favored children of a deceased spouse over a subsequent spouse, but this is no longer the case even despite the increasing incidence of divorce.

In addition, if you are not married to your partner, you may well receive nothing under the intestacy laws of your state or province, although this appears to be changing very slowly. It is still essential for unwed partners to do their estate planning if either wants the other partner to share in his or her estate.

In the US, every state has its own laws of intestacy. These laws differ greatly from state to state. You can check out the intestacy laws of your state by going to www.mystatewill.com.

In Canada, each province has its own intestacy laws. You can check out the intestacy laws of your province by going to www.professionalreferrals.ca/2005/10/if-you-die-without-a-will-rules-of-intestate-succession-in-canada.

4. Medical and End-of-Life Decisions

> **Who will make medical decisions for you if you cannot?**

As bad as intestacy is, not doing any estate planning can actually be worse. Suppose you're in a coma or you have dementia; if you don't have an *advanced health-care directive* or *power of attorney for health care* (these names are interchangeable — different names are used depending on where you live), your spouse, partner, parents, or children may have to make those decisions through a court procedure called guardianship. This adds complexity and cost to a situation that is already emotional and painful, and which could have been easily handled with an advanced health-care directive.

In a blended family, particularly one that is not close (e.g., the partners got together after the children became adults), health decisions can create a very difficult situation — your life is in the balance. For instance, your children may question your current partner's motives in making certain health-care decisions for you. It could get even worse if you aren't legally married. Your partner may have no say whatsoever; where the doctors might not even speak to your partner (due to patients' privacy rights

concerns); and where your partner may not even be allowed in your hospital room!

While disagreements could still occur with an advanced health-care directive in place, the directive states the person you wish to make the final decisions. Without an advanced health-care directive, you are doing your partner no favors.

Who will make a decision to discontinue life support if that is your wish? Again, your partner and your children may make that decision, but they could encounter difficulties if family members disagree amongst themselves or if the doctor or hospital balks at the decision without a court order. Cases involving these situations have gone all the way to the United States Supreme Court, which can get very expensive both in legal and medical fees, not to mention how emotionally draining and charged these issues are. If you and your partner aren't legally married, your partner, who may know what your intentions are relative to being maintained on machines, may have no legal right to make decisions on your behalf.

5. Financial Decisions

> **Who will handle your business and financial affairs if you aren't able to do so?**

Without a *durable power of attorney* for property management, your loved ones will be stuck with the onerous court procedure (called *conservatorship* in the US), which applies to the management of property for someone who can't manage his or her own property and who hasn't appointed someone to represent him or her. Conservatorship is not only expensive, but it makes all your financial and personal information a matter of public record that anyone can access. Conservatorship can usually be avoided by a good durable power of attorney and/or a *funded living trust*, the latter of which we discuss in Chapter 9.

There are things that a durable power of attorney can accomplish that probably can't be done in a conservatorship proceeding. Again, an unmarried partner may have no recourse if you become incapacitated because the incapacitated partner's children will have priority to be named conservators. Indeed, this contingency could render the unmarried partner homeless if the conservator sells the home in which the partner is living. (We wouldn't include this grim scenario if we hadn't witnessed it first-hand.) Our commitment is to educate, inform, and do our part to mitigate unnecessary pain and suffering in the face of grief and loss.

If you die without any estate planning, who receives your assets and in what proportion will depend on what type of property it is and how it is titled. Property that passes by will or by intestacy is called *probate* property. This makes up a lot of what people have, such as personal property, vehicles, most bank accounts, some real estate, stocks and bonds, and the like.

> **If your property is titled as joint tenants with rights of survivorship, the property won't need to go through probate.**

However, how property is titled will determine whether that property is subject to probate in your state or province. If property is titled as *joint tenants with rights of survivorship*, the property won't go through probate but instead will pass to the surviving joint tenant no matter what your will or trust says.

When you purchase real estate as a married couple, you're liable to get a joint-tenancy deed unless you specify that you don't want it. This is because realtors and escrow officers generally do not understand the potential ramifications in blended families related to the various methods of owning real property. It is important to note that whether you live in a community-property state or common-law jurisdiction makes a big difference. It is essential in good estate planning for your estate planner to review the deeds to all real estate in order to determine how that property will pass at death. The estate planner must see the deeds. He or she also needs to know how you want to go about addressing these very important concerns.

While joint tenancy helps take care of the surviving partner, it could also impact the surviving children because the children of the first partner to die could lose out entirely on their inheritances. The children who will most likely receive assets shared in joint tenancy are the children whose parent is the one who outlives the other. When animosity exists between partners and their stepchildren, this becomes a real concern.

The intestacy laws used to favor the children, but today, they generally favor the surviving spouse, which may seem odd given the rate, ease, and speed of divorce. Again, with very few exceptions, if you and your partner aren't legally married, the surviving, unmarried partner will generally receive nothing, even if that partner has been a partner for a long time. Probate property is generally divided between the spouse and children, although in several jurisdictions, the spouse could receive it all. Very few partners in blended families want to die intestate because intestacy is rough justice. Moreover, for estates that will owe federal estate tax, there can be adverse estate tax consequences to dying intestate, primarily through loss of a marital deduction.

5.1 Non-probate property

There is a classification of property commonly referred to as *non-probate property*. Non-probate property includes life insurance, annuities, retirement plans, and US Individual Retirement Accounts (IRAs). However, it can also include pay-on-death (POD) accounts (sometimes referred to as transfer-on-death [TOD] accounts).

Most non-probate property passes directly to the person named in a beneficiary form to receive the asset at your death. In other words, non-probate property doesn't pass by will. Quite often, clients sign these beneficiary forms without even realizing that they are doing estate planning, especially since most people don't save copies of the beneficiary designation, and usually almost never think through the ramifications of the beneficiary designation.

Take a minute and consider your current situation. Have you confirmed that your former spouse is no longer a beneficiary of your non-probate property, which you aren't required to and do not wish to leave to him or her? In most areas, if you die while a former spouse is still named as a beneficiary, that former spouse will be entitled to the proceeds of the account and there is nothing that anyone can do unless your former spouse willingly gives it up. Cases like this occur all the time so take action to prevent this from happening in your situation.

> **Name contingent beneficiaries for your non-probate property so that if your original beneficiary doesn't survive you, your non-probate property won't pass to your estate.**

One area of non-probate property that gets frequently overlooked is backup beneficiaries, which are called *contingent beneficiaries*. Many people don't get around to naming contingent beneficiaries at all. These asset documents usually provide, buried in the boilerplate language of the policy or plan document, that if your beneficiary doesn't survive you, the proceeds pass to your estate. In other words, they become probate assets. As such, these assets are subject to the same intestate problems discussed earlier concerning passing, pursuant to the state or province's estate plan for you, (intestacy), not yours.

If this isn't enough to get you motivated to get your documents in order, things actually can get worse. Usually, your creditors cannot reach non-probate assets. However, if these assets inadvertently become subject to probate because you didn't name a contingent beneficiary, your creditors could lay claim to these assets too. If these assets are retirement plans or IRAs, it gets even worse because income tax on the entire proceeds could be due a lot sooner than it would have had there been some thought given to contingent beneficiaries.

> **Obtain advice from a professional when naming beneficiaries of non-probate property.**

Although we discussed it earlier, it bears repeating: Property titled as joint tenants with rights of survivorship (or as tenants by the entirety) is also non-probate property. Again, if you want your children to get your part of that property, you better count on being the surviving partner for that to happen. Otherwise, your children will receive nothing unless the other partner, who will have no legal obligation to your children, agrees after you're dead to give them something. In estate plans that don't involve both partners and that don't take into consideration all the concerns, this very rarely happens.

When couples in blended families take the time to truly listen and understand each partner's motivations and concerns related to *all* the children in their lives, much can be done in the estate plan so that the surviving partner is well provided for, as are the wishes of how the estate could pass to the surviving children from prior relationships. We work with people to design scenarios and structures where there's a win-win feeling, as opposed to the more adversarial, protective, "mine versus yours mentality" that so often shows up. By keeping the "yours, mine, and ours" foremost in the conversation, new possibilities and solutions can emerge and everyone can have a sense of alignment.

6. What Makes Estate Planning for Blended Families So Hard and So Necessary?

Estate planning can be difficult even for people who have only had one partner. When people take on new partners, especially those who have children of their own, the complexities in estate planning multiply exponentially. While we know we're stating the obvious, it is somehow overlooked in terms of taking action — every one of us is going to die.

Many people believe that they don't have enough possessions to do estate planning. However, everyone has something that someone else wants when they are gone. This could range from family keepsakes to family companies. While we use the term "blended families," we're well aware that in many instances your family can feel anything but blended, where there may be little or no relationship between your current partner and your children from previous relationships.

Oftentimes, one of you may be the glue that keeps the blended family together. Guess what can happen after you die? Without a plan that is shared in advance in ways that honor all your loved ones, survivors often fight over virtually nothing of value. Despite the fact that many partners in blended families believe that they must make an excruciating choice between their partners and their children in their estate planning, spelling out who you want to get your belongings is far superior to doing nothing and letting them fight about it after your death. There are ways to include all of them so that there is a sense of valuing the people in your life and what matters to them; this will do wonders to minimize arguments about "things."

7. Action Steps

1. Review any estate-planning documents you have that are signed and legally binding. Do they reflect your current wishes and current family structure? Note any changes you see that need to be made and write down any questions that may have occurred to you by reading this section. You may be considering some of the following questions:

   - Is our real estate in joint tenancy and is this taking care of both of our most important values and concerns?

   - Who are the written beneficiaries of our individual and shared non-probate property? This includes life insurance, annuities, retirement plans and Registered Retirement Savings Plans (in Canada), IRAs (in the USA), and pay-on-death (POD) accounts. Are these the beneficiaries I want

now? Do we have backup beneficiaries named?

2. Determine the status of your power
of attorney and durable power of attorney or advanced health-care directives. Are they in place and with the
people you want to be in those roles
at this time? Are those people aware
of their roles and what is required of
them in those roles? Are they aware of
your expressed wishes?

3. Put all these relevant documents in a
locked, protected file and make copies for both you and your partner.
Make sure the relevant parties in
your estate plan know where these
documents are located.

4. Create a binder with tabs for each section so that as you go about your estate
planning, all the information you are
gathering is easily accessible in one
place for yourself, and for your family
members, should something happen to
you or your partner unexpectedly.

5. Schedule specific appointments in
your calendar where the two of you
can tackle your estate-planning questions and concerns. If it's scheduled,
you'll take action and it will get done!

We recommend one to two hours every two
weeks, or three to four hours once a month
where you dedicate your focus and attention
to your specific estate-planning questions until
you determine answers and strategies that you
can work with advisors in implementing. This
will expedite your work with your attorney and
accountant while also helping them do their
jobs more effectively and to your satisfaction
— and it will save you a great deal of money.
Make it a goal to have one aspect of your estate
plan decided and signed every two to three
months so that you are making regular, steady
progress towards your overall goals.

Most couples know how important it is to do
their estate planning and yet they tend to avoid
that which is uncomfortable and that which
they do not understand. Their fear of making
a wrong or poor decision often causes them to
take no action at all, which, as we've seen here,
causes them to make a default decision to go to
intestacy, which is not a choice anyone would
want to make given the ramifications.

One coaching strategy we have seen work
well for couples committed to making proactive
choices for their legacy planning is to incorporate fun and rewards in the midst of the estate
planning decision making. Some couples enjoy
scheduling time on a Saturday afternoon, and
then afterwards going out on a date as a reward.
Other couples take their notebooks and resources with them to a weekend getaway and
spend time planning for their future as they also
plan for what will happen after they die.

Couples that are serious and want to expedite their process often hire consultants to
keep them on target and to make sure they
are addressing that which matters most to
them in ways that they would not otherwise
be aware. By having a committed relationship
with ongoing scheduled meetings, there is accountability along with an investment of time
and money that helps you stay on track to get
your goals achieved, which is similar to hiring
a personal trainer when you want to seriously
get into shape!

The Basics

CHAPTER 1

The Human Side of Estate Planning

All estate planners and clients should be united in the search for and implementation of a *good estate-planning result*. What is that, you ask? To us, a good estate-planning result is one in which the people you want to get your possessions get them the way you want them to, taxes are minimized, and relationships after death are enhanced or at least not negatively affected. The tax part is easy (or relatively so). It's the relationships that can be elusive, as Illustration 1 demonstrates.

In Illustration 1, the factors above the line are factors with which heirs, estate planners, and folks such as yourself have to deal. Factors below the line are characteristics that you, your estate-planning advisors, and your heirs have.

This book will assist you in achieving a good estate-planning result, which, as you will discover, is usually more challenging for a blended family than a traditional family. Sometimes, the best you can do is not surprise anyone by the results of your estate planning.

1. Key Elements of a Successful Estate Plan

There are three key elements of a good estate plan that must work in unison in order for the plan to even have a chance. Illustration 2 best describes this relationship.

Every estate-planning tool or technique used must carefully match the "players" (you and your family usually), the assets used in the tool or technique, and the tool or technique itself. In our experience, virtually every failed estate plan contains at least one mismatch between the players, assets, and the technique.

Illustration 1
Why Is a Good Estate-Planning Result So Hard to Achieve?

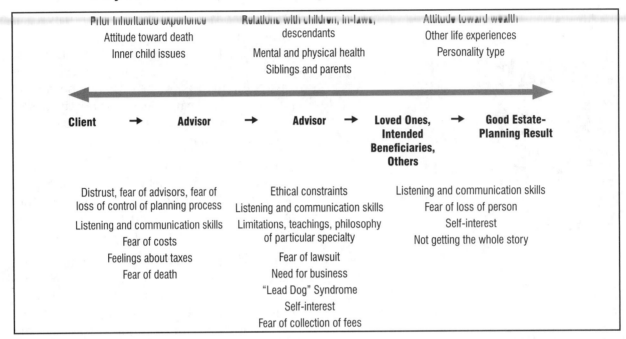

2. Common Fears Associated with Estate Planning

In our experiences as an estate-planning lawyer and a blended family coach, we have come to conclude that estate and will planning is not a favorite activity for most people. In a radio commercial, broadcaster Charles Osgood once said that, for him, estate planning ranked right up there with root canals! Why is that?

Although the statistics range a bit, it is estimated that 50 to 70 percent of Americans die without a will or without having done any deliberate planning. At an intellectual level, all rational human beings know that they are going to die eventually. So why not plan for death? While there are myriad reasons why people avoid taking the necessary actions related to sound estate planning, the majority of them relate to fear and the avoidance of pain. People tend to do things that are comfortable and avoid that which is painful or uncomfortable, no matter how good it might be for them to do it.

> What part of estate planning makes you the most uncomfortable? Whatever it is, don't let it stop you!

What are people afraid of? We have identified 11 of the most prevalent fears that we encounter when it comes to estate planning, all of which are valid and real:

1. **Fear of contemplating death:** While everyone knows they will die eventually, many people are uncomfortable thinking about their own deaths or the death of their spouse or partner.

Illustration 2
Key Elements of a Successful Estate Plan

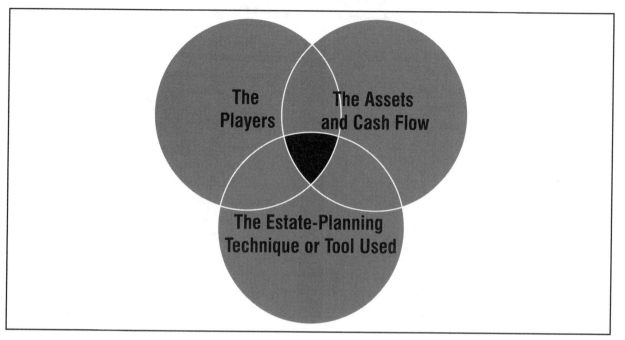

Estate planners think that fear of death is the main reason their clients procrastinate in their estate planning. However, we believe that this issue is much more complex than most estate planners ever consider. The other fears that we have identified also contribute as much or more to the procrastination or failure to act when it comes to estate planning. Many mask this fear of death with a feeling that "it isn't my time" or "I've got more time," which is somewhat irrational because no one knows their time of death in advance.

2. **Fear of not doing the right thing:** Some people are so afraid that they might make a mistake in their estate planning that they won't even begin to plan. What many people don't realize is that their state or province has an estate plan, called intestacy, for them if they die without a will. Whether consciously or from denial or avoidance, intestacy often is a much bigger mistake than any plan that a person could make on his or her own. To learn more about the pitfalls of intestacy, please review section **3.** in the Introduction.

3. **Fear of the unknown:** Estate planning requires some projection of future events. Some clients are so fearful of what the future may bring that they put their heads in the sand and simply do nothing with respect to their estate planning. This fear has a ring of irony to it, as the result of failing to plan *is* certain — again, the estate reverts to intestacy and all it entails.

4. **Fear of hurting someone's feelings:** The fear of hurting a loved one's feelings has caused many clients to procrastinate in their estate planning. For example, a parent may be fearful of hurting the oldest child's feelings because he or she believes it best to select the youngest child as successor trustee or as successor president of the family business. This fear becomes even more pronounced in blended family estate planning, where a partner may perceive estate planning as having to choose between his or her partner and his or her own children. This fear is one that robs people of being able to take effective actions that they know are in the best interests of all their family members. From an attorney's perspective, it is also irrational because the estate plan won't work well if you pick the wrong person or if you don't choose anyone at all.

The irony of avoidance continues here because intestacy grants certain persons priority to handle certain jobs, such as an executor, and these persons may not be who you envisioned for such positions. This can be particularly difficult for blended families, when there may be certain members of the family who would not be honored or acknowledged by intestacy, but you would have very much liked to have included. The subtle nuances and dynamics between family members that you know well and could plan for during your lifetime via communication and specific strategies are not taken into consideration with the law taking over the administration of an estate. The unfortunate result is that a blended family is more likely to become estranged upon the death of a parent.

5. **Fear of estate planners:** People often fear even the professionals that they have selected to help them. The knowledge gap between estate planners and their clients on estate-planning issues really bothers many clients. For example, a person who is not accustomed to being in a lawyer's office often is uncomfortable being there, even for his or her own estate planning. Many clients feel distrustful of lawyers and resent the costs associated with estate planning. When these emotions impact a person's ability to work collaboratively with his or her legal and estate-planning team, there is a much greater cost to the family at the time of his or her death.

The time of death is already particularly emotionally charged with the loss and grief of the loved one. Chaos and confusion are added to this emotionally charged situation when there is no understood and agreed-upon plan about how to adequately take care of the concerns of the person who is no longer there, and to learn what he or she wants to be done with his or her belongings and money.

A good estate planner should be able to estimate in advance a range of costs for most estate plans. With this book in hand, you can become knowledgeable about how to work effectively and efficiently with your advisors to maximize their time and minimize the monetary costs.

6. **Fear of the estate-planning process:** Some people fear the process of

estate planning. That Charles Osgood commercial associated it with root canals, even though there is not a bit of physical pain involved in estate planning. We've come to suspect that the reason for this is that clients fear losing control of the process to the attorney or to someone else along the way. Some people freeze when it comes to planning their own estates. The same people who can jump right in and make suggestions for other people's estate planning simply can't do it for themselves.

Paul fondly remembers a client who carried around drafts of estate-planning documents in a briefcase for almost ten years. Paul ran into the client in an airport after about five years, and he showed them to Paul, almost expecting praise from him for still having them. Paul firmly believed that this guy was concerned that concluding his estate plan meant that he was going to die shortly thereafter, and that by post-poning execution of the documents, he was somehow cheating death.

> **Completing your estate planning will ease stress and bring peace of mind that will improve the quality and length of your life.**

Emily's step-grandfather sold life insurance and often encountered this same strategy among a group of eager, genuinely motivated, and con-cerned potential clients who could not bring themselves to complete the final stage of the process by committing

to getting life insurance. They would speak about their superstition that if they insured their life, they would prematurely bring about their deaths.

7. **Fear of running out of money or losing security:** This fear is often as-sociated with suggestions by estate planners that the client engage in some sizable lifetime gift-giving or enter into a significant estate-planning tech-nique. As life expectancy has skyrock-eted in the past century and continues to increase, the fear of outliving one's assets has grown exponentially as well, especially with the looming specter of a loss or reduction in social security and potentially high medical costs towards the end of life.

Some people attempt to justify put-ting off all of their estate planning based on this fear alone. This fear is irrational when attempted to be used for this purpose because lifetime irre-vocable estate planning is but a small part of the estate-planning process. Indeed, where blended families are concerned, estate planning may not involve any irrevocable lifetime estate-planning strategies, as the odds make this a less than wise choice in most circumstances.

8. **Fear of law changes:** Some clients simply procrastinate because they are so fearful that the laws may change after they sign their estate-planning documents, which would result in having to revisit their estate planning. This stems from the erroneous belief that once an estate plan and will are completed that it is over and done. The reality is that the estate plan you

make now is for life as you know it now, with the understanding that as things change and you continue to live, your wishes and your estate will also continue to evolve, requiring you to revisit your estate-planning documents and make changes where necessary and desired.

We encourage clients to embrace change as a part of life and to incorporate change as part of their planning strategy. This often puts their minds and hearts at ease as they realize that they don't have to figure out every single possible scenario the first time around. There is freedom to address unanticipated events for their assets as they become aware of them and what they want to do about them.

Clients are reassured when they learn that most estate-planning documents are revocable and amendable. In Paul's experience, the unsettled nature of the federal estate tax since 2001 has caused many clients to put off their estate planning, and he's seen some terrible situations when well-intentioned people die without a good plan and leave a mess for their blended families.

9. **Fear of facing reality:** While they may not fear estate planners or death, many people simply don't want to face the reality of the importance of tending to their estate planning. The reality is that the law provides an estate plan (i.e., intestacy) for those who don't come up with their own, so this fear is irrational. People who don't want to face reality will nevertheless be subjected to it, or, worse, their families will.

For couples in blended family situations who are not married, relying on the default intestate plan option is really not an option at all, as your partner will not be acknowledged or honored in any way close to how you would like him or her to be. The law is focused on the legalities of situations and relationships, not on the level of care and commitment. Check out your state or province's laws on common-law unions and intestacy to get a sense of that reality.

For couples in blended families who are married, there are still other aspects to consider related to either of your goals about the stepchildren in your lives, or any birth children you may have. For partners who have been involved in the lives of their stepchildren and step-grandchildren, taking the time to specify how you would like them to receive your various assets would be a very wise and prudent way to proceed. If you do not declare what you want to happen in legal terms, it will likely not happen (or if it does, it may not happen as you would have hoped).

10. **Fear of loss of flexibility:** Some clients don't want to engage in any significant irrevocable lifetime estate planning for fear of the loss of flexibility relative to their future. Knowledge and understanding go a long way towards alleviating ungrounded fears such as this one. Irrevocable lifetime estate-planning options are something that you can research and learn about in this book and other books to see if they are a good, viable option for you or not. With so

many options to choose from and with estate tax laws changing frequently, there are pros and cons to using these. We are not strong advocates of irrevocable lifetime estate-planning options in blended family situations, and we will go into greater detail regarding each option in Chapter 9.

As mentioned earlier, some clients also believe that once they make their estate plan, it is set in stone and cannot be changed, which we have already shown is not the case. We are painfully aware of the irony here again that people who don't have their own estate plans get the one that the state or province has for them, which is usually more inflexible than anything they might design for themselves.

11. **Fear of loss of privacy:** Some people won't begin any deliberate estate planning because they are reluctant to divulge personal and financial information to an estate-planning advisor, or possibly to their partners.

Paul has seen many situations in which clients divulged less than all of the relevant asset information out of fears that someone else would learn about their financial situations. Emily has navigated a number of blended family situations where trust needed to be rebuilt between partners and among all the children involved before people were willing to be open about all the details of their estate with one another. The need to keep things hidden is a detriment to effective estate planning, as prudence dictates that all relevant information be given in order for the estate planner to prepare the most optimal estate plan.

Paul has seen some people attempt to hide behind false or incomplete information, such as an understatement of their own wealth, as a justification for not going forward with a suggested estate plan, even when it would be in their and their blended family's best interest. This self-defeating behavior stems from a belief that it is better to hide and keep some things secret than to have an open and honest way of approaching how they want life to look for their loved ones after their death. What we continue to find odd about this is that the specific details will all be known at that time, and the degree of regret and resentment the remaining family members encounter can take an extraordinary toll on their well-being and quality of life.

2.1 What do these fears of estate planning cause?

These fears prevent people from doing estate planning, or cause them to procrastinate in their estate planning. Fears lead to avoidance strategies that cause delays in estate planning. We have seen many an estate plan come to a screeching halt when a child did not want to discuss life after his or her parents' death. The parents simply decide to put off estate planning rather than make their child uncomfortable, which is almost always a mistake. Never mind the fact that their child may really either dislike or not be ready to handle what happens with intestacy. The "child" may actually be an adult with children of his or her own, with his or her own estate-planning needs to consider, which makes knowing his or her parent's plans that much more important.

When children are dealing with divorced parents who will both have different plans based on their assets shared with their current new spouses or partners, the children involved are even more in need of sound advice and guidance related to how to best address the desires, goals, and concerns of their parents.

Chapter 2 gives important background information, tips, and strategies for how to communicate when emotions are high and concerns are at stake. More often than not, people tend to avoid those conversations due to a lack of awareness about *how* to have the conversations effectively. Children in blended families often feel that what they want or care about doesn't really matter. Often, they refrain from speaking about their concerns out of fears of being perceived as entitled or greedy — when all they really want to know is what they can expect so that they can do sound planning for themselves. Knowing how to have these conversations makes a huge difference for all the family members. This is especially true when certain family members will have key roles to play in the estate plan, such as executor or trustee.

Emily knows of a stepmother and her stepdaughter who were co-executors on the husband/father's estate. The stepdaughter was the trustee on all the trusts for her full and half siblings, as well as on her stepmother's. These women had various levels of preparation prior to entering into those roles, with the stepmother knowing what the will said and the stepdaughter in the dark until the day her father died. The stepdaughter knew she had that role, but she had no idea what was involved. Even with her background in finance, she found the job daunting and challenging to such a degree that she began to wonder how it would be for a family member to find herself in a similar role without any financial background. This prompted her to go back and get her Certified Financial Planner (CFP) so that she could better understand her role, and possibly market herself in the role of trainer and advisor to others who found themselves thrust into that role unaware and unprepared.

> **Make sure your executor and trustee are prepared for their roles.**

3. You Are the Sum of Your Life Experiences

We are all the sum of our past experiences and feelings. We both love the quote: "Wherever you go, there you are" because it is so true. Give it some thought and you'll likely agree. What we have seen, heard, and done in the past all have a major bearing on our likes, dislikes, feelings, and opinions. So where have you been?

Where do you fall in the birth order in your family of origin? Birth order can play a significant role in how people perceive certain things in estate planning. Historically, it has not been that long since we got away from the oldest male heir taking the entire estate under the ancient doctrine of primogeniture. Today, birth order still subtly impacts estate planning through the frequent default use of the oldest child as executor or successor trustee. If you're an eldest child, this might suit you just fine. However, if you're not the oldest child, your view of selecting the oldest child as successor may be quite different. If you're the only daughter, you may find yourself as the primary caregiver your parents turn to for assistance and help, and they may rely on you more than your brothers, while still giving the oldest the responsibility of carrying out their wishes. This can be confusing when you may know and understand their wishes better than your sibling. You may even be very sensitive about this issue. Perhaps you had a past experience with an older sibling where that sibling was favored solely because of being older than you, and you resented it.

These are important areas to consider as you begin to wonder which of your children and stepchildren you see in various roles related to your estate plan. Knowing how to include them effectively in the conversation can be very helpful, and it can shed light in learning what it is that the various members of the next generation care about and what roles they would be open to considering. Two variations of the Golden Rule come to mind here:

- Do unto others as you would have them do unto you. Take time to think about how you would have liked to be treated by your parents when it came to their estate planning and how you'd like that to translate into your plans for your estate.

- Do unto others as *they* would have you do unto them: We're all different and what would work for you might not work at all for some of your children or stepchildren. Taking time to get them to discuss what matters to them and what they would prefer is a great way to honor them as you go forward, and can go a long way towards having the family stay connected and unified. This takes a great deal of skill and practice if you haven't opened up these sorts of conversations before. Coaching professionals such as Emily can aid you in having effective conversations that matter with all the members of your blended family.

4. What Constitutes Being *Wealthy* to You?

In James E. Hughes, Jr.'s book, *Family Wealth*, he describes a family's wealth as consisting "primarily of its human capital and its intellectual capital, and secondarily of its financial capital."

Do you see yourself as wealthy? What are some of the stories and beliefs you have around the term "wealth"? Some people have clearly defined wealth parameters. Others don't. Some people are ill at ease with being thought of as wealthy and do not want to be defined as such. It has been our experience that people who aren't comfortable with a definition of "wealthy" rarely do any substantial irrevocable lifetime gifting, even if estate-planning advisors think that gifting is a great idea and that there's more than enough liquidity in the estate to do so with ease and without adversely impacting the overall robust nature of the estate.

Liquidity: How quickly and cheaply an asset can be converted into cash.

How did you obtain your wealth? How you obtained your wealth sometimes gives clues about how you view wealth and how you will divide it. It is not unusual for people who have inherited wealth to view that wealth differently than those who made the wealth themselves.

People who made their own wealth often very much identify themselves by their property. In our experience, they are more often apt to demand to retain control of their property and they are more willing to take estate-planning risks with it. They also tend to feel more confident in the realm of estate planning and in learning about all their various options. Contrast this with the person who inherits significant wealth. With inheritors, we see two approaches most often:

- Those who are much more apt to view themselves as mere stewards of the property. They usually play it more safely.

- Those who may come across as feeling entitled and that the money is theirs to do with as they choose. Often they seem to be more irresponsible and free with the spending of their wealth and less competent and able to see themselves in the role of managing, growing, and furthering the wealth for future generations.

This is an unfortunate circumstance for many inheritors who were not given the opportunity or training to be competent with their finances. They often feel a great deal of shame and embarrassment around their lack of acumen with their wealth and finances, and these emotions keep them from seeking and accessing professional training, coaching, and advising that could allow them to truly flourish in their lives, where they build their competence and confidence. This often leads to the "shirtsleeves to shirtsleeves" in three generations that is so common — lack of preparedness on the part of inheritors is one cause of the assets and wealth being gone in short order.

5. Your Union

How many previous partners have you had? How many previous unions has your current partner had? Estate planning can be impacted by the number of times that a person marries or takes on new partners. Fears, doubts, and even cynicism about whether a relationship will last can creep in and impact the degree of trust you have in yourself and in your partner to go the distance this time around.

Estate-planning options vary in part by the quality of the current relationship. This is where we find working together as a collaborative team to be very helpful for blended families seeking sound estate-planning advice. The more safety there is to honestly share the reality of your current situation, and not just the positive (or negative) imagination you may have about your relationship, the more grounded and effective your estate plan will be for both of you.

We find that it is imperative that the two of you, as a couple, be candid with your estate planner about your relationship. For example, if the couple's relationship is rocky, the estate planner may be less inclined to recommend significant lifetime estate planning. Paul once had a couple hire him to create a family limited partnership. He didn't find out until after the plan had been implemented that they'd been legally separated for several years, and each partner had been dating other people. Had he known this pertinent information at the time the couple came to see him, he might have given some different advice or designed the partnership differently.

After Paul's experience, we make it a point when working with clients and their estate attorneys to ask direct and indirect questions about what they hope to accomplish. Questions we weave into the conversation include:

- Why does the couple think this is the best and right solution for their particular need or problem?

- What have they considered, if at all, should something happen to their union?

- Have they considered using other options, such as a Grantor Retained Annuity Trust (GRAT) (in the US) or sales to intentionally defective grantor trusts (both discussed in Chapter 9), as each can accomplish the same end goal, while not having the same degree of expense and challenge in the event that the relationship ends in divorce rather than death?

> **A Grantor Retained Annuity Trust (GRAT) is a creature of US tax law. In a GRAT, one creates a specially designed trust with property and retains a right to an annuity from the trust for a specified period of time.**

Consider how well you communicate with your partner. The quality and frequency of communication between the two of you as partners can significantly impact estate-planning advice. This is even more important in a blended family because people usually come into new relationships with their own way to do things and often a lot of their own property, as well as standing legal agreements from the dissolution of prior relationships. Generally speaking, couples who don't communicate often or very well should be represented by separate estate planners.

Indeed, some partners actually hide information, be it financial or family information, from the other partner, which can create ethical problems for the estate planners who represent both partners. This is a particularly challenging aspect to blended family estate planning, and points to the role that a communication coach can play in seeing how to bring the couple together in areas that matter a great deal to both. When a couple is already interacting with a desire to keep secrets from each other, there is likely a breakdown in trust that could be mended with some expert coaching, which could do wonders for the relationship and for the family as a whole.

Emily was referred to a couple by their estate-planning team when they had failed to sign their documents for more than two years. The team had done the best they could to address the concerns and estate-planning goals that the couple expressed to them. When they did not sign the documents over such a long period of time, the team noted that there may be some underlying problems that a trained coach could facilitate resolving.

After spending four months working with this couple on repairing breakdowns in trust and past resentments from more than 30 years of marriage, they came up with a strategy to address both of their seemingly disparate approaches to their estate plan. He had four children, two from a prior marriage and two from their marriage. She had her two children and she was a devoted stepmother to his two daughters. He wanted his part of the community property to be shared equally among his four children, after her death should he predecease her. She wanted her two biological children to get a greater percentage of her estate, as a way to signify her contribution and her value of bloodline when considering estate planning

— noting that his two children would receive benefits from their biological mother that hers would not. Their inability to have effective conversations that could open new possibilities kept them from signing their documents and contributed to a growing animosity and discord between the two of them. After their coaching experience, they were able to work with their estate-planning advisors to creatively implement their shared, desired results.

Knowing how to communicate the emotions, hopes, dreams, and desires you both have will allow you to be much more fluid and fruitful in your estate-planning process with your advisors.

6. Health Issues

How's your health? Health issues are significant in estate planning, as some people are more motivated to act on their estate planning after being beset with health issues; getting a diagnosis is often a potent wake-up call to get started when planning has been avoided. Unfortunately, once a diagnosis happens, it is often too late to take advantage of some vital estate-planning opportunities. Sometimes people are motivated to initiate estate planning by the loss or sudden illness of a friend or an acquaintance.

Historical life expectancy in someone's family of origin can also have an impact on what advice an estate planner gives regarding possible estate-planning techniques. Families who choose to take advantage of having their genome done in order to track hereditary issues should also bring this information to their estate-planning advisors for better awareness of how to best design their particular plan.

You can visit Complete Genomics (www.completegenomics.com) to learn more about genome sequencing. Fees at this time are approximately $10,000 USD per person.

7. Finances

Have you ever been involved with a bankruptcy or been sued for significant money? Do you owe on any promissory notes or do you have money loaned out to others? Do you have debts that your partner is not aware of by which he or she will be impacted at the time of your death? Are you aware of ways to protect your partner and your family members from debts and loans you may be liable for at the time of your death? Past experiences of financial issues such as a personal bankruptcy or having to defend against a large lawsuit, or being saddled with debts give people certain views on their estate planning. In Chapter 2, we provide a new perspective on the "innocent" and "fool" and how they contributed to the decisions that led to consequences you could feel ashamed about; this approach to patterns around money can be quite empowering and expand your options going forward.

Knowing the reality of your financial situation will be imperative for your advisors as they go about modeling your various options. You don't want them wasting their time and your money coming up with plans that would not apply to you given your current situation and obligations. You want your estate plan to be focused on what will make the most sense for you and your family. Knowing that, according to research from Lawrence H. Ganong and Marilyn Coleman of the University of Missouri, "just 20 percent of people discuss financial matters before they remarry." We are aware that your partner may not be fully apprised of all your financial details. Check and see what you may not have fully disclosed, and also consider how you might open the door to a more authentic conversation about what is true for both of you individually as well as goals for your shared finances in the event of one and then the other's deaths.

8. What Will Your Family Look Like at Your Death?

Have you ever envisioned your family at the time of your death? Does the idea of discussing your family after your death make you feel uncomfortable? These and many other questions should be faced because they can provide insight as to how things will play out, including how people will react at that time. In a blended family, this can be critical because relationships usually change after death — relations between your current partner and your children may be fine during your lifetime, but this can change dramatically after you're gone. Your children, who may be cordial and pleasant while you are alive, may ignore or become hostile towards your partner, and perhaps even their half-siblings. The fear of these scenarios becoming reality often keep people from addressing the underlying issues and concerns during their lifetimes, which more likely than not results in that which they fear coming to fruition.

> Brought into public awareness through Dr. Richard Warshak's book *Divorce Poison*, "parental alienation" is a form of emotional child abuse where a custodial parent belittles or vilifies the other parent to the child.

When parental alienation has entered into the mix, your birth children may have been turned against you by your former spouse and you may find your options for a unified family going forward dramatically impacted, which may sway you and how you look at your estate-planning options. For instance, birth children who think that they are entitled to a percentage of your estate may end up being written out of your will as a way of getting back at them for writing you out of your lives. This is the saddest and most painful way people approach estate planning — to communicate their pain, hurt, resentment, and anger at all the loss of relating during life.

We've also seen the reverse, where a conversation about estate planning can open a relationship that had been previously estranged and where important healing and re-establishment of trust can happen when using an approach aimed at responsibility, accountability, apologies, and amends. The overarching and long-lasting impact of parental alienation can be averted and reversed with a commitment to coaching towards a commonly shared goal. For better or worse, when there's an estate at stake, it can bring players to the table in ways that nothing else will.

> Knowing how to have uncomfortable conversations about death and dying can be very helpful when addressing estate-planning questions and ideas.

People rarely, if ever, face these questions, often because other family members are more uncomfortable discussing these issues than the person actually doing the hypothetical dying. Some key things to remember are to not take what your family members share with you personally. The more you can listen from a place of understanding that they are revealing themselves to you and what matters to them, the more you can be present for their concerns, even as you are sorting your own concerns. Communication strategies related to these and other emotions addressed in this chapter, including fear, shame, and guilt, are discussed in Chapter 2.

We have seen estate planning interrupted by the objections of children who did not want to discuss anything to do with a parent's death and the aftermath on the grounds that it was morbid or was (they figured) too far into the future to worry about. We've also seen the next generation balk at opening these conversations out of fear of repercussions. They have learned to keep their thoughts to themselves because their parents may have reacted in the past with upset or judgment when they risked expressing their particular desires.

In one family Emily worked with, a mother asked her children if any of them wanted something from their parents' possessions, and when a son expressed a desire for a particular heirloom related to the holidays, she immediately reacted with displeasure, saying that he couldn't want that because he wasn't religious. His response was to hide any other desires and choose to be silent and resentful rather than risk being judged.

With a blended family, we always advise that the couple seriously contemplate that the family relationships may go south or end after the death of one partner. We wish it wasn't the case, but we've seen it happen far too often. We both err on the side of realism over idealism. When you consider the statistic, from *Preparing Heirs* by Roy Williams and Vic Preisser, that 70 percent of the time families end up disconnected after the deaths of both of their parents, you can see the strong likelihood of that number being even greater if you're considering the added complexity in blended family situations.

9. Your Views on Life

Where did your views on life come from? Whether we want to admit it or not, we often obtain our views on life from our parents. This includes our views on estate planning. While we have a wide band of experiences with our parents, there is the specter of a parent remarrying, whether by reason of divorce from the other parent or of surviving the other parent. Many children disagree with their parent's decision to remarry or to take on a new partner, particularly after the death of the other parent. This can impact both the relations with that surviving parent as well as that child's views on remarriage for himself or herself.

Consider your formative experiences related to your parents' choices. Also consider how your choices may have impacted your children at their ages when the choices happened and the choices as they relate to their lives now. Obviously, in blended families, we are by definition talking about situations where one has taken on a partner who is not the parent of some or all of the children. Children have a variety of mixed feelings about their parent remarrying or taking on a new partner at whatever stage of development. In many instances, adult children can view new partners or stepparents as interlopers to their inheritance. If their other parent is now deceased, some children view a parent's remarriage as somehow disloyal to the memory of the deceased parent, almost as if the surviving parent must remain in mourning forever. Their own conflicting feelings around loyalty to their deceased parent can create a barrier to engaging with their stepparent in an authentically loving and connected manner.

> For a detailed discourse on how adult children can feel about their stepparents, read the book *Step Wars* by Grace Gabe and Jean Lipman-Blumen.

Did your parents discuss their estate planning with you? Another trait that we often get from our parents pertains to whether or not they discussed their estate planning with us. Children whose parents did not discuss their estate planning with them generally are far more likely not to discuss their estate planning with their own children. Some parents "discuss" their estate planning by telling their children and stepchildren various aspects of what they will be doing, even if this information changes or conflicts with or leaves out pertinent information that the parent might have told someone else. We have found that many parents do not discuss estate planning with a child until that child is also a parent. In our experience, the best estate planning includes input from all who are concerned, especially if everyone has a sense of safety and freedom to openly share their thoughts and desires.

Sharing information can be very important when it comes to family businesses, because parents usually look to the children to take over. If the parents don't have frank and open discussions with children and stepchildren in this situation, they run the risk of miscommunication, and the children could end up selling the business after the parents die, even though this is not what the parents would have wanted.

Sometimes it is a matter of two ships passing in the night. Paul recalls a situation where a father lived cash poor for many years because he was paying the premiums for his life insurance policy that was to be used to redeem his shares in his family business, thereby passing control to his son, who also worked in the business, so the son could keep working in the business. The father told Paul that had his son expressed no interest in working for the business, he would have sold it and never bought the insurance. The father was undergoing some lean times so that his son could keep the business going.

When the father died, the son immediately took the life insurance proceeds and then sold the company. The son emotionally related to Paul that he had hated the business and that he had never wanted to work there. However, he felt obligated to his father to do so out of a sense of loyalty. When Paul asked him if he had ever expressed those sentiments to his father,

he said that he had not because that would have demonstrated disloyalty to his family. This was a very sad situation because had the father and son had such a discussion, the father could have lived a lot better for a long time. Dad also could have sold the company during his lifetime for a lot more that what the son received in the sale. This illustrates costly scenarios that occur far too often due to a lack of open, effective communication related to significant decisions that have a great deal of impact on loved ones during life and after death.

10. Past Experiences with Estates or Trusts

What past experiences do you have with estates or trusts? Our experiences with prior estates and trusts often inform our views on our own estate planning, particularly if it involved our own parents. Paul once had a successful man break down in tears in his office over the fact that his parents only left him half as much as they left his siblings. He wondered if his parents only loved him half as much. This gentleman was significantly wealthier than his parents, so it was not an issue of money — it was about love. This was a situation where the parents could have saved their son a lifetime of worry and shame by simply telling him that they were giving more wealth to their other children because they knew that he did not need it, but that they loved him just as much. Nevertheless, this same gentleman was about to treat one of his children differently in his own estate plan by giving that child, also very successful, less than some of his other children. He was not going to tell that child either that he loved them all the same until Paul pointed out to him that what he was about to do was repeating what his parents did to him. Once he saw it, he changed his mind.

Children often are upset by what can be very effective estate-tax planning (where estate tax exists) by their parents, especially where the parents "skip" them and leave significant wealth to their children's children, (i.e., the parents' grandchildren). It's not that the children are opposed to their parents saving them estate taxes. It's that the children want to have their cake (i.e., the estate-tax benefits) and eat it too (i.e., enjoy the property). In other words, the children either want to have control over what their children receive or they want direct access to the wealth itself for personal reasons. Again, what the children want more than anything is to be somehow included in the planning so that they have awareness and understand the basis for decisions being made. This goes a long way towards averting resentment and pain that ends up looking like entitlement and greed.

We have found it somewhat curious that people often want things in their estate plans that differ from their views for the estate plans of others. For example, Paul has asked clients if they believe that trusts should last forever, and they say no, they shouldn't, yet they want this result in their own estate plans. Other issues include whether co-trustees are workable, or at what ages trusts should be distributed to children. Many times their views in general differ significantly from what they want in their own plans. Other issues that clients view differently for their own plans are whether institutional trustees are desirable, whether estate plans should reward or punish certain behavior, and how much authority or discretion should be given to trustees. **Note:** If this paragraph causes you some concern (or overwhelms you completely with all of the jargon) don't worry; as you utilize this book, you will learn what all these terms mean so that you can understand them fully as well as see how they apply to your family.

All in all, the human side of estate planning plays a huge role in the process. The more your advisors have an honest, reality-based understanding of your family situation, the more your estate plan will be able to reflect your values, your intentions, and get the best results for your family with regards to taxes and asset allocation.

11. Action Steps

First, take a personal inventory of your —

- health,

- relationship to wealth and assets,

- relationship with your partner,

- relationship with your children and stepchildren, and

- relationship to estate planning.

Which fears stand out the most for you? Which ones are you surprised about? Which ones keep you from taking action? If you find yourself wanting to avoid taking action here, definitely stop everything right now and list your "what ifs" by answering the following questions:

- What if I don't take any action? What's likely to happen?

- What if I put this off and wait for another time? What's likely to happen?

- What if I take one small action step right now? What could happen? What small step can I take at this moment towards my goal of having a healthy estate plan for myself and my family?

- What's another step I could take? What if I took that next step?

If you find yourself feeling motivated, you could write out a list of the different steps you could take that you see as most important right now. By breaking down a big looming goal such as estate planning into small, bite-sized chunks, you'll have a greater likelihood of taking action, and an even greater likelihood of completing all the actions towards your goals. Think about the tortoise — slow and steady wins the race!

CHAPTER 2

Communication Strategies

Most advisors will encourage you to communicate and be open with each other; however, few give you useful strategies on how to do so effectively, and with the outcomes you desire. Our purpose in writing this book is to empower you with knowledge and tools to make it more likely that you will be able to access and put that knowledge to good use on your own, and when you are with your advisors.

This chapter is geared towards facilitating honest, authentic conversations that will allow tough choices to be made in ways that strengthen your relationship. Emily draws from more than 25 years of working with couples and families, and working with hundreds of clients in successfully navigating the emotional land mines that arise when contemplating transferring wealth, assets, and values to the next generation.

This chapter will show you how to communicate in powerful ways that enable you and your partner to feel heard and understood — not just in terms of the content of what you're sharing, but more important, in terms of what's driving the underlying concerns and how to get to the heart of the matter.

Couples who use these tried and true approaches find that their estate-planning process goes much more smoothly and enjoyably. Additionally, their relationship as a whole improves, their enjoyment of one another and *all* the children in their lives dramatically increases, and they have an overall sense of fulfilment and peace.

By reading this chapter, you will learn about key distinctions related to why couples in blended families in particular avoid conversations that are emotionally loaded. We will offer you a number of resources to use in different instances. We will also give an overview of specific strategies you can employ with each other when you feel like you're walking on eggshells, or when you've just stepped on an emotional land mine.

1. Money Types

Core concept: Who is doing the communicating?

A fundamental approach Emily has found to be a swift, effective, and surprising way to open new possibilities for relating to each other around conversations about money and estate planning is to understand the players in each of your "inner theaters." These players are the voices you hear when you are speaking and talking about money and planning.

Emily is a trained money coach from The Money Coaching Institute. She shows couples how to identify and work with their core *Money Types* when in conversation with each other about money, when making important decisions about their estates, and when discussing important concerns about their finances with their advisors and their children. Her company works with blended families in their entirety using a Family Legacy Retreat format that ties in the Money Types with communication strategies, which empowers family members to be successful in their roles in the family enterprise, the family estate plan, and in the overall stewardship of the family wealth.

Emily also works with advisors to facilitate their understanding of the different players that typically show up when working with clients around emotionally loaded topics in their estate plan. What follows is an explanation of Money Types and how they can be utilized with each other and within your blended family.

The concept of Money Types makes a lot of sense to people once they discover it. Simply put, we are each the directors of our lives, much like we are the directors of our estate-planning process. Over time, we forget that we write our scripts and we direct our plays as we go, and we give way too much power and control to the cast of players on our stage of life. This cast is the same for every person — who is front and center differs from person to person, from situation to situation, and over time for each individual. Knowing these players intimately allows you ease of directing them and taking care of their quirks and needs when situations arise so that *you* are in charge of who is center stage when it comes to what matters most to you. Once you have *awareness*, you then have a *choice* about how to move, and this allows you to take effective *action* when you want to.

1.1 Awareness of Money Types

Who are these characters? Before we answer that question, we want to make sure you understand what is meant by a "type." Archetypes have been written about and explored since Carl Jung first introduced the concept by that particular name, though they have been around a lot longer. Joseph Campbell made them even more accessible and understood in his writings and teachings. There are numerous books about archetypes in general for those who want to understand this concept more in-depth. For our purposes here, we'll explain them in a simple, straightforward manner.

Money Types are a way of describing common patterns and habits people develop over the course of their lives when relating to money and financial decisions. These patterns become ingrained over time as we repeat them again and again. They are familiar to us. They are our automatic ways of reacting and responding when the following happens:

- A bill arrives in the mail. Do you open it immediately and pay it? Do you set it aside for later and forget to pay it? Do you hand it to someone else to take care of it for you?

- A letter shows up from the trust officer. Do you open it, read it, and take the necessary action? Do you put it in a drawer, unopened with all the other ones?

- A check or payment is received. Do you open it and deposit it that day? Do you put it aside and misplace it?

- A check is written. Do you balance your checking account at that time? Does it end up bouncing?

- A document you need for estate planning needs to be located. Do you know exactly where it is and what it says? Do you have to search for hours? Do you call the advisor or institution and have them generate a new one for you?

- A conversation about money is opened. Do you have the information you need? Do you avoid the conversation? Does your stomach start to hurt?

As you read these examples, look and see what your approach most likely would be in each situation. These honest approaches are all valid and real, and they are each generated by one of the eight different Money Types. Each person has all eight types (and more — these are just the most common) and how strong or prevalent each type is depends on a number of factors including, but not limited to the following:

- Your upbringing and what patterns were modeled for you. What you saw, heard, and felt.

- Your own thinking and what meaning your mind made about what you saw, heard, and felt.

- Decisions you made about who and how you were going to be as a result of what you saw, heard, and felt.

- Societal and cultural stereotypes about gender and roles in the family.

- Birth order (i.e., oldest, youngest, or middle child)

- What situation you are contending with; for instance, you may be great at bargaining for small-dollar items but avoid making significant financial decisions.

- The time of day.

- The time of year.

- Your mood.

- Who you are with (e.g., women versus men, someone younger versus someone older, someone with more education than you versus someone with less).

Money Types go by different names depending on which book you read or whose approach you choose. Brent Kessel in *It's Not About the Money* writes about Guardian, Pleasure Seeker, Idealist, Saver, Star, Innocent, Caretaker, and Empire Builder. John Robbins in *The New Good Life* discusses the Saver, Innocent, Performer, Sensualist, Vigilant, and Giver. In Emily's *Special Report: Money Problems and the Best Way to Fix Them* she describes four basic money personalities: Spenders, Savers, Avoiders, and Monks, which she learned through training with T. Harv Eker and his work on the *Secrets of the Millionaire Mind*. (**Note:** You can get a free copy of this Special Report by going to www.blended-families.com/ebookstore.)

Having studied all of these various models, Emily has found the approach of Deborah L. Price, founder of the Money Coaching Institute and author of *Money Magic*, to be the most elegant, accessible, and useful way to work with people to break free of ingrained patterns, and support them in discovering new ways of being when it comes to money, wealth, finances, and estate planning. These are the Money Types:

- Innocent: A sense of confusion and of not knowing how to proceed.

- Fool: Leaping in before looking and gathering the relevant data.

- Victim: Feeling put upon and blaming others.

- Martyr: Righteously indignant, resentful, and bitter.

- Tyrant: Needing to control; infuriated and wanting to take action and state his or her case.

- Creator/Artist: In denial and avoiding anything to do with money.

- Warrior: Empowered, aware, and ready with the data.

- Magician: Aware, alert, and grounded in the current circumstance while able to access creative and new ways to deal with persistent problems.

One reason for this particular approach being especially effective is that the names of these Money Types are evocative and conjure up images that we may not want to look at. This tells us a lot about what our relationships are within ourselves when it comes to our financial lives. While no one would ever want to identify with being a *tyrant* or a *fool*, understanding how these characters show up in our lives, conversations, and decision-making is incredibly useful and revealing. Exploring your Money Types can make you feel quite vulnerable and, what Emily's clients find to be most surprising of all, it can be quite liberating too.

Knowing and understanding the elements of all the Money Types is liberating because as soon as you're aware of which character is driving you, you can direct it where you want to go, or you can put another one in the driver's seat and get there more quickly and competently, while also taking care of the concerns of the type that you caught steering you off course.

An example we often see in blended family estate planning is as follows: A second wife is meeting with her husband and their male estate-planning advisor. The advisor and her husband are talking about possible ways to avoid taxes and protect his key concerns as they relate to his children from prior relationships. The two men are using technical terms she does not understand. She also notices that she is not being actively included in the discussion and that there are aspects of the discussion that are not addressing her key concerns. Her *innocent* type keeps quiet and does not ask any questions. When she realizes that the decisions they are making will have a direct impact on her freedom to make financial decisions on her own if he should die first, her *victim* type then takes over and becomes quite hurt and upset, yet she still does not say anything.

If she had awareness of the *innocent* and *victim* and how they are driving her behavior in the meeting, she could access her *warrior* to step in and speak up. Her *warrior* would respectfully express her concerns, and ask that they slow down and describe what they are talking about and how it will impact her directly in ways that she can understand. The *warrior* would continue to slow them down each time they said a term she was unclear about and ask for further clarification and how it relates to the bigger picture.

Now imagine this couple leaving that meeting. If she did not have awareness and access to her *warrior*, chances are that her *innocent* and *victim* team would call her *martyr* to be center stage and her husband would have one resentful, angry, and hurt woman to contend with as they drove home. By being empowered to have her *warrior* step forward and make sure her needs get met and addressed, the couple has a chance of having a much more enjoyable and relaxed drive home, sharing what they both got from the meeting, and discussing the next steps for their estate-planning process.

If you find yourself intrigued about Money Types and want to know your predominant characters, as well as your partner's, so that you may begin to explore new ways of communicating with each other and with your advisors, go to www.blended-families.com to get your easy-to-use assessment and information packet.

On the accompanying CD we provided you with a modified version of an article on child support and Money Types by Emily that appeared in the October 2010 issue of *StepMom Magazine*. This article goes into more detail about the Money Types and shows you how each of them show up in the thoughts and conversations of people as they contend with money issues in their blended families.

2. General Communication Strategies and Approaches

> **Communication is more about listening than speaking.**

Now that you are aware of the predominant characters on the "inner stage" of estate planning, we want to give you some effective strategies for communicating with each other and shifting those automatic patterns of relating successfully.

Awareness is the key that unlocks the door to new possibilities. Simply having the awareness of which of these characters is taking cues to be center stage is a great start. Knowing that you are the director of these internal Money Types and that you can choose who to listen to and who should speak gives you many options.

2.1 Defining conversations

We often open conversations without having a sense for where they will go or what they are really about. Starting a conversation with a particular purpose can do wonders for opening new ways of relating and approaching estate planning successfully. There are a number of different sorts of conversations we can have in the course of estate planning (and in life in general). When approaching any aspect of your estate planning, we recommend the following:

1. Begin by **exploring the prospects**. In this type of conversation, all ideas are captured and welcome. All thoughts are treated as valid, and there's plenty of space for all sorts of options to be opened. The key in this preliminary conversation is to generate ideas and open the playing field. To do this effectively, it is important to refrain from voicing opinions like the following:

   - That'll never work.

   - Are you crazy?!

   - I don't like that because …

   - I think that's a bad idea.

   - So and so would never go for that.

   Opinions and preferences close down creativity and possibilities and that's not the intention. The purpose of this conversation is to generate ideas and possibilities, and to create the space for all sorts of creative thinking to be allowed. You never know what can show up when you're not concerned about getting it right or needing to defend.

2. The next step is to **explore the likeli-hood**. In this step, you look at the list of ideas you've generated and then narrow it down according to those that are likely, those that have the most amount of challenge, and those that might work if certain other pieces are addressed. As you go through each idea, it's important to be as objective as you can be.

If you find yourselves getting attached to one idea more than others, know that you will hamper the process and close down access to options that could work just as well, if not better. Take the ones you are attached to and place them in the "likely" section with a star by them so that they are honored. For each of your starred ones, be sure to note somewhere what specific concern you believe that strategy addresses and why you feel it is the best one, along with your specific fear of what could happen if that choice is not chosen. Then allow yourself to see other possibilities as viable options — not that they threaten your preferred choice, but that they may enhance or even more adequately address the same concerns.

Note: Key challenges you will face during your conversation for probabilities include:

- Taking the opinions expressed by your partner *personally*.

- Getting caught in being *right*.

- Being attached to one idea being the *best* or *only*.

> **Don Miguel Ruiz, author of *The Four Agreements*, shares the secret to not taking anything personally: "Nothing other people do is because of you. It is because of themselves."**

3. It's time to **determine actions**. Get a new sheet of paper and for each likely option, write a list of the actions that would need to happen in order to successfully implement each one. Also note any potential roadblocks and issues that will need to be addressed satisfactorily in order to use that particular method. Important elements for a conversation for action include being clear about who will be taking the actions and when they will have those actions completed and where the results will be filed or noted. Making sure these elements are all in place allows you to easily create an action plan that will support you in having this action happen the way you want it to and in the time frame you desire.

2.2 Setting the stage

Now that you have a sense of the types of conversations you can have and how to structure them, let's take a look at how to get started. A great way to begin is with the end in mind. As you consider opening a conversation about your estate-planning concerns that you know may be particularly dicey and emotional, instead of dreading it, see if you can set the stage for a great outcome.

You can do this effectively by stating your purpose in having the conversation and what you'd like to see happen as a result. Here are some sample approaches to give you an idea of what we mean:

- "Honey, I'd like to explore with you how we might set up the ownership and use of our house should one of us die unexpectedly. This is so that we can both have peace of mind that our needs are taken care of, while our desires for what we'd like to eventually happen with the house in the estate transition are also addressed."

- "Dear, would you be willing to have a conversation with me about powers of attorney? I'm feeling overwhelmed by the different ones and I would like to have a better sense of what you understand about them, how you see using them, and *who* we should consider as agents, so that we can feel more comfortable making those decisions together."

- "Sweetheart, I'm feeling particularly challenged by … "

- "After reading all of this, I'm beginning to feel motivated and scared. What about you? Where would be a good place to begin?"

- "There's so much to learn and decide. With all of this, I'd like to look at our calendars and come up with a plan so that we can be successful and accomplish our goal of getting our estate plan in place. When would be a good time for you to look at dates and planning and when we want this to be completed?"

If either of you finds yourselves getting bogged down by details and getting a bit snappy or irritable with the other, remember to touch into this strategy and remind each other about the purpose of all of this. You could say something like: "Hey, honey, I know this is unpleasant/a drag/not our favorite way to spend our time, but I'm so thrilled that we are taking steps to get this important aspect of our lives taken care of — for greater peace of mind, and for the sake of *all* of our kids' lives going forward after we're gone. Thank you!"

2.3 Gratitude and acknowledgment

Did you catch the *thank you* at the end of that last example? There's an important reason for this. When faced with things that are important and not necessarily pleasant, drawing on heartfelt appreciation of each other will fuel you more than just about anything else you can imagine. When you are feeling resigned, frustrated, or stuck, nothing will shift your mood faster in a positive direction than feeling authentically grateful.

With estate planning, it's easy to access a positive direction by touching into the gratitude you have for having an estate to plan! There are plenty of people who would love to have an estate to plan. This is the sort of challenge that comes with having resources and access to money and assets; it is what many call the "price of privilege." Touching base with each other about all the gifts you have in your lives and what a blessing it is to get to look at how those gifts can benefit those you love is an extraordinarily rich and wonderful place to reside, as is having the autonomy and power to choose. To get to decide and know that your wishes will be carried out is another huge thing for which you can be grateful. There are many people who may have access to a certain degree of opportunity and money, and yet have absolutely no say or control about who or what or when it will be given to someone else.

When you are communicating about what matters to each of you, creating a space where there is generosity in your listening with each other is a wonderful gift you can both experience and be truly grateful for. Taking a moment to *acknowledge* this gift will invite more of that sort of listening.

Whether training a puppy or raising a child or teaching a student, we know that much more is accomplished through genuine acknowledgment and recognition of incremental steps along the way than by pointing out what's not happening. Focusing on what you're getting is a great way to set a positive experience and mood. Focusing on what you're unhappy about and wishing it were different is a recipe for pain and displeasure for both of you.

The thing that amazes us time and again is how very simple it is to acknowledge each other and yet how seldom people do it, especially with the people they love the most. Given that research has repeatedly shown that people are more interested in acknowledgment than money when it comes to the workplace, it continues to baffle us that what we want and seek the most is what we give the least in our most caring relationships. If you want to start cultivating rich, meaningful, and open conversations about money and estate planning, start bringing authentic acknowledgment into your everyday language and conversations.

Here are some examples to show you just how simple this is:

- "Thank you for putting the bills in the mail today."

- "Thank you for listening when I needed to vent about how the advisor spoke to me."

- "Thank you for being my partner in all of this; it makes it so much more enjoyable!"

- "Thank you for being so strategic and keeping us on task with this. I know I grumble about it, and I want you to know I really appreciate you for making this a priority for us."

When an acknowledgment comes from your partner, take a breath in, pause, and simply say "thank you" in return. By acknowledging that your partner's appreciation of you was heard, you're much more likely to receive more. If you give an acknowledgment and find that it is not received or that he or she pushed it away, take a breath, and ask if he or she heard you and if you should repeat it — and if he or she might let it sink in for a moment. It can take practice to give and receive acknowledgment from each other; especially if that's something you haven't really experienced much of in your life.

Note: This one little strategy will do wonders in your relationship with your stepchildren too. They may take a while to recognize your "thank yous" as authentic, but once they get it that you really mean it, you'll start to see a difference in how they relate with you. When people feel valued and recognized for their contribution in your life and in the world, they want to show up more, they want to engage more, and they tend to trust you more too.

> **What are you thankful for right now?**

2.3a When you don't feel grateful

One thing that can get in the way of accessing authentic gratitude is when the *martyr* Money Type is lit up and feels that everyone else is ungrateful for all the hard work you do and all the ways you show up for them. If this is the case for you, know that you are not alone, as many parents and stepparents in blended families feel this way.

If the *martyr* has been building up a lot of resentment and anger over years of going unacknowledged, it can be very difficult to access any desire to acknowledge others; especially if you have felt taken advantage of and taken for granted. If this is where you are right now, we encourage you to start this section with acknowledging *yourself*. Instead of waiting for others to recognize you for all your sacrifices, see where you can acknowledge yourself for how you keep showing up. Being a stepparent can largely be a thankless role for a long time, as can being a parent who is in a noncustodial role.

When it comes to estate planning, you may have to contend with ungrateful, entitled, and spoiled attitudes that don't seem to take you into consideration at all. Years of underlying, seething resentment can get stirred up and this is when we often see those "emotional land mines" go off as the *martyr* turns over control to the *tyrant* that's had enough and is going to seize the opportunity to take control and not allow himself or herself to be run roughshod anymore. This can be quite surprising for others who have been used to a *victim* or "doormat" character who has quietly endured without saying much aloud.

If you find that this dynamic is derailing your process, you may find great value and relief in working with someone trained in helping couples break free of these dynamics to re-experience the magic and creativity that filled their hearts and lives when they first got together. Know that this is definitely accessible to you again and that those underlying hurts can be healed.

3. Communication Strategies for When Emotions Flare

If a conversation about estate planning turns sour, you can shift where it is heading easily and effectively by applying some important tactics (this is true for any conversation that takes a turn for the worse), which are discussed in the following sections.

3.1 Slow down

There are obvious clues as to when a conversation isn't going well:

- Tempers begin to flare.
- The same topics are repeated.
- There's a sense of growing frustration
- Eye rolling occurs.
- Interruptions occur often.
- Tone shifts to defensiveness.
- Voices are raised.

The moment you're aware that your conversation is not going well — **stop**! It's useless to continue. You will only do more damage and neither of you will have the sense of being heard or getting your point across. Better to simply understand that emotions are flared and rational thinking is no longer present. It's the reality of the situation at the moment. There's nothing inherently wrong about it. It just won't get you where you want to go. You definitely don't want to be making decisions from that place because those decisions won't be coming from an aligned, centered, and mutually beneficial place.

We all know about calling a "time out" when our children are small and they are too emotional to have a talk. The same holds true in adult partnerships when one or both partners feel that something that matters to them is at stake and threatened. By asking for or calling a time out, or to slow down, or pause, you give each other a chance to regroup, and to get back in touch with the fact that you are both each other's partner and care deeply for one another — and that you are not adversaries. Ways to slow things down include using phrases such as "Hold on a minute," or "Could we take a break?"

3.2 Breathe

Take some slow, deep breaths in and out. When we get upset and emotions get triggered, we tend to hold our breath. This actually heightens the distress, anxiety, and reactive response and makes it harder to shift. When encouraged to take a breath, most people take a big breath in and continue to hold their breath, which can only make things worse.

Once you have a sense of resolution about something that's been on your mind, don't you usually let out a big sigh of relief? That sigh is you finally exhaling after holding your breath a long time. By making sure to take as long an exhalation as you do an inhalation, you activate the other aspect of your nervous system that allows you to think more clearly, to relax more deeply, and to access other options to which you would otherwise be closed off.

Our breath is one of the most useful and effective tools we can use in managing our mood and our choices in the midst of strong emotions. The best part is that we can all do it and use it; it really is quite simple. By inhaling for a count of five and then exhaling for a count of five you are already shifting things for yourself and opening up new possibilities.

The other thing about the breath is that it brings us to the present moment. A lot of times when we are triggered, we are either in the past with all of the emotions related to something that happened a while ago that is unresolved or we are in the future and caught by anxiety or fear of what might or will happen if we don't hold on tightly to our position. Neither of these has to do with the present moment and the present is where all the options, creativity, and possibilities are for designing the future that you want.

You can use your breath to get present. Being present allows you to see that in this moment you are safe and that you are not threatened, and that you have access to all sorts of resources, love, and support to get you where you want to go.

Another aspect of using the breath is that it helps the two of you get back into alignment. If you're feeling at odds with each other, and if you're both willing to take a time out and breathe in and out together for even just three deep breaths, you will find that you are more in tune — more in sync — with each other and what matters to you both as a couple. Couples that are having a particularly hard time may find breathing together for five to ten minutes can be very helpful.

3.3 Seek to understand

When there is an upset, typically what's happening is that each of you feels right about a particular position, and there's a sense of defending and convincing, without much success. Shifting your approach will really help to open your options as you look at what's in front of you.

Seeking to understand the position of the person in front of you comes from a place of discovery. It will take a bit to let go of being right about your position. Just to clarify, this is not about giving up your position, this is about allowing for another way of relating where neither of you has to be wedded to a particular position.

Seeking to understand where your partner is coming from will give you a lot of data about what matters most to him or her and why this is so important to him or her. Asking open-ended questions that bring forward what your partner sees and what he or she cares about gives you the underlying, core reasons for why he or she is taking a stance at all. Whoever has less of a charge around the current issue can choose to listen and seek to understand what is going on for the other person. You may want to ask open-ended questions and begin statements like the following:

- Tell me more about …

- What about this matters most to you?

- What would it look like to you if we did … ?

- How would you feel if we didn't do … ?

- What is it you hope to accomplish by seeing it that way?

- What is it you worry will happen if we do (or don't do) it that way?

While you're in this curiosity mode, it's crucial that you truly are seeking to see things from your partner's point of view. This approach will backfire if you then use what he or she has shared to show him or her how wrong he or she is and why. This isn't about blowing holes in what the person cares about; it's about joining your partner in what he or she cares about — there's a big difference here! If your partner feels that you care about what he or she cares about, he or she will be much more open to listening and caring about your perspective too.

One of the ways we go sideways in relationships with our significant other is when we believe that our partner should think and approach the world like we do. We all have distinct styles and approaches to life that make us unique and wonderful. Appreciating and valuing our differences is an essential component of life and it also opens up the greatest likelihood of new, creative, and exciting options. However, we tend to limit our possibilities when we want everything to come from our preferred approach only. Because of this we tend to create discord and resentment from our partner who feels misunderstood and not honored or appreciated for his or her approach to life. When there's a shared understanding about how each member of the family approaches problem solving, takes in information, and communicates in general, there's a greater sense of ease and enjoyment of each other.

Emily works with couples and blended family members to understand each other's learning styles and strengths, and she shows families how to maximize those natural gifts and talents with one another. Two resources Emily highly recommends are the Kaleidoscope Profile® from Performance Learning Systems (www.plsweb.com) and *StrengthsFinder 2.0* by Tom Rath. (When you purchase Rath's book, you get a code to do the inventory online to get your top ten strengths (www.strengthsfinder.com.)

Another way we can get offtrack is when we get caught by the content. Let's say you're having an important conversation about whether or not to do lifetime giving. As the conversation gets more heated, you find yourself talking about details and specifics related to why certain choices are good or bad ideas, and you keep going on different tangents that get brought up in the course of the conversation. Before you know it you're having an argument over child support and how you're also paying additional money for private school. This is a classic example of how a well-intended conversation about one topic ends up in a fight about something that seems completely unrelated to one partner and feels totally relevant to the other partner. There are two things you can do in this instance:

- Use the *shelf* strategy. If one of you brings up something that seems to be a tangent that could really take you in a different direction, the other can ask that, while that is an important conversation, you shelve it for now with the commitment to address it later. You can even put on the calendar when that topic will get addressed. Or you can keep a running list of what gets shelved and pull it out and make sure those items get addressed at another time.

- Explore the *context*. Ask about how your partner sees it as relevant. Express what you're hearing.

For example, when a stepmother brings up her distress about the child support in light of lifetime giving, her partner may be curious and wonder aloud: "I'm imagining that you may be feeling a sense of disparity between what my kids are receiving already versus what our children may get and that you have a concern that if we do lifetime giving that there may be even less for them. Is that right?"

The key to sharing a curious exploration like this is to not be attached to being right. The goal is to get to the person's core concern so that he or she feels understood and taken care of, as that will help to decrease the amount of negatively charged emotion in the space. To take this example further, the stepmother could easily respond: "No, that's not it. I'm more worried about how I'll be taken care of and I have a fear that we will run out of money as it all seems to go towards your kids whenever there's a request from your former wife. I have this underlying 'what about me?' feeling that really worries me." This willingness to share her concerns could open his heart to her and allow them to connect in a way in which she trusts that she will be well provided for as they move forward with their estate-planning goals.

> **When you let go of needing to be right, you open a space for more connection.**

3.4 Recognize when you are full

When you take time to listen, and you haven't really listened like this before, your partner may use the opportunity to dump a whole lot more than you were expecting. Even with attempting to shelve certain things along the way, there's a strong likelihood that you will only be able to listen so far before you get "full" and need to let off some of your steam as well.

The things that your partner says may trigger you in all sorts of ways and it is very important to take care of yourself and to not keep listening if you are finding yourself getting hooked or upset. A good clue that you're still thinking about something that he or she said that was shelved is that you are no longer listening or being present. Owning that and saying that you're full is a very wise thing to do at this point. You may want to shake it off, do a couple of jumping jacks, take a brief walk, or otherwise move your body to shift your mood. You may need for your partner to listen to you for a while about what was triggered for you. One person's upset does not supersede the other person's; it has more to do with how present each of you can be for the other in a given instance. Whoever has the least charge or upset about a certain topic is probably more able to listen and try to understand the other person.

Another key element to letting go of what's got you triggered is to *not* take it personally. Remember that even if the other person is saying it's about you, it's really about him or her and something that he or she cares about. You can listen from his or her perspective: "I wonder how that is for him even as he thinks it's about me." Some simple tools that can assist you in not taking what your partner says personally include the following:

- The Reversed Pointing Finger: If you have the sense that your partner is blaming you and pointing his or her finger at you, remember that three other fingers are pointing back at your partner! See if you can find what he or she is pointing at to be true in your world about you — it's usually not that hard — and then, you can be curious about where that might be showing up for your partner.

  A frequent example we see with couples is where the wife might complain to the husband about how disorganized he is in his office and how messy everything is. He then takes it personally, gets defensive, and starts justifying why he likes it that way, even when he might not actually like it at all.

  With this approach, that same complaint could be met by the husband with total agreement that his office could definitely be more organized. For the wife, she might be feeling particularly disorganized or frustrated with herself when it comes to locating needed paperwork related to the estate-planning process. Allowing for both to discuss the situation, it creates more intimacy, fewer fights, and a lot more likelihood of forward movement.

- The Work: If you want to take the "turnaround" in the previous point to another level, or if it is too hard to get your partner to see how what he

or she is pointing at you may be more about him or her, then "The Work" by Byron Katie can be very effective. In situations where there's a strong attachment to an opinion or a story you or your partner have as being right and true, The Work helps you understand that thinking and helps you begin to open up. In a nutshell, The Work is composed of four questions and a turnaround:

1. Is it true?

2. Can you be sure it's true?

3. How do you react when you believe it is true?

4. Who would you be and how would you be different if you didn't believe that it was true?

After answering these questions from your heart, you then take whatever statement or story you have and turn it around so that you put yourself into the story. An example of this is: "You should take care of me and my needs before everyone else." This statement would be turned around as: "I should take care of you and your needs before everyone else." And, "I should take care of myself and my needs before everyone else." These statements open new possibilities about what you might not be attending to in terms of taking care of yourself and others, in the same way that you expect them to do for you. This tends to shift couples out of the double standard that can often be felt during estate-planning proceedings, and give you both a chance to step into what it's like for the other person.

3.5 Strive for alignment

Often we get quite stuck in believing we need agreement when what we're really looking for is alignment. Agreement seeking tends to create gridlock and stymie your estate-planning progress. This is what happens when you each take a position that you feel *right* about and, by definition, the other must be *wrong*. The problem is, both of you are attached to being right, and as long as you hold tightly and unwaveringly to your stance, you are deadlocked, with no way of moving without one of you feeling like you are going to lose and the other will win. This is a common occurrence and often leads to resentment, or even outright hostility.

While this issue shows up in the course of our daily lives, when it comes to estate planning, it can really waylay the whole process. Someone who has built up a lot of resentment over the years may be unlikely to sign a document that sets in stone something that he or she honestly does not want to happen, or something with which he or she doesn't authentically agree.

As you learn more about what truly matters to both of you (using the other techniques, especially seeking to understand), you will also begin to see where you can be aligned as you go forward with your planning. We recommend you take note of where you see patterns of concerns, jointly held areas of possibilities, and where you have distinct differences. As you discover what you both care about and you tap into the love you have for each other, you may begin to see ways of using the various options available to you to take care of key concerns — even if it means each of you gives up a little of what you ideally want. Coming to a place of alignment does a great deal towards bringing peace to your interactions, and can smooth over where there would otherwise be resentment if one of you pressured or forced the other to agree when the person truly did not.

The most vital component of all of this is to remember that you two are partners and you are truly on each other's sides. As you embrace that you have each other's best interests at heart and you can work things out as they come up, you will gain greater confidence in yourselves as a couple and as a united front when communicating with all the children in your blended family. When you two are united, the pressures from other forces, such as the "yours, mine, and ours" in your lives, will not tear you apart.

4. Communicating about Prenuptial and Property Agreements

More often than not, conversations about prenuptial and property agreements are handled in a way in which the partner being asked to sign the agreements feels pressured and that he or she has no choice.

When couples seek coaching support on how to handle these types of agreements differently, Emily works with them using a profound and effective system known as the RichLife Portfolio™ (www.wealthlegacygroup.net) to explore their historical patterns and Money Types; to envision their future desires and plans in a specialized format; and to determine clear actions in the present that will support them in successfully achieving their goals. With this foundation in place, the couple can then begin to address the concerns that a prenuptial or property agreement is designed to handle, and they determine how they will honor their union as it successfully reaches various milestones so that the partner asked to sign the document feels that his or her future is being invested in as they design their life together.

If a prenuptial or property agreement was signed under duress, this may be a time to use the tools in this chapter, perhaps with the assistance of a trained facilitator, to express, explore, and heal the underlying hurt and resentment that may be lingering and perhaps poisoning your relationship.

5. Communicating about Commingling Property

Given how important it is to have separate property in blended family situations, we want to support you in having effective conversations about how to separate property that has been commingled while also honoring and acknowledging what the two of you have built together.

Begin by looking at all that you possess and see what has been accumulated since your union began, as opposed to what each of you had initially. Then, celebrate all you have accomplished and what you have built together. Perhaps this will be your beautiful home and furnishings. Perhaps it will be a business you started together. Or maybe it is the children you had together and how proud you are of them as they grow and develop. There's so much to be grateful for when it comes to your partnership and all you have been able to have and do as a result of being together.

From this place of love and gratitude, begin to explore what aspects of your commingled

property should be separated. Use the tools described in this chapter to help you navigate this part of the conversation if things get heated or emotional. Always remember to keep returning to the topic of all that you have together.

This is where your creativity comes in as you begin to explore ways of possibly separating some of your currently jointly held property into each of your estates, so that all of your children are honored in ways that feel fair and respectful of how both of your lives have been augmented by being together.

6. Withholding Information

As you do your estate planning, you may find yourself quite uncomfortable with the recommendation to be honest with your partner about all of your financial obligations and holdings. If you have chosen to withhold information from your partner until now, and you believe you are ready to trust and share these details with him or her, here are some ways to go about it that you may find helpful.

Along with using the concepts outlined in this chapter, you may also consider *apologizing* and *making amends*. You'd be surprised what an authentic apology will do for a relationship. This is not about saying "I'm sorry, please forgive me" and it's over. This is about honestly and openly showing your partner what you withheld and why you felt you needed to until now — using "I" statements as much as possible. Let the person know that you genuinely apologize for taking as long as you did to trust yourself to tell him or her without it backfiring on both of you.

> *Love Story* had it wrong; authentically apologizing is one of the healthiest things you can do for your relationship.

We often do not share information with a loved one because we do not have the competence and confidence that we can do so in a way that will strengthen our relationship. By letting your partner know up front, as you frame the conversation, that you want to —

- share more openly and freely with him or her,

- deepen your trust and intimacy,

- create room for even more sharing on both sides, and

- open his or her heart to hear you and receive what you have to share as an invitation, not as a slap in the face.

If there is a fear of repercussions as a result of withholding, do what you can to mitigate the situation by making amends. Let your partner know what you will do differently in the future, and also how you want to make it up to him or her now and going forward. Be open to hearing your partner's feelings around all of this, and use this as an opportunity to get to know him or her even better. Find out the answers to the following questions:

- What is it about this that upsets your partner the most?

- What is it that he or she doesn't ever want to have happen again?

- What is it that he or she needs from you going forward?

If you find it too daunting to consider opening this conversation, yet you know how important it is to do so, you may want to consider hiring a trained coach to facilitate. Coaching is also a vital resource if you do initiate the conversation and it does not go well.

7. Communication about Funeral Planning

Let's start out this section by stating the obvious: No one wants to talk with their parents about their parents' funeral arrangements. Even though it is an important topic that they might be worried about and thinking about, they do not want to come across in any way as seeming to be looking forward to that day! With most blended families, there are some truly loaded scenarios to be addressed including the location, and who will be included.

When speaking with loved ones about what you want to have happen at this particularly emotional time — when you won't be around to see it happen — there could be lots of emotion in the anticipation of your funeral. Prepare yourself in advance by rereading this chapter's section **3.3** (seeking to understand). This will aid you in being able to listen to your loved ones as they express their worries, concerns, and questions about this aspect of your planning.

Being able to give them the space to cry, be angry, and withdraw as you listen to and love them will allow their hearts to open to new ways of seeing themselves with other family members that they may not want anything to do with now. Knowing how important it is to you that they make an effort can go a long way towards shifting things, especially if they see that you are taking the time to truly understand their perspective and why it is so hard for them to consider it to begin with. Staying open to future conversations about this with them will also help as it will give them time to digest what has been expressed and to see what else might be underneath their concerns.

8. Putting Children and Stepchildren in Key Roles

In some instances, a stepparent may want to put one of his or her stepchildren in the role of executor or trustee, seeing the stepchild as a better choice than one of his or her own children. In instances such as this, we strongly recommend spelling out very clearly why you made this decision. While it may be obvious to the stepparent, it may come as a surprise and be accompanied by a great deal of hurt by children who would have wanted to be in that role. Clearly stating requirements that the stepchild meets, which none of the birth children have attained, helps to take care of potentially hurt feelings.

We recommend that if this situation is one you are considering, that you speak with the stepchild first to see if he or she is willing to take on the role before telling your offspring. If the stepchild accepts, we strongly encourage you to speak with each of your children and let them know how you came to this decision and how you would prefer they work with their stepsibling. Make sure you listen to all of the objections and concerns of your birth children. Use the strategies in this chapter to see where your children can come into alignment with your idea.

Another tactic some parents take in this situation is to come up with other roles within the estate plan, and to develop milestones for those roles in a way that allows opportunities for every child to have a role, if they so choose. This can be a way to encourage them to step up and take on more responsibility in their lives — knowing that there are roles that they can step into if they are adequately skilled and trained.

9. Taking Care of Your Spouse after You Pass May Take Away from the Children's Inheritance

What do you do when taking care of each other takes away from the inheritance of children from prior relationships? The crux of the concern here is that for the surviving partner to be able to continue to live in his or her current lifestyle, the predeceasing partner's children will inherit less than they would if that partner received a certain share equal to what they receive at the time of the predeceased partner's death. This is the place where the couples we work with tend to get the most perplexed when it comes to finalizing their estate plans.

Partners usually agree that they want their surviving partner to continue to live a long, healthy life in the lifestyle and at the home that they currently are in at the time of the planning. Where they differ is in how to assure that the predeceased partner's children will receive the inheritance that their parent wants them to have, since there can be no assurances once the surviving partner receives the bulk of the estate; it is the surviving partner's to do with as he or she wants and chooses.

Thankfully there are a number of options that couples can choose to take care of all of these concerns, and structures can be put in place so that the surviving children receive some inheritance at the time of their parent's death, and the surviving partner continues to benefit from the estate while the children receive the rest at the time of the surviving partner's death.

The key to conversations of this nature is to seek to understand and let go of being right about how it is supposed to look — to allow for how it *could* look. See what creative options the two of you can come up with. If you get stuck in gridlock, investing some time and attention on this particular facet of your estate plan with the assistance of a trained coach or consultant will do wonders to make the rest of your planning go smoothly.

10. Discussion about Separate Representation When Creating Your Estate Plan

Now, take a deep breath as we tackle one of the most delicate and important topics in this book for you to seriously consider: when the need for separate representation is indicated. We will reiterate in Chapter 7 the particular facets of blended family systems that tend to call for separate representation when doing your estate planning:

- Where one of you is childless but the other has children; you are not in similar circumstances.

- Where there is a significant disparity in wealth or income between you and your partner.

- Where one of you is economically dependent on the other.

- Where one of you does all of the talking or appears to exert strong influence over the other.

- Length of the relationship. Generally speaking, the shorter the relationship, the stronger the suggestion of separate representation.

- The number of past relationships one or both of you has had. Generally speaking, the greater the number of past relationships, the stronger the suggestion of separate representation.

We ask that you take time now to honestly appraise each of these scenarios and determine where you are on the spectrum. Do you have a yes to more than one of the bullet points? Are they all a yes? Does one of you see that some of these are valid, real concerns, while the other does not? Use the strategies discussed earlier to have an open conversation exploring how each of you sees these.

This is where not taking it personally is critical. This is about connecting and seeing how each other views things — granting as valid each of your perspectives, even if you don't experience it the same way.

Some of this may bring up shame or embarrassment. This is when slowing things down and breathing in and out a few times can be very helpful. If you find that old hurts, fears, and doubts start coming up and out, you may want to stop for now and seek professional support to continue the conversation in a way that will bring you closer and unite you even as you consider using separate representation.

CHAPTER 3

Basic Estate Planning Considerations

Estate planning is a *process*, not an event, so you should always seek professional guidance when doing it. Paul has had to fix way too many "do-it-yourself" estate plans that actually cost more to fix than they would have to create from scratch. Even though you should get professional help, you and you alone must be in charge of the estate-planning process. This will require some work on your part, principally in reading documents and asking questions. Our intention in writing this book is to empower you to feel competent and able to take charge and be the director of your estate-planning process.

If you are intimidated by legalese or by estate planners, you can stay in control of the estate-planning process by knowing what you want to accomplish and by requiring your estate planner to explain it to you to your satisfaction. If your estate planner either can't or won't explain your estate plan to your satisfaction, then it is time to hire another estate planner.

The best estate plans that Paul was ever associated with involved hands-on clients who took an active role in the creation of their estate plan and who remained in control of the estate-planning process. Paul was always bothered by hands-off clients who basically abdicated their estate plans to him. Remember that the estate plan is *yours*, and not anyone else's.

> **For a successful estate plan you need to be engaged and in control.**

1. Your Estate-Planning Goals

The first step in the estate-planning process is to identify what you want to do — your estate planning goals. This step often befuddles people, and they almost always ask: What do other people in our situation do? It isn't that easy. Every family is different, especially blended families.

In order to help you along, we've included a list of possible estate-planning goals for you to consider, many in the context of a blended family. These potential goals are not in any particular order. Many of these goals can conflict with one another. You won't have all of these goals either. The following sections are intended to give you some idea of possible goals and concerns so that you can consider all of the possibilities. You may even have a goal that is not discussed here.

1.1 Retain control over assets and business decisions

First and foremost, most people want to retain control over their lives and their property as long as they possibly can, and decide who will be in control when they're no longer capable or no longer want to do so. The goal of control is a particularly important one in estate planning for the blended family because there are people whose interests can be divergent (e.g., children from a prior marriage and a current partner) and who are (or who seem to be) vying for that job. Therefore, a carefully thought out durable power of attorney, provisions for backup trustees for those who use revocable living trusts, and advanced health-care directives are a must, and even more so in the blended family. Details about these aspects of your estate planning will be covered in Chapter 6.

If you own a business, you may want to pay very close attention to your corporate documents to see what they provide regarding succession in office. Have the documents reviewed and coordinated with your estate plan. Failure to coordinate business documents with estate-planning documents can ruin or negatively affect the estate plan. For example, if you are being paid a salary by your own company and you get disabled, will your salary continue to be paid, and, if so, for how long? Who will make that determination? Who will succeed you in your office in your own company if you are unable to serve? Will it be a child of yours, who may be adverse to his or her stepparent? Can the new person in charge fire someone in your family, such as a child? These and others are all very critical questions to which you need to know the answers prior to disability or death.

1.2 Provide support for children and the surviving partner

Providing support for children and the surviving partner is not as easy to achieve in a blended family for many reasons, not the least of which are possible conflicts between children, stepchildren, and the surviving partner. Many people have a goal of wanting to provide support either for a period of time or through an endeavor such as the education of a minor child. The goal of providing support to someone in a blended family can conflict with other estate-planning goals, such as giving your children an inheritance. For instance, you might want to provide lifetime support to your partner (who may be depending on it), even if it means that your own children must take a backseat and possibly get nothing from you. There are no easy answers here. That's why you've really got to give this one some serious thought.

Sometimes, there are conflicts between older children, for whom you provided an education, and younger children, whose education may not have even started yet. This is often compounded in the blended family situation because the younger children might be with your current partner, whereas your older children may be from a prior relationship. You may feel obligated to support your child of another union even though your partner might also need (and expect) support. This situation would clearly be a conflict. However, do not allow these potential or actual conflicts to cause you to stop or procrastinate on your estate planning; remember, intestacy or an incomplete estate plan is far worse.

> Don't let conflict keep you from acting; use the communication strategies in Chapter 2 to help you resolve your differences.

1.3 Protect loved ones from predators and themselves

Loved ones who are young or vulnerable may need protection to ensure that their inheritance stays intact and is not reached by creditors or those who would unduly influence them and rob them of their money. In addition, with the high divorce rate, spendthrift trusts (a clause added to a trust that is intended to protect the beneficiaries from their creditors) may help otherwise capable loved ones from the ravages of a divorcing spouse even if they may not otherwise require trust protection.

In a blended family, this goal could be even more important because of the polarization that frequently occurs in these families after the death of a parent/partner. Some children are too young or immature to handle responsibility or money. There may also be a child who has special needs so management of that child's property is required. Other instances that suggest the possible need for financial management via a trust are when a child has a drug or alcohol addiction or financial problems.

1.4 Keep certain property in the family

Some families own property that has been in the family for a long time, and others own family businesses that they wish to keep in the family. This requires special planning and can involve buy-sell agreements (discussed in Chapter 5) or co-tenancy arrangements, the latter of which can provide a method of sharing property use, revenues, and expenses.

Some estate-planning goals may have to be changed to keep property in the family as opposed to it being sold. This is particularly true when estate or capital gains tax will be owed. In the context of a blended family, this type of property, more often than not, consists of antiques or heirlooms that have been in a family for a long while. We've seen lots of problems and litigation over family heirlooms and family pictures, especially in blended families. Sometimes, it is more important in a blended family to specifically provide who will receive the "emotional assets" (e.g., grandma's silver) — which often have more sentimental value than actual value — than it is to provide for the financial assets. People do fight each other in court over very little, and this is much more common in blended families. Chapter 4 goes into detail about what to consider and how to go about specifying what you want to have happen with such possessions.

1.5 Protect your assets from creditors, lawsuits, and undue influence

Many people don't consider asset protection to be an estate-planning goal, and a discussion of asset protection is beyond the scope of this book. However, the litigious nature of our society today demands that we consider insuring against many of the risks of life. Life insurance is important, as is property and casualty insurance, including umbrella coverage. You should consider insuring against insurable losses (there is no such thing as lawsuit insurance) by using corporations or limited liability companies, or, in some cases, trusts.

In blended families, the risk of undue influence, most notably from the other parent of the stepchildren involved, is even greater than in other families, and trusts can protect you against changes by others in favor of themselves late in life that you would have never done on your own.

1.6 Avoid probate

This may or may not be a goal, depending on where you reside. The probate process in most jurisdictions is generally streamlined and easy, but there are jurisdictions, such as California, where probate is costly and complex. In fact, in the context of a blended family, we frequently recommend that a client make sure that his or her estate would go through probate because of the supervision that a judge would give. We know that this seems like radical advice, but it is not. There are lots of situations that require oversight by someone, and we prefer that person be a judge rather than an interested family member who may not have the other member's best interests at heart.

> Do your research and find out the pros and cons of probate in your particular jurisdiction.

1.7 Maintain flexibility

In other words, one goal is to be certain your estate plan is flexible enough to work in changed circumstances, such as changes to tax laws or even family changes. Frankly, we really don't know what the future will bring. For example, will there be a federal estate tax in the United States in the future?

Sometimes, our desire to retain flexibility outweighs all other estate-planning considerations, particularly in the area of lifetime gifting, which often makes sense in estate planning. Good estate-planning documents build in as much flexibility as possible to anticipate reasonably foreseeable events. In a blended family situation, perhaps the couple is planning on having children of their own, which may prime other goals. The use of a trust protector can be very beneficial, and we'll briefly discuss this concept in Chapters 6 and 8.

1.8 Retain access to capital

This is no doubt one of the most important goals for clients that unfortunately many estate planners neglect to consider — estate planners often overfocus on estate-tax reduction. Gifting in *any* form, whether outright or in trust, causes the loss of access to the capital represented by the gifted property. Many people cannot really afford to part with access to capital, even though they may have a taxable estate. If retaining access to your capital is one of your goals, make sure that your estate planner knows that at the beginning. This will save time, narrow your options, and usually saves you money.

1.9 Make lifetime gifts

Another goal may be that you want to enjoy the satisfaction of seeing family members and others enjoy gifts during your lifetime. The bad thing about transfers at death is that the giver is not around to see the receiver enjoy the property. Some people like to see that and make significant gifts during their lifetimes. In blended families, the desire to make lifetime gifts can cause conflict because someone (e.g., your partner or one of your children, to whom a gift was not made) may be very unhappy that a gift was made for fear that this might work to his or her detriment.

1.10 Transfer future appreciation

Maybe you have property that is expected to appreciate in value, and you'd like to get that property out of your estate before it appreciates. This is an estate-planning goal for some. There are some very effective estate-planning techniques that can accomplish this, such as US Grantor Retained Annuity Trusts (GRATs) or installment sales; both are discussed in Chapter 9.

> In a technique called a sale to an intentionally defective grantor trust, a parent can sell property to an irrevocable trust in exchange for a promissory note that calls for installment payments.

1.11 Transfer an opportunity

Opportunities for wealth, such as an idea for a new business or a piece of property, often present themselves to us. For some, they would like to transfer that opportunity to a loved one before the opportunity is taken, which keeps the value out of their estate and they never have to estate plan with that asset.

1.12 Move property to grandchildren or more remote descendants

Some clients believe that their children are well-provided for, so they are more concerned with benefiting their grandchildren. Some like to make significant transfers to grandchildren or great-grandchildren. In blended families, this is definitely an area to discuss and consider how you want to plan, as you may have different grandchildren with different needs from each of your prior relationships.

1.13 Defer estate or income tax

Most clients' goals are to defer estate tax or income tax for as long as possible. This often makes no sense when it comes to the estate tax, but many people like to do so anyway because they lack the liquid cash to pay estate tax at the first partner's death. Deferring estate tax can *increase* the amount of estate tax due when the second partner dies when the US estate tax has graduated tax rates, which, absent a law change, will not be the case again until 2013. However, many people see this as the problem for their surviving loved ones.

Income tax deferral usually makes sense unless you are deferring income into periods where the tax rate will be higher. Income tax deferral most often comes into play in the setting of beneficiary designations and distribution options for retirement plans and Individual Retirement Accounts (IRAs). There are ways to stretch out receipt of benefits from retirement plans and IRAs to maximize the income tax deferral.

1.14 Avoid estate tax

Needless to say, a goal of most of our clients is to avoid as much estate tax as possible. In the US, the tax law provides very few breaks from the estate tax. One of those breaks, though, is the special use valuation break. However, this is a very complex provision and only applies to estates that have a heavy concentration of certain types of real estate (e.g., farms and closely held business property). Sometimes, it makes sense to plan to retain that benefit by continuing that use, as opposed to doing something else with the property, such as selling or leasing it.

There is also a break that can be found by paying estate tax in installments (it usually is due nine months after death). This break only applies to estates that have a heavy concentration of closely held business interests or real estate. Often, people lack the cash to pay their estate tax if they died today. Sometimes, it makes sense to plan your estate so that you retain the eligibility to pay the estate tax in installments. Of course, when the federal estate tax exclusion is high (i.e., in the US in 2012 it was $5,120,000), very few people have to worry about the US federal estate tax.

At this time, there is no Canadian nationwide inheritance or estate tax, although there is a tax on deemed capital gains at death in Canada.

1.15 Avoid gift tax

For clients who wish to make lifetime gifts, one goal is generally to pay as little gift tax as possible while making the greatest amount of gifts. The United States gift tax contains several handy breaks that the federal estate tax does not have. One of them is the exclusion for gifts of up to $13,000 (in 2011) to an unlimited number of people, who don't even have to be related to you. Another is the unlimited exclusion for transfers made directly to health-care providers or schools for someone else; this allows grandparents to pay for their grandchildren's tuition. It often makes sense for people to use these breaks.

There are some other breaks too. The big one though, is the US $5,120,000 exclusion for gifts made during 2012 (under current law, the exclusion is supposed to revert back to $1,000,000, but it will be indexed for inflation since 2001 in 2013; stay tuned for possible additional changes). You can use this exclusion during your lifetime or at death. There are possibly more benefits to using it during your lifetime if you can afford it. The biggest advantage to lifetime use is that all of the income and growth in value of the gifted property is out of your estate. This is also the downside: You no longer have that property in case you need it later in life.

1.16 Maximize usage of US estate tax exclusions

It always makes sense to fully use the lifetime gift exclusion (for people who die in 2012 — under current law, it will revert to $1,000,000 in 2013, but it will be indexed for inflation since 2001), which can be used either during your lifetime or at death. Use of this exclusion usually is a goal for most people once they are aware that it can keep their estates from being subject to the estate tax. You can learn more about gift exclusions in the US in Chapter 9.

1.17 Donate to favorite charities

Some people have an estate-planning goal to make significant transfers to their favorite charities. There are estate-planning techniques such as charitable gift annuities and charitable remainder trusts that assist in facilitating charitable pursuits (discussed in Chapter 9).

1.18 Achieve tax predictability or finality

If you are risk averse, it is important to discuss tax predictability and finality with your estate planner at the outset. Some estate-planning techniques are riskier than others. Some people are very risk averse. These people are not interested in estate-planning techniques that create any form of risk of running afoul of the taxman. This is similar to a risk assessment that you would do for investments. It is important at the beginning of the estate-planning process to tell your estate planner your risk sensitivity. Of course, some people want the most aggressive estate plan they can get, and these are also available.

1.19 Provide tax-deferred diversification

The estates of many people hold a significant part of their value in one or two assets (e.g., a family home or business). This is an undiversified estate, which is much riskier than a diversified estate because in the undiversified estate, all of the estate's money is invested in only one investment. As the lesson in an Aesop's Fable says, it is dangerous to put all of one's eggs in one basket.

At some point in their lives, some people want to reduce their risk of nondiversification. The major obstacle for those who desire this is the capital gains tax. There are estate-planning techniques, such as the charitable remainder trust, that permit diversification of assets without having to pay the capital gains tax up front. In other words, you can keep a significant part of the tax working for you.

1.20 Provide guidance and management for your children

A major goal of estate planning for many is to set up a system to protect loved ones from themselves when they are young or financially challenged. Or give them a soft landing by doling out the money in smaller portions. Trusts and some other estate-planning techniques can do a very good job of this. For example, instead of a child receiving all of his or her inheritance at once, a trust can be set up to pay out the inheritance in stages.

1.21 Encourage or discourage certain behaviors

Many clients do not wish to reward their children for relying on a possible inheritance, for not obtaining honest work, or for engaging in unsavory or illegal activity. State and provincial laws (which vary from state to state and province to province) permit people to give additional money or income to their loved ones for engaging in certain types of productive behavior, such as working in a socially useful but undercompensated field like law enforcement or the not-for-profit sector.

State and provincial law, within limits, also may permit delaying or withholding an inheritance to discourage certain types of behavior, such as not working, marrying outside of the family faith (although this one often doesn't work), or substance abuse. This doesn't matter to most people, but to those to whom it matters, it seems to matter a lot.

Paul has mixed feelings about these clauses and he usually counsels against their use because, in his opinion, they are inflexible and there are much better alternatives to achieve the same result. However, Emily has worked with blended families who come up with the standards for inheritance *as a family* so that there is buy-in from all those concerned and the family gets to promote their values in how they delineate the terms for beneficiaries. Families with a strong concern around entitlement issues find this process to be very helpful and they enjoy having their values tied into their estate plan.

1.22 Level the playing field

In many families, beneficiaries will have extremely different needs, so many clients wish to provide appropriately for those beneficiaries while not excluding the others. Estate plans should identify those who could be vulnerable after the death of a parent or partner and take some steps to anticipate and minimize this vulnerability to the extent consistent with their overall estate-planning goals.

Leveling the playing field can be crucial in a blended family. For example, a dad decides that his second wife will have voting control over a family business by virtue of being trustee. Dad's eldest son from his first marriage, who works in the business, is then subject to the decision-making and potential whims of his stepmother and could even be fired from his job with the family company. Paul has seen this happen. There are ways to ensure that this either doesn't happen or is made so difficult or costly that it is unlikely. Sometimes, if it is decided that a bank or other institutional trustee will be used, giving the trust beneficiaries or a trust protector the power to change institutional trustees could make a trustee more responsive to his or her needs. You can read more about trusts related to this concern in Chapter 10.

1.23 Provide a mechanism for resolution of disputes

Even among family members who get along during life, disputes may, and generally do, arise after the death of a parent. Providing a mechanism for resolution of disputes can be critical in estates in which a fight is possible or even expected. A system for either arbitrating or mediating disputes should always be considered in estate-planning documents for a blended family because court fights in blended families are far more likely than in other families.

1.24 Keep certain assets away from certain people

Some clients know that certain beneficiaries would not handle the inheritance of a particular asset well, such as an interest in a business. Some people would never want to see certain assets subject to the control of a former spouse. This is a very common estate-planning goal in blended families. People often shudder to think that their property could come into the hands or under the control of a former spouse and they are relieved when they learn about ways to keep that from happening.

If you are one of the fortunate few who has a good relationship with a former spouse or partner, you can always name the person in your estate plan if you choose to give him or her something. It's completely up to you.

2. Your Estate-Planning Concerns

After you have evaluated and chosen your estate-planning desires, it is time to consider possible risks and concerns in estate planning. In blended families, these concerns can be daunting.

2.1 Choosing between a partner and the children

Often, choosing between a partner and the children is the greatest concern in estate planning for blended families. Who should receive what and at what time? Trying to balance the interests of the children getting an inheritance and a partner being supported after your death usually is a matter of the size of your estate. If your estate is large, it may be possible to do both. However, if your estate is modest, you may well have to choose. Our best advice is, once you have decided how you want your estate plan to look, take time to explain your actions to all parties so that no one is surprised after your death.

Emily witnessed one instance where a couple agonized over how to divvy up their estate given that the second wife was significantly younger than her husband and would most likely survive him. He wanted all four of his children to receive an equal amount of his estate, and she wanted more to go to her two children with him. After they came to a strategy that made sense to them and honored both of their concerns, they shared their decision with all four of their children at the same time. The children varied in age by almost 20 years, with the two from his first marriage being 18 and 15 years older than the younger two. When the children learned of the estate plan, they felt honored and were relieved that they knew what to expect so that they could adequately plan for their own estate planning and needs.

What came to light as a result of that facilitated conversation is that the older two did not anticipate seeing any inheritance until well into their 70s, as they hoped their stepmother would live a long and productive life, and they expressed that they understood that they would have to plan for their retirements and their children's college educations without counting on anything from this set of parents. The parents had not considered this and began to look at ways to adjust their estate plan to possibly allow for some gifts to occur towards their grandchildren's education with the hope that it could happen during both of their lifetimes and that they could see the results of their gift-giving. They worked with Emily and their advisors in crafting a giving plan, that also took into consideration the long-term needs of the second wife who was going to live on the income of the estate should her husband predecease her.

2.2 Plan for the payment and apportionment of estate taxes

If your estate is taxable (due to changes in tax laws, your estate may not be taxable today but it may be tomorrow), how will the taxes be paid, and from which beneficiary's share will they be paid? Very few estates have to worry about paying the federal estate tax. However, for those who do have to pay, the federal estate tax presents a huge area for concern because of the amount of the tax and the speed at which it is due.

Some people whose estates will owe estate tax choose not to worry about it and leave the problem to their loved ones. After all, they reason that they'll be dead and gone anyway.

However, others realize that failure to minimize the estate tax could cause the sale of a family farm or business that they worked for years to build. These people are much more likely to make estate-tax reduction and funding a high priority. This is something that you should discuss with your estate-planning advisor because most just assume that everyone wants to reduce estate tax to the lowest possible amount, which isn't always true. In blended families, having the estate tax on the share of one heir payable out of the share of another heir negatively impacts one side over the other, which increases the likelihood of litigation.

2.3 Dealing with problem children

Should you leave assets outright to a child who has problems handling money or who has a problem partner or a drug or alcohol problem? Some people consider their children whose plans have not panned out in life to be problems. This usually means that a trust (which seems to really mean "don't trust") will be helpful to that child.

> **Problematic behaviors do not define a child as a problem. Address the behavior, not the person.**

2.4 Protecting young or disabled children

How can you make sure that the new baby's inheritance is not totally used up by higher education, which is the inheritance older beneficiaries are enjoying earlier? Also, how can you provide funds to support a disabled child without the child losing federal, state, or provincial disability benefits? These raise distinct and separate concerns. Perhaps a healthy youngster needs to be educated. However, a disabled child may need support and property management for the rest of his or her lifetime.

2.5 Caring for elderly parents

What if your parents outlive their own retirement savings? Suppose one or both of your parents survive you. Do you take care of their financial needs in your estate plan? Can you afford to take care of their financial needs? Elderly parents can present a serious impact both on your lifestyle and your estate planning.

3. Prioritize and Communicate

Once you have identified your estate-planning goals and concerns, it is time to prioritize them, from the ones that you are most interested in to the ones that you are least interested in by using Checklist 1: Identifying Your Goals and Concerns. (This checklist is also included on the CD.) Communication of these goals and concerns to your estate planner is essential because, otherwise, your estate plan might not achieve what you want.

Estate planning can be very complicated, but it doesn't have to be. If you properly consider your goals and concerns and communicate them to your estate planner, and then make sure that your estate plan does what you want, the outcome will be much better.

4. Action Step

Now that you've read through a number of possible topics that your estate plan can address, it's time to take action and determine your priorities and what matters to you. Complete Checklist 1 while referring to this chapter and see which sections speak to you and really touch on what you care about the most. This is a great exercise to do separately and then you and your partner share your results with each other afterwards. You will learn more about each other and your concerns as they relate to the estate plan. Once you have a clear picture of what you each want to accomplish, you can read the rest of the book with a sense of purpose around *how* to best achieve your goals.

Checklist 1
Identifying Your Goals and Concerns

You can use this form to rate your goals and concerns. You can give this form to your estate planners so that they know what is most important to you. Rate these goals on a scale of 1 to 5, with 1 meaning "most important" and 5 meaning "not important."

Potential Estate-Planning Goals

_____ Retaining control
_____ Providing support
_____ Protecting assets
_____ Flexibility
_____ Retaining access to capital
_____ Transferring future appreciation
_____ Transferring of opportunity
_____ Skipping a generation
_____ Deferring estate and income taxes
_____ Qualifying for tax benefits
_____ Using gift-tax exemptions and exclusions
_____ Maximizing usage of estate-tax exclusions
_____ Facilitating charitable desires
_____ Tax predictability or finality
_____ Providing tax-deferred diversification
_____ Providing guidance and management
_____ Encouraging or discouraging behavior
_____ Leveling the playing field between those in control and those not in control
_____ Providing a mechanism for resolution of disputes
_____ Other (identify a goal not listed here): _____
_____

Potential Concerns and Risks

_____ Choosing between your partner and the children
_____ Estate taxes
_____ Problem children
_____ Disabled children
_____ Elderly parents
_____ Risk of loss of control
_____ Risk of loss of access to capital
_____ Risk of doing nothing
_____ Risk of loss of flexibility
_____ Other (identify a concern not listed here): _____
_____

CHAPTER 4

Property Ownership: Means and Issues

This chapter introduces the different ways that people own property, either separately or together, as well as the various agreements that blended couples may enter into with respect to their property.

1. Marriage Contracts and Property Agreements

Partners in blended families often enter into marriage contracts (also called prenuptial agreements) prior to getting married, although these can be entered into after the wedding too (postnuptial agreements) if applicable state or provincial law permits. Additionally, unmarried partners often enter into property agreements that have many of the same provisions as marriage contracts. These agreements are usually signed and in place prior to a legal marriage. They are initiated for a variety of reasons and are about specifically determining who owns what going into the partnership. At times, these agreements are required based on prior estate planning on the part of one of the partner's parents or grandparents.

Marriage contracts and property agreements often deal with the following issues:

- Classification of property owned coming into the partnership (e.g., community, jointly owned, or separate).

- Division of property on divorce or separation.

- Whether property acquired during the marriage or relationship is to be considered community property, jointly owned property, or separate property.

- Designation, ownership, and/or use of the residences that the partners own.

- Responsibility for separate debts.

- Distribution of property on death, including placement of restrictions on changing the estate plan after death of one of the partners.

- Alimony or support in the event of divorce or separation.

- Financial responsibilities in the partnership, and division of household financial responsibilities.

- Applicable state or provincial law for interpretation or enforcement of the marriage contract or property agreement.

- Whether alternate dispute resolution measures such as mediation or arbitration are to be used.

- Whether the marriage contract or property agreement will terminate after a specified number of years of marriage or relationship.

- Waiver of the spousal election (if married).

It is imperative that your estate planner review your marriage contract or property agreement as it may limit your flexibility in your estate planning. You also may need to give your estate planner copies of all agreements that you have with former partners, as these agreements also may impact your estate planning. Many partners owe obligations to former partners. These obligations may impose requirements such as alimony or support, child support, or maintaining life or health insurance. These obligations can also impose restrictions on your estate planning, such as restricting testamentary freedom requiring legacies to certain

persons such as children of a prior union. It is very important that your estate plan be coordinated and consistent with your marriage contract and property agreement.

1.1 Agreement issues

If you and your partner have a prenuptial or property agreement, chances are there were some emotionally charged conversations that occurred prior to the documents being signed. In most cases, the less wealthy partner didn't want to sign a prenuptial agreement or a property agreement because for him or her it reflected a lack of commitment, love, and trust from the wealthier partner. In reality, it is the estate-planning professionals who are the ones who typically encourage the use of these agreements, because they are practical, safe, and sound business practices. It is their duty, as advisors, to do what they can to protect their clients from loss of property or other assets by anticipating possible breakdowns in the future. Given that in blended families the likelihood of splitting is greater than the chances of remaining together for life, the advisors are supposed to take care of that possible outcome as best they can. One thing we try to get partners who are considering these agreements to see is that if the roles were reversed, the other partner would be advised to do the same thing.

Without thoughtful communication and respecting each other's concerns in the course of signing these documents, there can be underlying hurt and resentment. This will be even more the case if there are no stipulations for financially honoring the relationship over time, as this pain can lead to litigation. More often than not, we see that these types of agreements are frequently challenged after a couple splits. The typical allegations that are made are that the wealthier partner misrepresented his or her wealth, or that one of the partners unduly influenced the other partner to sign the agreement. The closer to the wedding date that a prenuptial agreement is signed, the greater the likelihood of a successful challenge to the agreement. The same is true if the partners are represented by the same lawyer. This is why a careful estate planner should evaluate the likelihood of challenge to a prenuptial agreement and he or she will inquire as to the circumstances at the time of execution of the agreement, which is important given the higher probability of divorce in blended family marriages, according to the US Census Bureau.

1.2   Postnuptial agreements

A postnuptial agreement is an agreement that married partners enter into after they are married. The agreement contains the same types of provisions as prenuptial and property agreements. However, postnuptial agreements often deal with qualified retirement plan benefits. This is because a prospective spouse can't waive his or her interests in a qualified retirement plan (i.e., pension plan or 401(k)) until after he or she is married. Spousal waiver of right to be the life beneficiary of a qualified retirement plan would permit the plan participant to make any person, such as his or her children, the beneficiary of the plan benefits. This rule is not applicable to Individual Retirement Accounts (IRAs), so it is fairly common for a prospective spouse in a blended family to roll out of a qualified retirement plan into an IRA to permit freedom with the benefits.

2.   Co-ownership Issues

It is not unusual for partners to co-own property prior to marriage. That property might have been acquired during a marriage or brought into a marriage where the union began in an unmarried condition. This property often includes real estate and other investments such as stocks.

Jointly owned property can be owned as *tenants in common* or as *joint tenants with rights of survivorship*. Jointly owned property is frequently acquired as joint tenants with rights of survivorship. The estate planner must review account titles and real estate deeds in order to determine whether a survivorship condition is present.

In Paul's opinion, couples in a blended family relationship should not own *any* property with rights of survivorship because the property will pass to the surviving partner (i.e., surviving joint tenant) on the death of the first partner (i.e., first joint tenant). This result will bypass the children of the first joint tenant to die, which usually is against the true intentions of that parent.

If the property is retitled as tenants in common, the surviving partner will co-own the property with the deceased partner's estate. If the surviving partner desires and can afford it, the partners agree that the survivor between them be given an option to purchase the deceased partner's interest in the property, or he or she could be given a right to lease the property on favorable terms. The partners could also agree that the survivor between them would get to use the property for free for a period of time, such as two years.

3.   Community Property

At the time of writing, nine states in the United States have community property laws. These states are Arizona, California, Idaho, Louisiana, Nevada, New Mexico, Texas, Washington, and Wisconsin. Additionally, Alaska has an opt-in community property regime, meaning that you can have a community property regime if you want one. In Canada, only the province of Quebec has community property. Nevertheless, community property laws do differ from jurisdiction to jurisdiction. In other words, the community property laws in California differ from those in Arizona.

As a general rule, unless they agree otherwise, property that a married couple acquires during a marriage from wages that either earns is considered to be owned 50-50 by them as community property. It doesn't matter in whose name that property is acquired. Property brought into a marriage and property gifted or bequeathed to a spouse is separate property. Generally, each spouse can pass off his or her half of the community property at death. However, a few community property states such as Texas and California have introduced a survivorship feature into the community property mix, so it is important that your estate planner review your community property titles as well.

It is not unusual for blended family couples to have community property regimes with respect to property acquired during their marriage and have separate property that each brought into the marriage or inherit during the marriage. People do move periodically to another state, whether it is to a community property jurisdiction or out of one. It is imperative that you give a relocation history of your moves to your estate planner so that he or she can check to see if there is community property in your estate. Use the Relocation History form, provided on the accompanying CD, to make this task simple and straightforward for you and your advisor.

Community property has benefits for US income and estate tax purposes that co-owned separate property in noncommunity property states do not have: The ability to get a new tax basis equal to the then fair-market value for the entirety of the property at the death of the spouse who is first to die. Contrast this with co-owned separate property in a noncommunity property state, where only the deceased spouse's interest gets the new basis. Consider the following example:

Bill and Mary live in a community property state, and Bob and Alice live in a noncommunity property state. Each buys a home for $100,000 in 1978. In 2011, each home is worth $1,500,000. In 2011, Bill and Bob both die. Mary's new tax basis in the home is $1,500,000, while Alice's tax basis will be $800,000 (Bob's new basis of $750,000 — one-half of $1,500,000 — plus her original basis of $50,000). If each widow decides to downsize in 2011 and sells her home for $1,500,000, Mary will have no capital gains tax to pay, but Alice will not be so lucky. She'll probably have to pay capital gains tax on a part of the gain on the sale of the home.

4. Separate Property and the Perils of Commingling Property

Property that is neither community property nor jointly owned property is considered separate property. The difference between separate and community property is that generally one spouse is not able to make substantial gifts of community property without the consent of the other spouse. In blended families, most couples come into the marriage with each person owning their own separate property. It is easy to spell out the separate nature of the property in a prenuptial or postnuptial agreement, and this can bring clarity going forward with your estate-planning goals.

For the sake of ease and freedom of decision making with each other's personal property, we recommend that blended family couples who marry have either a marriage contract or property agreement. We further recommend that a marriage contract expressly state that both partners agree that each is totally free to do whatever estate planning he or she wants to do without any need for input or consent by the other partner. Of course, this does not preclude communicating with each other and giving each other feedback and input. It is a way to honor that each of you has your own property and that you have the ultimate say on how it will be distributed. If property is neither jointly owned nor community property, it is your separate property.

What follows is probably the most valuable advice in this book, so pay close attention. Keep your separate property *separate*. Do *not* commingle your accounts or keep "informal" track of things.

> **If you do nothing else, you would be wise to keep your property separate and avoid commingling.**

While we're well aware that the vast majority of you have already commingled property and will continue to do so, we feel it is our duty to inform you of what you are potentially putting at risk as a result. For example, Jack has two sons from a prior marriage and Jill has two daughters from a prior relationship. Jack and Jill commingled all of their separate property in the course of their marriage and at the time of Jack's death, Jill's daughters were able to successfully win a battle of classification of property and receive more than Jack had intended, and Jack's sons did not receive the lion's share of Jack's estate that he owned prior to marrying Jill.

If you and your partner have been together for awhile and have commingled your property, see if you can agree on a division of the property between the two of you now and at least identify what property belongs to whom. If this subject is too sensitive, or if the two of you can't reach an agreement, start keeping track going forward and write down what you consider to be your separate property and what you consider to be community or jointly owned property. For techniques on how to navigate this conversation more smoothly, review Chapter 2.

How do these disputes over the classification of property arise? There are usually two ways that this can evolve into a dispute. The first is separation from your partner. If this unfortunate event should arise, at least you would both be present to give your sides of the story, each with supporting proof. The second way that a dispute arises is after the death of a partner. The surviving partner often has the authority to initially say what belonged to the deceased partner if the surviving partner has been named the executor or administrator of the deceased partner's estate.

However, if the surviving partner's stepchildren (i.e., the children of the deceased partner) or the deceased partner's creditors disagree with the surviving partner's determination, they can contest it in court. Because the surviving partner made the initial determination, the court may be skeptical, particularly where the determination favors the surviving partner. That's why it is imperative that you maintain good contemporaneous financial records and keep them. Financial records are usually difficult if not impossible to reconstruct after the fact. Don't make that mistake.

Keeping accurate and correct financial records requires some discipline, but we find that the online record-keeping tools offered by many financial institutions and by bookkeeping programs such as *Quicken* and *QuickBooks* make this task simpler. Don't pay expenses from one account that should be paid from a different account. Take the time to properly classify income and expense sources or pay someone else to do it. The most important thing is that this gets done regularly.

> **Put a note in your calendar for the first of each month to track and reconcile your finances to mitigate painful disputes in the future.**

Another big mistake that many people make is relying on a marriage contract or property agreement alone to dictate the result. Just because you have a separate property agreement doesn't mean that your property is separate — it is up to *you* to keep it separate. If you commingle your property with your partner, it muddies the water as to who owns what and it could look like you weren't both living by the agreement. You can't expect a court to uphold an agreement that the parties themselves didn't follow.

5. Contracts to Make a Will and Joint Will

Contracts to make a will are contracts whereby one party or the other, or both, agree to make a party's separate will in a certain way. A *joint will* is a will that is made by two people that generally can't be changed by the survivor.

Contracts to make a will as well as joint wills are governed by state or provincial law. Some jurisdictions don't permit either contracts to make a will or joint will or restrict their use to married partners, so you will need to check with your estate-planning attorney to see what the law is in your jurisdiction. These agreements may provide for certain provisions to be contained in any will that a partner executes and also sometimes restricts a partner's right to subsequently revoke or amend the will. Sometimes these types of provisions are included in a marriage contract or property agreement.

We see more desires to sign contracts to make a will or joint wills in blended families because the situations are generally more complicated than in single union situations. While we're not particularly big fans of these arrangements because, in our view, they unduly restrict surviving partners from addressing changes in circumstances that arise after the death of a partner, they can be helpful in situations in which a partner will only agree to give his entire estate to the other partner if she agrees to give it to his children after her death (and vice versa).

There are other ways to protect the testamentary intent of the first partner to die, namely, a lifetime trust for the benefit of the other partner as income beneficiary, with the children of the first partner to die being the principal beneficiaries. Using a life estate instead of a trust subjects the property to claims from creditors of the surviving partner after the first partner dies, which you wouldn't want to see happen. A lifetime trust would keep this from happening, and would also take away the need for a contract to make a will.

6. Prior Relationship Obligations and Benefits

It is not unusual for one or both partners in a blended family situation to bring either obligations or benefits from a past relationship into a new union. These might stem from divorce judgments, or they can originate from separate agreements or contracts with former partners. It is imperative that your estate-planning lawyer review all of these documents.

> **As you plan for the future, you must share your obligations from the past with your partner and estate-planning advisors.**

These arrangements may restrict what a partner can do in estate planning. For example, a divorce judgment may require a partner to maintain life insurance for the benefit of a former partner or children from a prior union. These are important details for your current partner to be aware of as you look at your present circumstances and goals and obligations in the future. If you have kept these from your partner out of fear of repercussions, know that sharing with him or her now, in an effective and humble way, will do much to strengthen your relationship going forward. You may have some upset to contend with around lack of trust in not telling your partner sooner, and this may cause him or her to wonder about what else you might be keeping from him or her. This is an opportunity to come clean, to treat your partner with respect, and to show him or her that, as you plan for your deaths, you're ready to take an important step towards greater trust and intimacy in your life together. You can refer to Chapter 2 on communication for some strategies for how to have this conversation effectively.

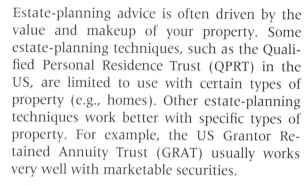

CHAPTER 5

Types of Property

Estate-planning advice is often driven by the value and makeup of your property. Some estate-planning techniques, such as the Qualified Personal Residence Trust (QPRT) in the US, are limited to use with certain types of property (e.g., homes). Other estate-planning techniques work better with specific types of property. For example, the US Grantor Retained Annuity Trust (GRAT) usually works very well with marketable securities.

Analysis of property and debts is probably more important in estate planning for blended families than in estate planning for traditional families. In the typical blended family relationship, the partners tend to bring separate property and debts into the partnership. This can differ quite a bit if the partners are not legally married.

Property can be owned in several different ways. It is imperative that you have it titled correctly and that this be in accordance with your wishes and your estate plan. As a general rule, it is not necessarily wise for blended family couples to have pay-on-death accounts (discussed in section **6.**) or to own property as joint tenants with rights of survivorship (as stated in Chapter 4). Nevertheless, this is what a lot of blended family couples have because they didn't pay close enough attention when they were opening an account or buying a property. Don't make that mistake. If you have already made that mistake, you should correct the title immediately. This is one of the benefits of estate planning: catching and correcting mistakes before it is too late to do so.

1. Family Home

Your house may be much more than just a home to you and the members of your blended family. We address the family home as a specific asset because for many people it represents the most significant property that someone owns. We've also run into many situations where the family home is a huge emotional issue for children of a prior union, especially if they were raised in the home.

There is usually a lot of tension in estate planning around the family home. For example, there could be tension between wanting your partner to live in the home after your death and wanting to limit your partner's ability to live there after taking up with someone else after you are gone. There could also be tension concerning your children's right to inherit the home. The family home should be treated as an asset just like any other piece of property, but it is one with some real emotional ties, especially if your children from a prior union are being raised there or were raised there. It is highly unlikely that if you die before your former spouse or partner, that your children with your former spouse will continue to live there. They will probably live solely with your former spouse and have to relocate and even separate from their half-siblings and stepsiblings, with the emotional changes such as switching schools or moving to a new city.

The issue of ownership of the home or homes that a blended couple lives in is one of the biggest issues in blended family estate planning. There are at least four possibilities:

- The home may be owned by one of the partners alone.

- The couple may jointly own the home.

- The home may be co-owned by one of the partners and that partner's children.

- In some instances, the house may be co-owned by one of the partners and his or her former spouse.

The home situation is further complicated by whether or not the couple or either partner has a child who is living in the home. There is also the issue of whether the owning partner wants his or her partner to continue to live in the home after his or her death. Finally, if the home is an emotional asset for the children of one of the partners, that can also make estate planning for the family home more challenging.

It is not unusual in single-marriage estate planning for the partners to leave their interests in the home to each other so that the surviving partner will solely own the home. However, this is often not what a partner wants in blended family estate planning, although the other partner may well exert pressure on the owning partner to leave the home to the other partner for security and peace of mind.

There may be a situation of one partner lacking the physical or financial ability to maintain ownership and upkeep of the property after his or her partner's death. In this situation, it is important for the financially challenged partner to realize this and to plan in the estate plan for alternative living arrangements after his or her partner's death. There are several ways to deal with the issue of the family home other than for the surviving partner to simply plan to move out after a partner's death. For example, the partners could agree that the surviving partner could stay in the home rent-free for a specified period of time after the partner's death in order to allow for an orderly transition.

2. Living Arrangements and Support

We've seen living arrangements in blended families that run the gamut, from one partner essentially paying for everything to the partners judiciously keeping track of house and living expenses between themselves. Paul has seen division of expenses go so far as phone bills being divided with long-distance calls charged to the calling partner. A prenuptial, postnuptial, or property agreement also frequently provides instructions for living expenses.

It is not unusual for the couple to be living off of the income of one partner. This is a situation that calls for some serious discussion about how the wealthier partner wants his or her partner to live if he or she dies first. Will the lifestyle change? How much income will the wealthier partner want his or her partner to have if he or she dies first? Clearly, your partner will want to retain the same standard of living. However, these are serious questions that must be answered and implemented in the estate plan.

The situation is somewhat exacerbated if the couple is living off of the salary of a partner, which will obviously go away if that partner dies first. How will this income be replaced if the earning partner dies first? How much salary should be replaced? These are all questions that you must answer, and we admit that there aren't any easy answers. Your partner will want to keep living the same lifestyle to which the two of you are accustomed and this is something you may want for him or her as well. The issue that you may encounter is that this desire will be at odds with another desire

to pass some of your estate to your children, because it may have to be at a lesser degree than you would like. There are tools such as life insurance and annuities that can be used to address both of those desires.

You two may find yourselves at odds around conflicting desires in this area, and may feel pressured one way or the other. This becomes particularly challenging (and potentially contentious) if the surviving partner continuing to live his or her current lifestyle means that the predeceasing partner's children get less. This subject needs honest and direct communication between the two of you. If you're up against this one, you can review Chapter 2 on communication strategies, and if you're unable to reach a conclusion that is satisfactory, you may want to seek some coaching prior to visiting your attorney to effectively sort this before preparing documents.

Emily worked with a couple in a blended family situation who would not sign their estate-planning documents because of just such a concern. Together, with the use of money coaching, they were able to sort their differences and come up with a plan they both felt good about. Their advisors were then able to provide them with the necessary structures and tools to carry out their wishes.

> **Don't get bogged down if an issue has you stuck. Speak with a professional who can help you explore all your options and come up with a strategy where all concerns are addressed fairly.**

3. Family Business Issues

Family business issues can confound and complicate any estate planning. However, in blended families, these issues magnify exponentially, especially if the couple is living off of the family business. Suppose one partner owns a closely held business. If the owning partner dies first, the other partner may need to continue to live off of the company after the owning partner dies.

Accordingly, special estate planning that may involve contracts such as buy-sell agreements (discussed in section **3.2**), salary continuation, employment contracts, or other types of agreements will need to be done in order to protect the partner who does not own a share of the business, if that is what you want to do. Issues become even more complicated if you own most, and your partner owns some, and you have children from a prior marriage in the business, and your partner's offspring with you are also interested in working in and owning part of the business. If, for instance, you own most of the business, and any of your children either work in the business or may work in the business in the future, this will impact who you will likely give or sell the business to or put in the role of trustee should you choose to put the business in a trust (which is one estate tax avoidance strategy). You may also want to consider how the different options you could choose might impact the job security and ongoing income of your loved ones at the time of your passing.

Lawyers tend to approach estate planning from a stance of how to protect assets, and also how to protect people. You may want to consider the use of employment agreements, if for no other reason than to keep your children working for the business. Usually, if relations between the children and the surviving partner (i.e., their stepparent) are strained, the parties don't realize that they may need each other. If, for instance, the stepmother is put in charge of the business, but she was not involved in the business during her partner's lifetime, she will need the children who have experience working in the business. Likewise, the children who work in the business need their stepmother, who is now their boss, whether they like it or not. If this is the governance that is chosen, it would be wise to make sure everyone is aware and on board ahead of time so that any potential grievances and resentments can be aired and cleared prior to the emotional impact of the loss when the owner dies.

> **Employment agreements can take care of major family business concerns.**

We've seen blended family businesses of every kind; from those that remained successful to those that experienced financial ruin after the death of an owning partner. The latter seems to happen more often when no comprehensive estate- and business-succession planning were done. You will need to seriously and independently evaluate your potential successors as the boss. Quite frequently, children either aren't yet ready to run the business (if their parent should die in the immediate future) or the children are not boss material. However, your partner also may not be competent as the boss either, especially if he or she has never been involved in the business or has no business experience.

People don't often realize that if their business interests are left in trust and they make their partner the trustee, they've essentially put the partner in charge of the business, which usually is not a good idea, especially if the deceased partner's children work in the business.

Indeed, this could cause the business to flounder, especially if there is animosity between the surviving partner and the children of the deceased partner who work in the business. If half-siblings are involved, there can be favoritism to contend with as well. If stepsiblings and in-laws also work in the company, you've got an exponentially more complicated situation to contend with.

When people discover their roles as they are described in the estate plan at the time the will is read, there is the double impact of being ill-prepared to fulfill that role they were not informed of *and* the loss of the person they would have wanted to mentor them and show them what was expected of them. For those of you in this situation, we encourage you to take time now to think these things through, to discuss them with all relevant parties to get their input and concerns, and describe your decisions when there's a chance to express them and your reasons behind them. This will go a long way towards bringing more unity and harmony into your blended family's experience when the estate is transitioned.

3.1 To sell or not to sell

For someone who is the sole owner of a family business, as you ponder how to protect both your partner and your children who are working in the business, consider that you have an even tougher situation to ponder: Should you sell the company during your lifetime?

Many businesses are best sold during the owner's lifetime because the business is more valuable with the owner still around to assist the new owners if need be. Other owners choose not to sell while they are alive, hoping that their legacy will live on and be furthered by the family, and that the business continue to sustain and support the family. Another reason they may choose not to sell is because

their identity is so intertwined with being the originator, owner, and leader of the business that they cannot imagine what they would do without that role.

As advisors who have seen what happens so often after the death of an original owner, we believe it is important for you to make an objective determination about selling. Do a valuation of the company with you at the helm and without you at the helm. Get the data. This is a very tough decision, especially if you have children working in the business who may be expecting to run it after you are gone and who may not be welcome to keep working for the business after a sale. You would be wise to include them every step of the way so that they understand your thought process, and so they know you are aware of their concerns.

If you have decided to keep the business, or for some reason can't sell the company, you must put together a business succession plan that provides for your partner as much as you want him or her to have, and that also takes care of your children, especially those children who are working in or who are dependent on the business. We discuss buy-sell agreements next, while also noting another key element of a business succession plan is the identification of the successor owners and managers of the business.

3.2 Buy-sell agreements

It is advisable for all closely held businesses to have a business-succession plan. One key element of a business-succession plan is a buy-sell agreement. A buy-sell agreement is a legal written contract between some or all of the owners of a closely held business that details what happens upon the occurrence of one or more events, called "triggering events." Death, divorce, bankruptcy, attempting to sell an interest of the company, disability, and competing with the company are common triggering events, but they are not the only ones that can be made triggering events in a buy-sell agreement.

A key element of a good buy-sell agreement is that it must prohibit transfer of any interest in the company except as provided in the buy-sell agreement. The buy-sell agreement must clearly set forth the applicable triggering events and what is to happen upon the occurrence of a particular triggering event. It is customary for a buy-sell agreement to permit transfers to certain persons, often referred to in buy-sell agreements as "permitted transferees," despite the buy-sell agreement. Permitted transferees typically include certain family members. In blended families, it is rare for the uninvolved partner to have any interest or involvement in the business. However, even if they aren't parties to the buy-sell agreement, we strongly recommend that uninvolved partners, particularly married partners, should acknowledge the existence of the buy-sell agreement in writing and sign off on the buy-sell agreement in order to prevent challenges after the involved partner's death.

3.3 Less than all of the children working in the business

Possibly one of the most difficult estate-planning assignments is dealing with a closely held business owned by one partner in a blended family, where less than all of the owning partner's children work in the business. It's usually a mistake to leave a business to all of the children (including both those working in the business and those who are not) because the children who work in the business often come to resent the children who don't work in the business. This is because the two sets of children have different interests. The children who work in the business usually view the business as their own and want to have the same liberties and same compensation that the parent enjoyed. The problem with this view is that the children who don't work in the business are fellow owners and also want money and other goodies from the company.

We've also seen another contentious issue between involved and uninvolved siblings, half-siblings, stepsiblings, and their respective in-laws where, those in the company wish to reinvest earning back into the company for ongoing growth and those not in the business want to have more liquidity and distributions. It usually makes more sense to give the business to the children who are working in it and leave other assets or life insurance to the other children and your uninvolved partner.

If the couple owns the business together but they have separate children, the issues can be even harder. Perhaps the hardest situation is where only one partner has children who are working in the business. Suppose the parent partner dies first. The question is whether to or how to protect the jobs of the children who are working in the business, especially if the parent partner leaves his or her interest in the business to the other partner. Hopefully, the situation won't change drastically between the surviving partner and the employee children. If the parent partner wants to leave his or her share of the business to the children, how do you protect the interests of the surviving partner? Quite often, buy-sell agreements can be devised to navigate these treacherous waters.

Issues related to buy-sell agreements become even more important when the couple in a blended family situation co-own a business. At the time of this book's writing, Emily was working with a couple where one partner had four grown children from a prior marriage and his former wife got a great divorce settlement. He'd sunk all his savings and leveraged his assets to build a new business and life with his current wife. They had no children together, and they owned the business together. How should he work his estate plan if he predeceased her, and he wanted a share to go to his kids who don't work in their business? Paul's recommendation for this couple would be to insure the husband in an escrowed buy-sell agreement and have the two enter into a buy-sell agreement whereby the wife is obligated to purchase his interest at his death. Paul would never have them co-own the business, as there is too much chance for friction, and the children may claim that their dad put up more of the capital than his interest reflects.

4. Retirement Plans

The interests of a partner in a qualified retirement plan can be a very difficult issue to deal with in estate planning for the blended family in the US. This is because US law requires that the nonworking spouse be the beneficiary of a qualified retirement plan. This is often contrary to the desires of the working spouse, but the only way that the working spouse can name his or her own children as the beneficiaries of plan benefits is if the nonworking spouse waives in writing any interest in the plan, which rarely happens. This waiver can't be made in a prenuptial agreement as it has to be made after the wedding occurs.

Retirement plan interests are fraught with their own challenges, even in traditional families, due to the fact that the benefits are taxed when they are distributed, which significantly reduces their value. If the partners are not married, there is no requirement that the nonparticipant partner be named a beneficiary,

freeing the participant partner to name anyone as beneficiary.

> **Do you know who the beneficiary is in your retirement plan? Is your plan up to date?**

4.1 US Individual Retirement Account (IRA)

Individual Retirement Accounts (IRAs) also make up significant portions of many people's estates in the US. While traditional IRAs have the same income tax issues as qualified retirement plans, IRAs have a lot more flexibility with respect to estate planning than qualified retirement-plan accounts. The married partner does not have a federal right to be the beneficiary of an IRA. This is important in blended family situations because the IRA account holder can use a trust that benefits both the partner (whether married or unmarried) and the children of a prior union.

5. Tangible Personal Property

The category of property that probably creates more hard feelings and fights in all types of families than any other category of property is tangible personal property. This category can create significant litigation even if the property is not worth much financially. This category of property includes things such as family pictures, memorabilia, furniture, jewelry, crystal, silverware, and china.

In blended families, these issues often are not carefully addressed in estate planning. As a result, the surviving partner gets this property even though the deceased partner may have understood that the surviving partner would give the family property to his or her children. There is no guarantee that this wish will be honored.

If there is any advice that we would give about this type of property, it is to consider giving it to the persons that you want to have it during your lifetime. Waiting until your death often doesn't accomplish your goal without very careful planning. If you give it away during your lifetime, and its value is within the $13,000 US federal gift tax exemption (in 2012) that you are allowed each year, you also help mitigate some estate taxation of those particular items.

6. Bank Accounts

Money can be held in a number of different ways, including an option to have a "pay on death" feature in which the bank account holder names someone to get that account upon the death of the account holder.

We don't usually recommend pay-on-death accounts to couples in blended families because this often conflicts with their estate plans. Remember, the account title trumps your will. For example, if your will gives your bank accounts to your children, but the accounts are held in pay-on-death or joint tenancy with rights of survivorship, your will may be meaningless in this regard. (You probably didn't realize the importance of dealing with bank tellers, did you?)

7. Action Steps

For business owners who have an uninvolved spouse, take five minutes right now to have the uninvolved spouse acknowledge the existence of the buy-sell agreement in writing and sign off on it in order to prevent challenges after the involved partner's death.

If you own a business and do not have a buy-sell agreement in place, that needs to be your very next action item. Once that is completed, be sure to complete the acknowledgment of the uninvolved spouse as recommended.

Now's the time to take a good, honest look at your property, by answering the following questions:

- What is it you own individually and as a couple?

- What would each of you like to see happen with that property at the time of your deaths? Give space for each other to be heard without having to go into agreement with each other. Enjoy learning more about each other and what you both see and care about for the other partner and for the children in your lives.

- What are the components of this chapter that are most relevant to you that you'd like to begin to address?

Come up with a plan that includes not only what you plan to address here, but just as important, *when* you plan to address the issues. See if you can plan something fun to do after each step as a little reward for all the great progress you're making. Each small step is getting you closer to your goal!

CHAPTER 6

Estate-Planning Documents

In the course of estate planning you will be reviewing, editing, modifying, and signing a number of documents. Most of these are legally binding documents that will put into effect that which matters most to you at the time of your death. This chapter will give you a clear understanding of what the different documents are that your advisors will be working with you on completing, as well as key considerations related to those documents. Our goal is to give you clarity about what your advisors mean when they speak about these different documents, while also giving you a leg up when it comes down to the decision making ahead of you.

1. Wills

Wills are sometimes called "testaments" or "last will and testament." Believe it or not, a long time ago there was a difference between wills and testaments: You gave away real estate by will and personal property by testament; hence the phrase "last will and testament" for documents that transferred both real and personal property at death. However, this distinction is no more, so the two terms are virtually synonymous.

Most people know something about wills, yet it is estimated that the majority of people don't have one of their own. We delineated some of the fears and reasons why this may be the case in Chapter 1. Whatever the reason, we hope that you see as we do that everyone should have a will because a will is a formal legal expression of your wishes as to who will receive your property, who will manage your property, when your property will be delivered to the recipients, and who will look after your minor children (subject to the limitations discussed in section **1.1**).

One of the best things about a will is that you can change it at any time before your death (or until you become mentally incapacitated to such an extent that you lose legal capacity). While there are many books about wills, including *Write Your Legal Will in 3 Easy Steps* (available from Self-Counsel Press), we'll cover the basics before focusing on the issues related to wills that are most important to blended family partners.

First and foremost, the laws of the state or province of the person (i.e., the testator) who is putting together a will generally govern it. Subject to some very broad limitations that are a function of applicable local law in your jurisdiction and a key limitation on married partners that we discussed in Chapters 4 and 5, you can do whatever you wish with your property in your will. Subject to the same caveats in the preceding sentence, you can leave your property to whomever you want, in whatever amounts and subject to limitations as you wish.

Whether or not a will is valid depends on the place in which it was executed, and valid wills executed in one jurisdiction are almost always valid if you move to another jurisdiction, so that if you didn't change your will before death, the will would still govern. This is important given that people often move between jurisdictions whether they be from state to state or province to province.

> Testamentary trusts can contain any provision that you want, subject to the laws of your jurisdiction.

You can leave property to a trust that is set up in your will. These are called *testamentary trusts*, and they don't come into existence until you die even though the will exists. Testamentary trusts can contain any provision that you want, subject to the laws of your jurisdiction. Some types of clauses in wills or trusts (e.g., restrict a beneficiary from marrying outside of his or her faith) are found invalid as some courts deem them to be contrary to public policy of the applicable jurisdiction. Your estate-planning attorney will be able to advise you on these matters.

1.1 Wills and minor children

In your will it is important to designate who will be the guardian of the minor children who are your offspring from your union if something should happen to both of you at the same time. One area of great concern to blended family partners is whether or not they have the ability in a will to designate who will take care of their minor children from prior relationships if they want it to be someone other than the child's surviving birth parent. This is very difficult to do unless the other parent has a significant problem such as drinking, abuse, or drugs.

If the other parent has been largely absent from the minor's life, you can see if he or she would be willing to relinquish parental rights because this opens the possibility of adoption, or at least makes it easier for the stepparent to be the legal guardian should something happen to the minor's primary caregiving parent. Barring having parental rights willingly relinquished, the best that most blended family parents can do in this instance is to state their desires in their wills and see if the court will go along. This is particularly unfortunate as it presents a possible significant life change for the minor child, who may have younger half-siblings or stepsiblings with whom he or she is being raised. These are all factors for the court to consider and are not automatic determinants.

There are many blended family situations in which the partner who is not the parent is the best option for the child, particularly when that partner has been very involved in the child's life and care for an extended time and when the other surviving birth parent has not played an active, engaged role. In this instance, another option is to get a memorandum of understanding from the child's other birth parent stating that he or she understands and agrees with the choice of the stepparent as guardian should something happen to the child's birth parent and primary caregiver. This can be added to the will for additional consideration by the courts.

> **Be proactive and make sure who you want to care for your minor children is designated and communicated the best way you can.**

1.2 Wills and probate

Many people believe that probate is a bad thing, but probate simply means supervision by a court. In the vast majority of jurisdictions today (California being a notable exception), probate is a very streamlined, efficient process of gathering the decedent's assets, identifying the decedent's debts, and passing the remaining property to the heirs according to the will or the laws of intestacy. That's all it is.

In blended families that have a lot of animosity in their family dynamics, probate is often a good idea because it protects everyone involved. Otherwise, if someone partial to one side is in charge, the chances of costly and unnecessary litigation are greatly increased. Probate allows for a neutral third party (i.e., the court) to preside over your will and make sure that your wishes are carried out appropriately.

2. Trusts

A trust is a means of property ownership and management whereby the "grantor" or "settlor" transfers property to someone to manage for the benefit of the beneficiary. Trusts can be established during lifetime or at death.

Trusts are divided into several basic sections. One section clearly describes the identity of the beneficiaries of the trust and what they are to receive and when they are to receive it. A significantly large section of most trusts is the part that deals with the authority and powers of the trustee.

2.1 Revocable living trusts

A revocable living trust is a trust that you establish during your lifetime. You frequently see these types of trusts referred to simply as "living trusts." By its very name, it is revocable, meaning that you can change it or get rid of it at any time. While most people don't need the additional complexity of a revocable living trust, they are much more common in jurisdictions such as California where probate laws are antiquated, costly, and burdensome. In the overwhelming bulk of jurisdictions, people use wills instead. Revocable trusts can have their place in any estate plan, and we see them used with more frequency in blended families because of the additional formality and protection that a trust can provide.

A revocable living trust contains many if not most of the same provisions that are in a will. Revocable trusts are just as easy to change as a will. Just because you have a revocable trust doesn't mean that you don't need a will to put into the revocable trust the property that you failed to put into the trust while you were alive.

Revocable trusts are often chosen over wills based on a mistaken belief that revocable trusts avoid probate and save taxes and costs. Unfortunately, with the exception of only a few states and provinces, it is less expensive to use a will than a revocable trust, which is why wills are so much more prevalent. You can ask your local attorney about which option is the wisest to use in your particular jurisdiction, and why you might want to use one over the other, or both.

2.2 Irrevocable trusts

Unlike revocable living trusts, which can be changed, irrevocable trusts, by their very name, are irrevocable — meaning that they can't be changed. Nevertheless, a well-drafted irrevocable trust should contain some flexible provisions that permit amendment, either by the trustee or by someone named in the trust as a trust protector or special trustee, to address unforeseen changes in circumstances. An irrevocable trust is a very broad topic, as irrevocable trusts can be established to do many different things, such as holding gifts of property for another either for a lifetime or for a specified period of time.

The most important matter in the institution of a trust is the selection of a trustee. Remember, documents don't do the work; people do. In blended families, the selection of a trustee is a very difficult decision if there is or could be tension between your partner and your children. We strongly advocate the use of an independent third-party trustee for irrevocable trusts for blended families, especially if the beneficiaries include your partner and your separate children.

2.3 Beneficiary designations

Beneficiary designations are related to non-probate assets. They are extremely important because a significant amount of a person's wealth is tied up in non-probate assets such as life insurance, Individual Retirement Accounts (IRAs), and retirement plans. Your will won't govern the transfer of these assets because they are non-probate assets. The beneficiary designation governs, even if you attempt to leave those non-probate assets to a different person in your will. It won't count and won't matter

what you want. This is why beneficiary designations are so critical. In blended family estate planning, it is imperative that your estate planners review actual copies of all of your beneficiary designations — operating from memory here is dangerous and ill-advised. It is not unusual for a review of beneficiary designations to uncover stale beneficiary designations, such as a designation of a predeceased parent or an ex-partner. You may also have had additional children who aren't named as beneficiaries.

It is very important to name contingent or backup beneficiaries in case something happens to the originally named beneficiary. Note that financial institutions have been known to not be able to locate beneficiary designations and to have made errors in the naming of a beneficiary, so it is always a good idea to check with your bank to see what is actually on file because that is what will count.

> **Double check who your beneficiaries are and be sure to designate contingent ones as well.**

Depending on the terms of the plan, it may be possible to prevent beneficiaries from withdrawing the entire amount at one time; thereby protecting the beneficiary from improvident spending. Usually there is a selection of options in this regard, and your estate planners can assist you with sorting them and picking the ones that are right for your situation.

3. Powers of Attorney for Property

A power of attorney is a legal document in which you appoint someone to act for you for whatever reason. These are very common in real estate transactions. In a power of attorney, you (i.e., the principal) dictate what activities your appointee (i.e., the agent) can do on your behalf. Your agent only has the authority that you give him or her, and no more.

In estate planning, the powers that are typically given to an agent in a property power of attorney are broad as the purpose of most estate-planning powers of attorney are to try to prevent the principal from having to be subjected to court supervision in a conservatorship or guardianship.

Your power of attorney can come into effect anytime you want it to — either immediately or at some point in the future — such as when you are no longer able or willing to act on your own. These latter powers of attorney are called springing powers of attorney.

Springing powers of attorney can be problematic if the event that springs the power of attorney into effect isn't clearly described. Paul rarely recommends springing powers of attorney because it is frequently difficult to prove that the event springing the power into effect has occurred. Often, the approval of medical doctors can be difficult to obtain.

The overwhelming majority of powers of attorney are drafted to go into effect immediately at incapacity and to survive your incapacity and last until your death. This type of power of attorney is referred to as a continuing, enduring, or durable power of attorney. Durable powers of attorney are very important in estate planning because incapacity is a much bigger problem to deal with and much more likely than death. Therefore, a carefully planned durable power of attorney is a must, even more so in a blended family, as we will show next.

By carefully "planned," we mean that the "regular" (if there is such a thing) powers in a durable power of attorney may be inappropriate in the blended family context. For example, many durable powers of attorney authorize the agents a lot of flexibility to make broad changes in their estate plans by revoking or amending trusts, by exercising powers of appointment, by giving away precious family heirlooms (e.g., silverware, china, artwork and photographs), or by changing beneficiary designations.

Such powers given to an interested party could cause your estate plan to be radically changed to the point of not being recognizable, in other words, not what you wanted. It is appropriate to put limits on an agent's authority in a durable power of attorney, particularly in a blended family context in which there may be conflicting agendas related to what will be done with the estate after each of you passes away. Clearly, the power of attorney given to a partner should automatically be revoked on separation or divorce.

Local law governs the legal form required for powers of attorney. Many powers can be generally given. However, some powers must be expressly included in the document. These powers include:

- To donate or give property to others.

- To settle a lawsuit or refer a matter to arbitration.

- To sell, buy, mortgage, or lease.

- To accept or renounce an estate or trust.

- To contract a loan, acknowledge a debt, or become a guarantor of a loan.

- To draw or endorse promissory notes and negotiate instruments.

- To enter into contracts between the agent and the principal.

- To deal with the tax authority (i.e., Internal Revenue Service or Canada Revenue Agency) and state or provincial and local taxing authorities.

- To waive an accounting by the agent. (This is something we would never recommend because it is unwise to allow an agent to not be responsible for his or her actions.)

The powers required to be expressly included is a matter of local law. Your estate-planning attorney can assist with this.

The most important thing to consider when choosing who will be your agent under a durable power of attorney is: How much do you trust that person? Once a person is your agent under your durable power of attorney, he or she has the capacity to purchase real estate, sign contracts, or enter into other legal commitments on your behalf and, in theory, without you knowing about it, although he or she is obligated to act in your best interests.

4. Powers of Attorney for Health Care and Living Wills

Sometimes *health-care powers of attorney* and *living wills* are combined in documents called "advanced-care directives" or "health-care proxies." We usually recommend that the two separate documents, which serve very different purposes, not be combined, especially if you want to select different people to handle each of the tasks.

To clarify, a living will, also known as an advanced-care directive, health-care directive, or a physician's directive, is a legal document that a person uses to make known his or her wishes regarding life-prolonging medical treatments. A living will informs your health-care providers and your family about your desires for medical treatment if you are not able to speak for yourself. It is an essential document for anyone in the position of agent under your health-care power of attorney so that he or she is informed as to what decisions you want made on your behalf relating to discontinuing extraordinary life support. In your living will, you can designate who you want to carry out your wishes, and that person's role can be separate from the person who is your agent under your health-care power of attorney.

The person you name as your agent under your health-care power of attorney is in the role of making all your health-related decisions (see detailed list below). The rules for health-care powers of attorney are a matter of local law, so your estate-planning attorney can guide you on these matters.

Of all the documents you are considering, the health-care power of attorney and the living will are by far the most imperative for unmarried blended family partners, as it assures that the two of you can be there to make each other's medical-related decisions (or be part of the process, if you choose to appoint your partner and another trusted friend or family member who has a background in medicine and health care). Without a health-care power of attorney, and without a legally acknowledged relationship, your partner may be kept in the dark about important aspects of your health care and will be unable to participate in key decisions that may have a direct impact on his or her life (e.g., the caregivers who may be coming into the home; the location where you will be cared for such as rehab, assisted living, or nursing home care; and whether or not measures will be taken towards keeping you alive).

In a health-care power of attorney, it is customary for the person who signs the documents (principal) to give the following powers to the person of your choice (your agent):

- **Engagements and termination:** Some important powers that the person with your power of attorney (agent) should have are the ability to select, contact, and discuss your health-care needs. It also is very important to grant the agent the right to pay and/or terminate employment or discharge insurance companies and other health organizations, physicians, dentists, nurses, sitters, and other professional or nonprofessional medical assistance; to select or change hospitals, health-care facilities, hospices, selection of insurance companies, or other health organizations, institutions, home care, nursing home, custodial care, or other places for medical treatment for the principal; and to make decisions as to the manner and nature of treatments and services to be performed by any physician, nurse, hospital, or other institution for the principal.

- **Represent the principal before federal, state or provincial, and local governments and governmental subdivisions:** To represent you before any federal, state or provincial, or local health-care bodies, including, without limitation, medical plans and veterans' plans on any matter that involves your health-care and living arrangements.

- **Emergency care and general power to consent:** To consent and arrange for emergency care and other medical treatment for you, including, without limitation, ambulance and other emergency medical transport.

- **Medical records:** To have complete access to all medical records in any form pertaining to your physical or mental condition, and to reproduce and discuss the same with anyone, as well as the power to execute those consents and releases as may be necessary

to obtain medical information and to discuss them with anyone.

- **Power to consent:** To make and execute all consents, refusal of consents, or withdrawal of consent to any care, treatment, service, or procedure, including, but not limited to, cardiopulmonary resuscitation, and to execute all releases from liability for any health-care provider which acts on your behalf.

Health-care powers of attorney can be very specific in the types of care that the principal either wants or doesn't want, including the following:

- **Artificial nutrition and hydration:** This is where you state under what circumstances you would choose to have life-sustaining procedures withheld (e.g., length of time in a coma without responsiveness, length of time in hospice care without hope of recovery). This can be a very controversial part of a health-care power of attorney with religious overtones as certain religions such as Roman Catholicism prohibit withholding nutrition and hydration.

  This issue is also dealt with in a living will. This is why some people opt to not combine their advanced-care directive with their living will, so that one person can take on this particularly challenging aspect of your wishes, and someone else can take care of the rest. Other people choose to combine the two in the hopes of not creating any confusion.

- **Religious restrictions:** Some religions, such as Jehovah's Witnesses, forbid blood transfusions. Other religions may have other restrictions. Stating your faith and how you see it being implemented is important to describe for whoever is asked to be your health-care power of attorney, as he or she may likely face legal pressures in some instances.

- **General intentions about mental health treatment:** This is where length of stay as well as the frequency and total number of treatment options that can be utilized would be described if this is an area of concern and likelihood. This includes options such as addiction care and psychotropic drugs.

- **Organ and tissue donation:** Some people are clear that none of their organs should be donated, while others want to donate their entire bodies to science. You get to state to what degree you would or would not like your organs to be donated. If this is a pertinent concern, explore with your attorney how to delineate this particular area in a separate document, since these matters often are set out in a separate document.

In today's complex world of government regulation of personal matters, federal and state governments put restrictions on who doctors and other health-care providers can share information with, so it is prudent to execute something known as a Health Insurance Portability and Accountability Act (HIPAA) Release in the United States, which will allow release of your medical information to persons other than your agent under your health-care power of attorney. This is particularly important for blended families and especially for unmarried partners who aren't the agent under the health-care power of attorney.

5. Ethical Wills

Your ethical will is your way to convey what you care about most to your loved ones. It is the time-honored tool for enduring personal expression that is nonbinding, but can accompany your will and/or trusts as a permanent place for loved ones to hear your "voice." The resource that sets the standard for ethical wills is Susan B. Turnbull's *The Wealth of Your Life*. In it she shows you in five easy steps how to go about crafting your ethical will:

> **Step 1: Identify those you wish to address.** This could be anyone from your children, your stepchildren, grandchildren, descendants (both through blood and through love) yet unborn, siblings, nieces, nephews, parents, spouse or partner, friends, guardians of your children, trustees, and even your agent under your health-care power of attorney.

> **Step 2: Consider your intentions and draft your opening lines.** Many people treat this like a letter and start with a simple salutation and a brief statement saying what it is about. Start with the end in mind as you consider what you would like the readers of your ethical will to have, and to feel, as a result of seeing your words.

> **Step 3: Reflect on what to include in the body of the letter.** Make notes for reference. People find this part easier to address by breaking it down into themes. Some themes Turnbull suggests as possible starting points include: your history; values; perspective; estate plan and financial plan from a personal context; and your feelings of love, hope, and concern for your loved ones.

Step 4: Integrate your thoughts into an outline.

Step 5: With your notes to guide you, compose your ethical will.

Taking the time to do this will not only bring you and your loved ones peace of mind, but it will also go a long way towards mitigating potential hurt feelings and allowing for greater understanding related to why you set up your estate plan the way you did. Having a context that is clearly expressed may allow the content of the will and other documents to be respected and honored more fully. See the CD included with this book for more about ethical will preparation.

6. Letters of Instruction

A letter of instruction, while not one of your formal estate-planning documents, can be one of the most valuable legacies that you can leave to those who will administer your estate after you are dead or incapacitated. It will give your executors and trustees a road map to follow and make their jobs much easier, less costly, and less time consuming.

In the letter, you can give detailed instructions and data related to where things are located and what exactly you want done with those things. As you write your instructions, you will also want to make it easy for your trustee and executor to find what they will need in order to fulfill your wishes easily.

You could identify in one document all of your various banking and other financial accounts and retirement plans, along with the names and contact information of your bankers and advisors who handle these accounts and where the checkbooks and related cards are located. Don't forget to include your passwords for all online accounts. Remember, this should be printed and put in a safe, secure place that is spelled out in your letter.

If you are a beneficiary of a trust or an heir to an estate, provide those details as well as the contact information for who has been assisting you with those matters. Take care that this information is held by your estate-planning attorney and/or in a locked box and do not share it with anyone else.

List the names and contact information for your estate-planning professionals as well as for those people who you would like to be personally notified of your death; you can even say who you would like to contact them.

You could also make an inventory of your most valuable personal property such as diamonds, heirlooms, antiques, and artwork, and place this with your other important details. You will want to label sets of keys to all locks, vehicles, and designate where these and the safe codes can be found easily when necessary. Also note the location where expensive watches, jewels, and memorabilia are stored. If you have safety deposit boxes, foreign accounts, or property, it is advisable to list those as well.

Some people choose to specify how they wish the rest of their possessions to be distributed at the time of a surviving spouse's death. Blended families need to be particularly creative in this arena because of the different levels of attachment to things from childhood for some family members that their stepsiblings and half-siblings may have grown to enjoy and love but that don't hold the same lifelong meaning.

One strategy that we've seen work well in blended families where there is a degree of amiability among all family members is to ask what they'd like. Couples who can be open to learning about what truly matters to their children when it comes to possessions can allow their heirs to inform them as to how to proceed with divvying up their possessions when the time comes. Sometimes, that time happens prior to death, such as when both parent and stepparent, or when a surviving partner has to go into an assisted-living or nursing home facility — thereby downsizing to a great extent.

The key here is that when you ask *all* the children in your lives what matters to them and what it is that they want, assure them that you will not be offended and that you will not see them as feeling entitled or greedy (these are common fears that keep beneficiaries from speaking up about what truly matters to them).

When blended families approach Emily to work with them in sorting out this particularly sticky situation, Emily recommends, after coaching the couple about how to be open and receptive, that the couple notify all the children in their lives that they will be receiving a letter with a very unique request. They then send a letter reassuring their children that they want their input and to learn about what they care about and then ask each of them to list up to ten items that the couple has in their possession that they would each want. The children are instructed to take time and think about why those items matter to them and to share those stories along with each item. The letter also explains that while there is no guarantee that everyone will get everything on their lists, the couple assures them that they will all get at least five things that matter to them when the time comes — and that they are not to ask and not to expect or anticipate when that time may be. They assure their offspring that they will do their best to be as fair as possible, and that they understand that they are asking a lot of them by having them take the risk and share this information with their parent and stepparent.

The couple then works together (and with Emily if it becomes emotional or challenging),

comparing the various lists that they receive. The couple is instructed to not share the lists with anyone else and to not discuss what one child has listed with any of the other children. They can discuss with each child more in-depth about what they've discovered as a result of the lists, especially if there's one item in particular that everyone wants.

The couple writes their determination of what five items each child will receive in their letter of instruction and also in the will so that there is no question. Then, they come up with other ways to have the children go fairly through the rest of the belongings that have not been designated to anyone in particular. Some couples have their children meet together (which in blended families can be a big deal) and draw numbers (either highest to lowest, or lowest to highest) with a neutral third party (i.e., someone who is not a child of either of the two partners) observing and moderating the proceedings. The child who wins gets to select his or her first choice, and then they go in order until each child has chosen one thing. The third party notes each item that is chosen and keeps track of the siblings and their numbers. The siblings then reverse order, with the one who chose last getting to choose first, and going down the line again. They then have the next to last go first and go down the line the opposite way again, and so on. Other families that like to keep things more competitive and charged have the siblings throw dice each round, so it is random who will go first each time. Families with a high level of play, fun, and tolerance of each other can have a lot of fun with this. Families that already have a breakdown in trust should shy away from this completely.

7. Burial or Cremation Instructions

While many of us have some idea of what we would like to have at our funeral or memorial service, very few of us actually describe our wishes as well as our preferred burial instructions. In many families, this doesn't matter. However, in blended families, failure to provide burial instructions could lead to very bitter fights between your children and your partner about what type of service and burial you wanted. Therefore, it is advisable to describe your funeral plans in writing and to let everyone know in advance exactly what you want.

It is not unusual for family members, who are already stricken by grief at your passing, to want control of your funeral, ostensibly under the guise of doing what they think you would have wanted. Unfortunately, this often conflicts with what other family members think that you would have wanted. Memories can change over time, as can desires and wishes. For example, a father may have had a conversation with his oldest son years ago where he expressed a desire to be cremated. Since that time, he has remarried a second wife who does not believe in cremation. If his wishes are not written, and if specific arrangements have not been made, that son is likely to hold as true and important the initially, long ago stated wish as a way to still feel connected to his father. The son may want to demonstrate that he knew his father better and was closer to him than his second wife. That father could have averted a lot of unnecessary pain and conflict by simply writing down exactly how he wanted his body treated at the time of his death.

Some other fights we have witnessed over the years have been over where a person will be buried, and what kind of memorial service to have, along with where it will be held and who will make the funeral or memorial service arrangements. This is why we advise you to take the time to describe in writing exactly what you want, and even make your arrangements in advance.

> **Do key members of your family know your specific wishes for what you want to happen with your body after you die?**

7.1 Appoint someone to be in charge of your funeral arrangements

We recommend that you put in writing whom you want to be in charge of your funeral arrangements. Advance funeral planning is a great idea, because if you don't do it, you run the risk of a dispute between your surviving partner and your children. It is not unusual for children of a deceased partner to want their parent buried next to their other predeceased parent. This gets even more complex if the partners lived in a different city, state, or province than where the deceased partner and his or her prior partner lived. Purchasing your plots (or urns) and settling all the arrangements well in advance will keep the agendas of others from creating conflict during a time of deep loss and grief.

7.2 Write your own obituary

Surprisingly, more feelings are hurt in obituaries than perhaps any other area of estate planning for blended families. The culprit often is the person who writes the obituary. Some write it with malicious intent, while others may have inadvertently left out someone.

On the more malicious side, in situations where relations between the surviving partner and the deceased partner's children are strained (or even hostile), we've seen one side or the other left out or even criticized in obituaries. These slights create hurts that often never heal and can permanently end relationships. We suggest avoiding this problem and writing your own obituary in advance. That way, you can name the people that you wish and say what you want to say about yourself. That way if anyone's slighted, it's your choice and you're the one to blame.

If you're taking the time to write your own obituary, you could also name the publications you would like it to appear in, and make that job easier for the loved one you put in charge of executing that little detail — giving him or her a role and explaining how to fulfil it is one of the most thoughtful things you can do.

7.3 Delineate mode of interment or inurnment

Just like obituaries, we've seen knock-down-drag-out fights over burial and cremation. Burial issues often involve the place of burial. Children may want a deceased parent to be buried in their hometown of origin and next to a predeceased parent. Funeral homes often are left in a precarious situation right after death when there are warring sides over the style of bodily disposition (burial versus cremation), place, and style of memorial service, and even what the deceased will wear in the casket. There can be arguments over whether a casket will be open or not. It is not unusual for families to argue for days over these and other issues, which delays the memorial service and interment or inurnment.

We recommend avoiding these arguments by delineating everything that you want for your funeral and disposal. While we realize that is not an easy task for you to face, we've seen the ramifications when it is left up to the loved ones to figure it out on their own. Not only is it not easy for them, it can be excruciating and painful. In instances where there is discord among stepchildren and their surviving stepparent, this loving action can save a lot of squabbling after your death.

7.4 Delineate who is to be invited to the memorial service or funeral

One of the saddest and unnecessary tragedies is what happens at a lot of funerals or memorial services where there are blended family dynamics. If there is animosity between your partner and your children, you must assume the worst, which is that one group or the other will be excluded from your funeral or memorial service. This is very rarely what people want, since the overwhelming majority of them hope against hope that the two sides will come together at least for the funeral or memorial service. Paul's experience is quite the contrary. He has seen surviving partners excluded from funeral or memorial services and surviving children excluded too. There are few things more sad than to have any family member miss a funeral or memorial service of a parent or a partner, because this is a one-time event. This is a slight that will linger forever and could likely make a rift between two groups permanent.

If you believe that there is even a remote chance that hard feelings will happen at your funeral or memorial service, give strong consideration to delineating who is to be invited. In this way, you will bring together all of your loved ones for your funeral or memorial service, even if some of them don't want others there, and vice versa. Sometimes, people allow short-term anger or long-standing resentment to cause them to make choices that they later regret that can never be rectified. We've seen that these can have long-term traumatic ramifications. You can avoid or at least minimize problems by listing who is to be alerted of your death and by whom, and to encourage everyone to be invited to your funeral or memorial service.

We strongly recommend having a conversation with the various members of your blended family system while you are alive and well about your wishes for your funeral or memorial service. During those conversations, if you can give them the chance to express their reasons why it would be painful or difficult or unthinkable to have certain people there, you may be able to begin to heal some of the pain that is keeping your entire family from being together during your lifetime, as well as smooth the way for them all to be together at the time of your death. You will be amazed at what can happen when someone feels truly heard and understood — his or her stance can shift and he or she can begin to see new possibilities. You can refer back to Chapter 2 to learn more about how to have this kind of conversation effectively.

8. Action Steps

First and foremost, breathe in and out! This chapter is filled with a lot of information and many action steps towards taking care of all your concerns. As a way to further support you, we've included a supplement section to this chapter that explains how to collect the necessary information, get your thoughts and preferences in order, and capture your wishes in a way that will make the drawing up of the specific documents easy and efficient. You can find the supplement entitled "Document Preparation" on the accompanying CD where you can directly type your responses.

We have also provided a form on the CD called "Vital Information for Executor and Trustee" on which you can record all the necessary information your advisors and loved ones will need to know at the time of your death. Taking time to complete this form will give you and your loved ones peace of mind. Be sure to store it in a safe, confidential, private place that only key, trusted people know.

CHAPTER 7

The Estate-Planning Players

In Chapter 2, we talked about estate planning being a life play. Who are the players, you ask? The star of the show, who also must be the director, is you. There are different schools of thought regarding whether your partner should be your co-star, as there are pluses and minuses to both of you sharing everything regarding your planning together. While there is great value in working together in approaching your estate planning, it is important to be aware of the cautions against including your partner in your planning. As discussed in Chapter 2, the following signposts definitely indicate the need for separate representation, and hopefully an estate planner will point these out to you:

- Where one of you is childless but the other has children. You are not in similar circumstances.

- Where there is significant disparity in wealth or income between you and your partner.

  - Where one of you is economically dependent on the other.

  - Where one of you does all of the talking or appears to exert strong influence over the other.

- Length of the relationship. Generally speaking, the shorter the relationship, the stronger the suggestion of separate representation.

- The number of past relationships you both have had. Generally speaking, the greater the number of past relationships, the stronger the suggestion of separate representation.

These are not easy points to consider and we ask that you neither gloss over nor ignore them. The more uncomfortable they make you, the stronger the indication

that you should do some serious looking at what is at stake and what is causing you to feel ill at ease. We also want to reiterate here that there are ways to do your planning with separate representation while also staying in communication and connection around *all* the planning that you are doing. We encourage both of you to recognize that this is not personal and that it is sound legal advice, and that you can take care of the concerns you each have as you go forward.

The goal in having separate representation is so that what you put in place is most likely to be done effectively. You can share with each other along the way, and you can ask for each other's input. You can do your plans in tandem, where you can cheer each other on as you both go forward. You get to choose the mood and the tone you set related to how you approach your planning — whether you do it individually or as a couple.

Estate planning is a play that involves lots of people other than just you. It is important to understand that your estate-planning decisions will impact the lives and relationships of a number of people long after your plans go into effect at the time of your death.

1. Characteristics of Blended Family Partners

The more details you can lay out for your estate-planning attorney about your mix and makeup, the more able he or she will be to create a plan that suits your unique needs.

Partners in a blended family couple can be very different from each other. They can be close in age, or there can be a wide age difference between the two. They can have different health issues and concerns. The partners may have vastly different sophistication and education backgrounds. There may be significant differences in the wealth and earning capacity of the couple. Some partners may have children while other partners may not. Some partners may be interested in having more children. The number and ages of the children may be vastly different, as may be the particular needs of each partner's children. Some couples may have joint children. A partner may have at least one living parent, while the other partner may not. One partner may have financial obligations to a former partner, but the other partner does not. Some partners may have several prior unions. Some partners may have children who have special needs.

While most blended family couples are married to each other, an increasing number of couples are not married. Some may have significant legal obstacles that prevent them from marrying. Some partners have to coexist or contend with former partners. Some blended family couples have been together for a long time, while other unions may be of short duration. In some blended family couples, one partner may have significant financial or emotional control over the other partner, while other couples are more evenly balanced. Partners may differ with regard to the relationships that each enjoys with the children of the other partner. This could range from no relationship to a poor relationship to a great relationship.

You may want to take a few minutes and complete Worksheet 1 (also included on the CD). This worksheet will help you record this information for your advisors.

2. Estate Planners

The second set of players in the estate-planning play is the estate planners. Estate planners are human and bring their own perspective (i.e., personal biases, personalities, and preferences) into the estate-planning process. Some estate

Worksheet 1
Our Key Characteristics

Features	Partner 1	Partner 2
Length of partnership		
Marital status (If you're not married, what is the intention and capacity?)		
Age		
Current health condition		
Health history		
Children from prior relationship(s) (Include names, ages, special needs, and status of your relationship with them; for example, daughter Sally from first marriage, 15, healthy, close relationship.)		
Number of children we have together (i.e., "ours").		
Interest in having more children		
Status of parents and stepparents (if applicable) (e.g., still living, state of health, needs)	Mother: Father: Stepmother: Stepfather:	Mother: Father: Stepmother: Stepfather:
Education and training background		
Socio-economic background (e.g., middle class)		
Level of personal wealth (this is separate from current partnership)		
Level of obligation to former spouse or partner		
Level of financial responsibility (e.g., dependency with each other)		

planners are biased in favor of certain estate-planning techniques and they are biased against others. Many estate planners make judgment calls in the so-called boilerplate of their estate-planning documents without discussing options with the client, whether those documents are beneficiary designations or legal documents such as wills or trusts.

You will like some estate planners as people; and others you won't like. Estate planners will feel the same way about you. Some estate planners will remind you of someone in your past you may like or dislike. You may remind the estate planner of someone in his or her past, which can be either good or bad. Some estate planners are better listeners than others. Some are better at explaining themselves, seemingly having an innate ability to speak in understandable layperson's terms.

Estate planners have no formal training in the "human side" of estate planning. In their formal education, they are taught the intricacies of their particular area of estate planning, with little or no education in critical areas such as how to interview clients, and how to deal with the emotions that clients can experience during the estate-planning process. They have to pick up the "bedside manner" of the human side of estate planning on the fly. The vast majority of estate planners purposefully shy away from the human side of estate planning, opting instead to focus on a limited area such as document preparation, life insurance sales, investment analysis, or estate-tax reduction, which may not be in their clients' best interest. There is a big difference between an estate planner and an estate-tax specialist. That difference is knowledge and awareness of the human side of estate planning.

There are usually multiple estate planners working for you at any given time, such as an estate-planning lawyer, a certified accountant, and a life insurance agent. There may also be others, such as an investment advisor, trust officer, or a planned giving professional. These people need to keep in touch with each other so that each knows what the other is doing for you. This often gets missed when people like yourselves forget that *you* are the director. The advisors may vie for which one of them gets to replace you as the director of your estate-planning play. This can be dangerous if left unchecked because some of them may be at odds with what another has proposed, and it is up to you to make sure all the choices being considered and utilized fit together and that they are not at odds with each other. It is important to find estate planners who can work well together and actually do so. It is imperative that you give all of your advisors the same information and that you give them the right to talk to each other and to exchange information relevant to your estate planning. The success of your estate plan depends on communication.

Perhaps more than any other estate-planning professional, estate-planning attorneys face some significant and tricky ethical issues when representing a couple in an estate-planning engagement, particularly when a blended family couple is involved. Any good attorney will require you to sign a document frequently referred to as an "engagement letter," which describes the terms of representation. It may include what the attorney will do for you, and how much the attorney will charge you for services. Some jurisdictions require attorneys to have written engagement letters.

One of you may already be represented by an estate planner, and the other may not be. He or she may simply agree to be represented by the same estate planner. This frequently happens. However, just know that this estate planner may be biased in favor of the original client, even if he or she is not supposed to be.

Other estate-planning disciplines have ethical rules too, and those rules may well impact those estate planners' abilities to represent you together. As we indicated at the beginning of this chapter, there are a number of instances where it would be wise, and it is very much expected, to hire separate representation. We realize that this effectively doubles the cost financially, and can take a toll emotionally.

Paul's experience with blended family joint representation has led him to see that there are a number of potential areas of conflict for joint representation to work; namely, disparities in age, children, and wealth. Unfortunately, hiring separate representation has proven to be sound advice with the statistics showing the separation rate among partners in blended family situations are even higher than the first marriage divorce rate. The truth is that separate representation keeps things cleaner.

3. Children

The next set of players in this estate-planning play is your children. Like the couple, your children are different people. You may like some of them, but not like others. Some you can trust when it comes to money; some you cannot. You may or may not agree with choices some of them have made, such as careers or partners.

Children often differ in their ages and in educational levels. Some children have finished their education, while others may still be in the process. Some children live with you, full time or part time, while others may live on their own. Some children are dependent on you for their livelihood, while others are self-supporting. Some children may have financial troubles. Others may have problems growing up or even a problem such as drugs, alcohol, or gambling. Some children may have issues that require special attention for the remainder of their lives, such as disabilities. You may be the primary caregiver for such a child, or someone else might be.

Some children may have partners, while others may not. We always counsel clients that a partner of a child always plays a very influential part in the life of the child. In other words, blood is not always thicker than water, or, in this case, marriage.

You may perceive your children's needs from your estate planning as different, even from child to child. Many parents slavishly maintain a "treat them all equally" posture. Children tend to expect this, which is a product of the "what about me" syndrome growing up. Other parents evaluate each child based on what the parent perceives the needs to be, or even whether the parent likes or trusts that child.

Some people will want their children to at least be aware of their estate plans while they're alive, while others will keep their estate plans a secret. We don't recommend the latter as surprises tend to create hard feelings between the surviving siblings, not to mention a greater sense of loss around not being able to talk with you about it. Your estate-planning decisions can definitely impact how your children interact with each other after your death, so think about that when you're trying to figure out what to do.

Children also vary greatly in their relationships with your partner. Some children, especially young children, may view the other partner as another parent. Many children greatly detest and resent the other partner. Other children, particularly grown children, may have little or no relationship with your partner. Your children's relationship (or lack thereof) with your partner will impact your selection of fiduciaries as well as estate-planning techniques.

3.1 Stepchildren

Why should your stepchildren be players in your estate plan at all? Because they may have significant influence on your partner in the estate-planning process; especially if you two are using the same estate-planning team.

> Including your stepchildren in your planning will do remarkable things for your relationship going forward.

You may be among the stepparents who want to provide for stepchildren, perhaps because they are young and may even see you as a parent, or possibly because they are the only children you've known and you have raised. However, you may not even know your stepchildren. You may get along well with your stepchildren, or relations may be strained. Another thing to consider is that your children may or may not know, and may or may not get along with, your stepchildren.

All of this is important because it can influence your choice of estate-planning techniques or even whether you want to do joint estate planning with your partner. You may find that one of your stepchildren would make a good trustee or executor, and perhaps even a better choice than one of your own children, although this can be problematic for the stepchild if not handled properly with him or her and with your birth children. In Chapter 2, we give some specific ways to go about approaching a conversation of this delicate, and potentially inflammatory, nature. Once you read Chapter 2 and get a sense for what it will take, you will see whether this is something you want to pursue on your own, or whether it might be better to hire a trained professional to facilitate the conversation.

3.2 Partners of your children

Partners can have significant influence on their spouses or partners who happen to be your children, and this influence may in turn have a significant impact on what estate-planning techniques you may want to enter into for that child. For example, if you are concerned about a child's partner having a bad or disruptive influence on your child, you may want to set up a trust with a third-party trustee for that child. Another consideration is how solid your child's relationship with a partner may be. If your child is in a short-term or rocky relationship with a partner, a trust may be needed in order to protect that child from his or her partner's possible malcontent.

> You may want to use a trust if you find that you don't trust your child's choice of partner.

4. Your Parents and Possibly Your Stepparents

It is not unusual for a parent of a partner to have a role in your estate-planning play. Many people have an elderly or infirm parent to care for, which must be factored into the estate plan in case the parent survives you.

In some instances, stepparents can play a vital role in estate planning as well. Emily knows of one family in Canada where a step-grandmother left a sizeable inheritance to each of her stepchildren and step-grandchildren, as they were the only family she had. Emily's own estate plan includes her two stepdaughters and three step-grandchildren.

It is also not unusual for a parent to have a significant estate of his or her own that could be factored into your estate plan, if for no other reason than to ask the parent to fashion his or her estate plan to allow you to disclaim your share so that it goes to your children. **Caution: In the US**, this must be done *very* carefully and according to the strict dictates of the Internal Revenue Code. Essentially, the Internal Revenue Code doesn't permit you to expressly disclaim in favor of your children without the disclaimer being considered a gift by you to your children. Disclaimers are more fully discussed in Chapter 10. Suffice it to say here that disclaimed property must pass without any direction by the person making the disclaimer.

5. Grandchildren and Step-Grandchildren

Your grandchildren and step-grandchildren might play a role in your estate-planning play. You may want them to receive a significant amount of your estate, you may want to pay for their education, or you may want them to play some role in the management of your estate, particularly where the grandchild's parent has made some problematic lifestyle choices or has predeceased you.

Caution is always advised when skipping a generation down to grandchildren as there could be generation-skipping transfer tax. The rules are complex. This should only be done with the guidance of competent counsel.

6. Other Players

Third parties can play significant roles in your estate planning. Perhaps you would like a good friend, a professional advisor, or a bank to consider serving in a fiduciary capacity such as executor, trustee, or guardian for a child. You should communicate with third parties in advance in order to make sure that they will accept the role that you want them to have and

will do it the way that you want it done. It is important to make sure that individuals you are approaching thoroughly understand what would be required of them in the particular role you would like them to consider. Having this conversation before they serve is imperative because they could easily spoil your plan by stepping aside. That's why it is important to name backup fiduciaries. Some friends who may have made great trustees, guardians, or executors could encounter difficulties in their own lives down the road that make it impossible for them to serve. They also may not survive you. This is a very common problem with naming someone in your own age bracket (or even an older person such as a parent).

> **Be sure to name contingent fiduciaries just in case!**

You could also approach a potential third-party trustee such as a bank to see if the bank will take on your trust. Some banks have minimum size restrictions for trusts; they will not take on trusts below a certain size. Banks are often particular about what your trust document says, so it is prudent to review the draft document with the bank's trust department to make sure that the bank will accept the document as written before you sign it. Just because you named the bank as trustee doesn't mean the bank is required to serve. If it doesn't like the terms of your trust, or if your trust will be small, it can decline to act. Banks are not necessarily opposed to taking on trusts with complicated scenarios (and perhaps even contentious parties) that can be in blended families, if the trust instrument is clear, and if the trust is large enough to warrant the difficulties. However, the last thing that a bank trust department wants is a small headache. Individual third parties such as professional fiduciaries, certified accountants, and other advisors also could be considered for a fiduciary position. More on the selection of fiduciaries, which can make or break your estate plan, is contained in Chapter 8.

7. Action Steps

Now that you know the players involved in your estate-planning play, it's time to sort them all out. We've provided Worksheets 1 and 2 in this chapter and on the CD to help you record all of this information, for your own records, and for the benefit of your advisors.

If you cannot take time right now to complete these worksheets, we strongly recommend you put an appointment in your calendar to adequately capture this information. Set aside 20 minutes and set a timer. Then, see how much you get accomplished during that time. If you need more time, set the timer for another ten minutes, or schedule another appointment in your calendar to finish this step. Once you are done, put your completed worksheets in a place where you can easily access them when working on your estate plan. Be sure to celebrate in some little way when these worksheets have been completed and put away.

Worksheet 2 will allow you to evaluate a potential estate-planning advisor.

Worksheet 2
Characteristics of a Potential Advisor

Name of advisor and his or her role (e.g., Don Smith, Estate-Planning Attorney):

_____

Office phone: _____

Cell phone: _____

Fax number: _____

Email address: _____

Mailing street address: _____

_____

City, state or province, zip or postal code: _____

Characteristics to Consider	Yes	No	Notes
Does the person listen?			
Does the person ask questions?			
Does the person understand blended family issues?			
Do I like the person?			
Does the person explain things in ways that I understand them?			
Do I, or would I feel comfortable asking him or her questions when I don't understand something?			
Does the person use a boilerplate approach? Does the person think we only need that kind of approach?			
Is the person more interested in documents and avoiding taxes, and less interested in other concerns?			
Can the person (or will he or she be able to) manage if we get emotional around the planning process?			

PART 2

Planning
Issues

CHAPTER 8

Reasons Estate Plans Fail

You may ask why we included a chapter about the reasons estate plans fail. We believe that this is one of the most important chapters in this book because the simple fact is many estate plans fail. According to research reported by Roy Williams and Vic Preisser in their book *Preparing Heirs*, 70 percent of estate plans fail. While unfortunate, failed estate plans provide golden opportunities to learn lessons from the mistakes that these people have made. Read the following reasons carefully; one of them can happen to your estate without proper planning to navigate the even more treacherous waters of blended family estate planning.

1. Failure to Complete and Implement the Estate Plan

The best estate plan ever devised is worthless if it is not completed and implemented. This seems rather self-evident, yet in our experience, many people walk around with incomplete estate plans. In other words, these people have started the estate-planning process but haven't put the estate plan into effect. Many others blithely say mañana and have done nothing at all but think about it. Too often, tomorrow comes earlier than anticipated. Don't be one of those people.

In our experience, estate planning is a matter of inertia: Once you start, you need to keep going until it is finished. Unfortunately, we see an inordinately high number of blended family estate plans go uncompleted. We suspect that this is because some tough choices have to be made that require forthright communication. That is why we chose to put a great degree of effort and attention on Chapter 2 on communication, so that you could get the tools and support you need to successfully complete your estate plan — and likely strengthen your relationship in the process.

> **Plan for success. Take out your calendar right now and, if you have not done so already, sit down with your partner and decide when you will both have your estate plans completed.**

1.1 Actions for success

Pull out your calendar and make a date with your partner to plan both your estates. When will you have your estate plan competed? Six months from today? A year from today? We invite you to be realistic and ambitious. One recommendation we have to make the process seamless and structured is to choose a date that is the same number of weeks away from today as the number of chapters in this book: 13 + 3 = 16 weeks. (The "+3" buffer takes into account that some chapters will require a bit more time to gather the data and other chapters will have more thought-provoking work to contend with.) Note each week which chapter you will tackle and the date by which you will complete the action steps. You can still go forward with the next chapter as you keep putting attention on the actions from the previous chapter. If you get bogged down, re-examine your intended date of completion and see what it will take on both your parts to complete by that time. Pushing the date ahead again and again is not an option, as you'll likely get caught in the mañana scenario mentioned earlier.

2. Failure to Provide Complete and Accurate Information to Estate Planners

It is axiomatic that you should provide complete and accurate information to your estate planners. However, the simple fact is that many people neglect, withhold, or refuse to turn over key pieces of information that, had the estate planner been apprised of that information, he or she would have changed the advice or recommendations given.

Why would someone intentionally withhold important information? Perhaps you think that the information is too embarrassing or will give too much financial information that will alert the taxing authorities. Whatever the reason, it is the wrong approach because it has been our experience that all of the information comes out after you're dead. Just like you can't take your property with you when you die, you can rarely take what you know about your affairs to your grave, especially if it affects someone still living. We also see a higher than average number of blended family estate plans fail due to withheld information, and we suspect that some of this is due to a number of different factors, including the following:

- There may not be enough trust and transparency between the two partners who choose to use only one estate planner.

- The complexities of the estate-planning process get the couple bogged down so they choose what they believe is enough information as a way to try to streamline the process, instead of digging up all the information and data that is needed.

- There may be sufficient shame and guilt about past choices and decisions that have one or both partners unwilling or unable to openly share all the sordid details with their advisors.

- The individuals may not know what to do about aspects of their estate so they end up not talking about it because they don't know where to begin.

Emily worked with one stepmother who purchased a piece of property in a foreign country with her first husband, and in the course of her estate planning the woman realized she still owned that property with him even though they had been divorced for three years. Her estate planning came to a grinding halt because she didn't know how to proceed, and this caused a great deal of frustration for herself and her current partner who both wanted to move forward. There was a lot of shame and embarrassment as she could not locate the needed documentation related to the property in order to even begin the process. Emily worked with her using the Money Types described in Chapter 2, to empower the woman's *Innocent* that wanted to ignore and hide the facts about the property because of her shame around how the *Fool* had jumped in to purchase it without adequately tracking everything.

They worked together to strengthen the woman's *Warrior* so that she could take the necessary actions to get the documentation and find out how to go about changing the ownership of the property into her former husband's name, as that was her wish. They broke down the process into small, incremental steps, and each day the woman took one small action towards her goal. They also found an advisor who understood this

particular scenario and was able to help them break down the steps even further and locate the needed information. During the process, Emily helped the woman navigate effectively when her *Victim* and *Martyr* would show up feeling angry and hurt and resentful towards her former husband and his *Fool* who had "gotten them into this situation." Emily showed her how to tap into gratitude for all that she had and how her life had improved since her divorce.

The woman saw how taking care of this on her own was an important step towards her goals of claiming her own power and not being a victim or blaming others for things. She was committed to becoming more empowered and effective in her financial life, as this was a lifelong pattern she was ready to shift. The relief and joy this stepmom felt when she completed this project was beyond what she had imagined, and she used it to fuel the rest of the estate planning that became effortless and much more fun as a result. She and her new partner benefited from increased intimacy and understanding, and he saw how much she grew and learned as a result.

2.1 Actions for success

- Take an honest look at the reasons above for why documents and needed information do not get provided. Could any of the reasons be true for you? Now's the time to get real and clear and determine if you will have the ability to work with one estate-planning advisor together, or if you will need to work with separate ones.

- Use the Vital Information for Executor and Trustee and Document Preparation forms (included on the CD and discussed in Chapter 6) to easily locate and collect all your documents and data for your advisors.

- If you hit a roadblock to getting some necessary data or documentation, see if you can access your *Magician* or *Creator/Artist* to come up with creative solutions and alternatives that will support you in getting the data you need in the time frame you desire.

> What one document would help support this process in flowing even more easily? Write it down and make a goal for when you will have that document in front of you.

3. Failure to Coordinate

People often try to do piecemeal estate planning (e.g., a life insurance policy here, a will there) but no coordinated estate plan. Here's an example of a failure to properly plan in a coordinated way. Suppose your wills are drafted to pay estate tax at either death, but your life insurance policy is a second-to-die life insurance policy, which doesn't pay its benefits until both insured parties die. Your will needs to be coordinated with *all* of your other estate-planning, whether it's your life insurance, lifetime trusts, or buy-sell agreement. It is imperative that all of this estate planning be coordinated.

3.1 Actions for success

After you have chosen all your advisors and created your list with all of their contact information (use the Estate-Planning Team Contact Information sheet, which is included on the CD), you can do the following:

- Give each advisor copies of the information along with permission to coordinate and speak with your other advisors.

- Convene a roundtable meeting with all of your advisors together where you do the overview of the goals and the data and create a plan together.

- Have regularly scheduled, brief conference calls where you are in the loop with all of your advisors at one time, learning what has been completed, what the next action items are, and what is required of you.

4. Failure to Communicate about Your Estate Plan

It may not be evident why communication of your estate-planning intentions with your loved ones is so important, but our experience and research has shown us unquestionably that it is. The research from Roy Williams and Vic Preisser in their book *Preparing Heirs* showed that the number one reason why 70 percent of estate plans fail is a lack of communication and trust among family members as it related to the family's wealth, assets, finances, and estate plan.

Family members and perhaps others have expectations about an inheritance from you, whether or not they should. When these expectations are not met after your death, many of them leap to some conclusions that may not be true and they may take some actions that are unnecessary.

For example, Paul has had very wealthy and powerful men break down and cry in his office when telling him that they didn't receive an equal share of their parents' estates, even when the men were several times wealthier than their parents. Their conclusion: Their parents didn't love them as much as the other children.

Emily had a client whose stepmother made him executor of her will while leaving everything to his three brothers and nothing to him. He was determined not to allow his second wife to do the same thing to his children from his prior marriage.

Had these parents in the above examples simply told these men either during their lifetime or by a letter at death (or inclusion in a will or living trust) what their reasons were, the men might not have been left for years wondering why their parents did what they did. One simple communication could have staved off years of not only heartbreak but possible resentment of their siblings, neither of which the parents probably intended.

Other possible unnecessary outcomes that could occur after your death include resenting some or all of the receivers of power or property as well as litigation in contesting or simply prolonging the matter. We firmly believe that good communication can prevent or at least minimize these types of actions by reducing animosity and creating buy-in with all family members so that everyone is clear about what to expect at the time of your death.

When we say communication, we mean exactly that. You don't have to ask your family for their input, although we have found that this is a good idea most of the time. Your estate plan is yours alone: It is not a democracy. However, communicating *why* you're doing what you are doing in your estate plan can prevent broken relationships after your death as well as costly litigation where no one wins but the lawyers. In blended families, because of the complexity and tenuousness of some relationships to begin with, communication is even more encouraged because, again, more blended family estate

plans seem to fail on this score. Communication can be made during your lifetime or shortly after your death. It can be in writing, recorded, or merely oral. The big thing is to just do it.

> **The communication tips and strategies in Chapter 2 can support you in having a conversation effectively.**

Paul experienced pushback from clients when he enthusiastically encouraged communication. Some thought that it was simply none of their heirs' business. Others were scared at the prospect of confrontation. However, after relating some horror stories of the things that can happen if they don't communicate the reason for the estate-planning decisions, the overwhelming majority did so, and most of them actually found the experience to be pleasant and it gave them significant peace of mind. Emily has also seen that with a few key strategies to effectively open up a sense of safety in the communication process, couples learn things they were unaware of that had them re-evaluate and adjust their planning in ways that worked even better for all concerned.

4.1 Actions for success

- Review Chapter 2 on communication and see which of the strategies discussed seem the most relevant and doable for you and your partner (you may find that you each choose different ones).

- Look at one aspect of your estate-planning process with which you'd like to begin to open a conversation with *all* the children in your blended family. Perhaps it will be about education or maybe about the family home.

- If you feel that communication is needed but you do not feel skilled enough to proceed on your own, consider hiring a coach to work with you to build skills and to facilitate one or multiple family meetings, depending on how large and complex your estate is. (The Resources file on the CD includes a list of estate-planning and wealth coaches.)

5. Incomplete or Incorrect Beneficiary Designations

As we've said several times in this book, and it can't be said enough, deficient or even missing beneficiary designations are the culprits for many failed estate plans. Too often, people don't give a lot of thought to the ramifications of their decisions about beneficiaries of life insurance, retirement plans, and Individual Retirement Accounts (IRAs), even though these constitute the majority of the wealth of most people. They are often hurriedly completed. The first step is to gather all of the beneficiary designations that are on file with the company or plan provider. You can't work from memory here.

Paul has experienced some horror stories where companies lost the original beneficiary forms, which caused some serious and unfortunate chaos. After you gather all your beneficiary designations, you need to sit down with your estate-planning attorney and coordinate your beneficiary designations with your overall estate plans. You should also have contingent beneficiary designations in case the original beneficiary dies before you do. You need to describe with specificity what is to happen if, for example, one of your beneficiaries dies but leaves children. Who gets that share? The surviving beneficiaries (which is what most plans provide)? Or do the children of the predeceased beneficiary, who often are your grandchildren, get the share?

Consider the following example: Suppose that Bill has three sons, Moe, Larry, and Curly, and Moe dies before Bill. Moe has a son, Shemp. When Bill dies, it is discovered that he has not changed his beneficiary designation to reflect Moe's death. What happens to Moe's share? Is it simply divided between Moe's surviving brothers, Larry and Curly, or does Shemp step in and take Moe's share? Your beneficiary form should describe your intentions in this regard, or the terms of the retirement plan, which you probably don't know, will govern. The bottom line: Describe what you want to have happen and don't leave it up to chance.

You must give this significant thought and seek competent professional advice with these matters. Unfortunately, blended family estate plans are more deficient in this area than most, again because of the complexity and often torn agendas with "yours, mine, and ours" to look after.

5.1 Actions for success

- Pull together your beneficiary designations that are on file with the plan administrator or plan provider.

- Review all the designations and make sure that they are up to date and reflect what you want your estate plan to do. These must be in alignment.

- Make these fully available to your estate-planning team and make sure key beneficiaries are aware of designations if their being a beneficiary will have an impact on their estate planning as well.

6. Failure to Keep Estate Plan Current

Even the best estate plans can go stale if not revisited regularly. Sometimes this is due to law changes. Usually, though, it is due to life changes. In blended families, we've seen many situations where a former partner received a large share of the deceased partner's estate (i.e., the decedent), life insurance, or retirement plans because the decedent failed to update the estate plan after the separation. Some jurisdictions have laws that automatically remove a spouse as an heir at the time of divorce, but these laws may not apply to life insurance or retirement plans. However, these laws only apply to married partners. Unmarried partners who separate are at a greater risk of having a former partner share in their estates without affirmative action on their part to change their estate plans on a split.

As Emily was working on this chapter with Paul, she met a woman who shared a relevant story with her. This woman's third husband got sick two weeks after he spoke with her about needing to review their documents. Unfortunately, they didn't review their documents prior to his death, and his well-thought-out and well-designed trust was broken due to the fact that the beneficiaries he named on retirement documents at work superseded his trust documents and the intention he expressed in his will. She didn't put up a fight, as she was fine with his kids getting a third of the estate and not being a trustee — and she mentioned that one of his sons still has nothing to do with her and blames her. She found it sad that her husband's wishes were not carried out due to an oversight. The woman commented on how important this book is and how she hoped her story might encourage people to double and triple check that their documents all work to fulfil the same goals, and they do not contradict one another.

6.1 Actions for success

If you have not done so already, now's the time to review the beneficiaries of all your various estate-planning documents. You may be surprised by what you find. As you do the review and make any updates and changes, keep track of this information in an easy-to-locate place so that you have ease of future changes when the time comes. We recommend putting this information in your estate-planning binder so that it is with everything else and easy to find.

7. Choosing the Wrong Trustee or Executor

Many people ask what the difference is between an executor and a trustee. The ultimate difference is that almost always the job of trustee lasts much longer and requires more ability than the job of executor.

The executor's role is intended to be temporary and only lasts while the estate is being administered. The executor's administrative tasks include, but are not limited to, the identification and gathering of the assets in the estate, payment of the decedent's debts, taxes, and distribution of the assets to the ultimate recipients — whether outright to individuals, to trustees, or pursuant to the laws of intestacy. If the executor is guided by an attorney who possesses the requisite skill in estate administration, not much skill may be required of an executor. This couldn't be further from the truth for a trustee. Trustees must possess much more skills, which are discussed in the next few paragraphs.

Ultimately, estate plans are administered by people. The best estate-planning documents on earth won't save an estate plan that is managed by the wrong people. How do you know who the right people are? The first thing to consider is whether someone is very competent in financial matters. The most well-intentioned, good-hearted soul who can't manage finances is an accident waiting to happen as a trustee or executor. Good evidence of financial ability is how the person manages his or her own finances; one who can't manage his or her own finances is more likely to be tempted to access the money under his or her control that belongs to other people.

The prospective *fiduciary* must either be a great record keeper or be willing to farm that out to professionals. We also suggest that a prospective fiduciary be independently wealthy or, at least, more than self-sufficient, to prevent the temptation to poach the property of the estate or trust and also to be able to cover any mistakes that he or she makes in the administration of the estate or trust. People frequently don't consider the need to have a bond for a fiduciary, but it often is a good idea to require one, especially for trustees unless you choose a corporate fiduciary such as a bank or trust company. For more information about bonds for fiduciaries in the United States, go to www.suretybonds.com/surety-bonds.html.

You will need to consider a prospective fiduciary's age. Someone who would be a terrific choice but who is older than you are is probably not who you want because chances are that he or she won't survive you. If you're considering a corporate fiduciary, you probably want to investigate the experience of the prospective fiduciary in estates and trusts, meaning the experience of the employees of the corporate fiduciary. One thing to be aware of as you make your considerations is the degree of turnover in the corporate environment, as you may choose a great employee who ends up leaving the company prior to your death.

You need to consider whether the prospective fiduciary will have a conflict of interest that might cause him or her to favor himself or herself over the other beneficiaries. While this is not a totally determinative factor in traditional, nuclear families, it can be a real problem in a blended family. Stepchildren tend to be more demanding and more litigious when a surviving partner serves as a fiduciary for the stepchildren.

You should consider how the prospective fiduciary is as a communicator because a very frequent source of conflict between fiduciaries and heirs is miscommunication, or incomplete, inadequate, infrequent, or otherwise poor communication.

How flexible is the prospective fiduciary? This is especially important if you're going to give the fiduciary significant flexibility, which usually is a good idea so that he or she is able to address unforeseen future changes.

One significant criticism of corporate fiduciaries is that they are rigid, poor communicators, bureaucratic, and fail to exercise the discretion given to them, especially when it comes to distributing property or income to a beneficiary. Frequently, the best option is to have a person and a corporate fiduciary as co-fiduciaries, with the corporate fiduciary taking care of the investments and taxes, and having the individual fiduciary taking care of the needs of the beneficiaries, although this is truer in our experience for trustees than executors.

Another quality that we look for in a fiduciary is that he or she must be strong enough to withstand what can be very belligerent beneficiaries who want all of the money now. If the trustee capitulates to the haranguing of beneficiaries (or their lawyers), the purpose of the trust can be compromised, which can be devastating.

> **Your fiduciaries need to have strong _Warrior_ traits.**

It is usually a good idea to put a system of checks and balances on fiduciaries in order to level the playing field, particularly with a corporate fiduciary or where a beneficiary also is a fiduciary. This also is particularly true for blended family situations. We usually recommend the following:

- Require accounting records to be provided no less than annually (local law often requires this).

- Allow the beneficiaries to replace a fiduciary with another fiduciary under specified circumstances.

- Require the consent of beneficiaries or others prior to the fiduciary taking certain significant actions (e.g., selling a family business).

- Impose a trust protector (who is almost always an individual and who is sometimes called a "special trustee" or "trust advisor") between the trustee and the beneficiaries for both flexibility as well as to rein in a wayward fiduciary or to remove a fiduciary.

Note: There are myriad significant tax reasons for naming an independent trustee depending on how you want to structure the trust. You will need to be assisted in this area by your estate-planning attorney.

Finally, and this could be its own separate mistake, is a failure to name successor fiduciaries or, at least, a means of appointing successors.

This is particularly true in blended families where a beneficiary, be it your partner or one of your children, also is serving as a fiduciary, and he or she either passes away or is no longer able to perform the duties. Consider who will take over the person's role and specify your choice.

7.1 Actions for success

- If you have already selected your executors and trustees, congratulations — this is a major accomplishment in and of itself. Now, use this section to make sure that the people you have chosen are right for the position. Do they meet all the criteria? Is there a conflict of interest?

- If you have not selected your executors and trustees, now's the time to do so. You are empowered now to know how to select the right person. Consider all your options of people and make sure they meet all the requirements given above to assure that your estate will be managed well and with minimal challenges.

- Once you've narrowed down your choices, consider who will be your first choice and who your alternatives are. Once you get firm commitments, you need to choose the successor fiduciaries and approach them to get their commitment as well.

8. Bad Estate-Planning Advice

Unfortunately, many estate plans fail because people picked the wrong estate planners or the estate planners that they selected gave incorrect or bad advice. Sometimes this is malpractice, but quite often it is not. You want a balanced and experienced estate-planning team working in unison for you at your direction. Don't hesitate to bring in another member of your estate-planning team or to change estate planners, although you should have good reasons for doing the latter, knowing that not liking their advice often isn't a good reason. Estate planning is not a job for the dabbler. You need and must have a team of people who do almost nothing but estate planning.

Too often, people want to use their divorce lawyer, or a lawyer who helped them in a lawsuit, or a family member who might be less expensive than hiring a professional. This is usually a bad idea. Using the same lawyer in a family situation might be a conflict of interest for the lawyer. In blended family situations, it may be problematic for you to use your partner's estate-planning attorney because of the possibility of divided loyalty for the attorney or favoring the longer relationship.

8.1 Actions for success

In Chapter 11, we go into detail about how to select the right estate-planning attorney for you, including resources, questions, and areas to consider. Study Chapter 11 and use it as a guide in finding the right advisors for you. Make sure your advisors understand the complexities of blended family issues and they have had experience in this particular area when it comes to estate planning.

9. Elections against a Will

This section applies to married partners only. It is especially relevant for those spouses who cannot agree on how to divvy the estate in ways that feel fair to both of them. Depending on your jurisdiction, a spouse may be able to claim rights in up to one-half of your estate unless that right has been properly waived in a valid prenuptial or postnuptial agreement. You'll have to ask your estate-planning attorney the ins and outs of this area (e.g., how much the spouse can get, how he or she can get it, and what is covered in your estate that is potentially exposed to a spousal election). It's also imperative that you get good advice from an expert in nuptial agreements since these are often challenged at death if the spouse doesn't get what he or she thinks that he or she deserves.

9.1 Actions for success

- Consult a local estate-planning attorney who is well versed in the phenomena of elections against a will. Not only will you learn more about this aspect of estate planning, but you will also learn a lot about how that advisor works with clients by how he or she answers your questions. Does the person explain the answers in ways you understand? Does he or she understand why something like this might be important to consider? Does the person listen to you or does he or she steer you towards what he or she thinks is right and better before getting all the relevant facts?

- Review your marriage contracts and property agreements with the same attorney and see if they cover your concerns adequately, or if there is vulnerability. If you do not have either of these contracts or agreements, consult with the attorney about how you might get a postnuptial agreement at this stage, or whether there other documents he or she recommends that would be better.

10. Post-Death Will and Trust Challenges

Few things delay the administration of an estate longer than post-death challenges to the estate plan. As we've discussed at several points in this book, it has been our experience that a significant amount of post-death challenges almost always arise from a failure to meet the suing person's expectations of inheritance. However, there are people who, out of pure spite, will challenge an estate, will, or trust. We see far more of both categories in blended family situations.

The vast majority of post-death challenges fall into two basic categories:

1. Challenges based on a claim that the decedent was not in his or her right mind when he or she made his or her estate plan.

2. A claim that someone unduly influenced the decedent to make the estate plan the way that it was made.

It is the latter category that more blended family estate-planning partners have to be concerned about due to the frequency of discord between stepparents and stepchildren. This is one reason partners in blended families choose to do their estate planning independently of each other and their children. While this choice may cause the "undue influence" claim seem unfounded, it does not preclude a disgruntled heir from suing anyway. As we've shown already, effective communication is the key to mitigating litigation in the end.

10.1 Actions for success

- Review Chapter 2 on communication and see if it seems feasible to apply these techniques with your blended family members. If so, you have a better chance of getting buy-in from all your children (and hopefully their spouses too). If they are honored and respected during your lifetime, and they have the sense that you

understand what matters to them, they will be much more likely to go along without contention.

- If you see the value of open communication, and also see that your family needs additional support in having these conversations, you would be wise to hire a facilitator or coach who specializes in estate planning and family dynamics. A list of possible resources has been provided in the Resources section on the CD.

- If you believe there's no way your family will ever be in the same state or province together, let alone the same room, and that open communication is out of the question, speak with your advisor about possible clauses you can utilize in your estate plan to minimize the likelihood of litigation.

11. Too Much Joint-Tenancy Property

Joint tenancy can be the prime enemy of estate plans because property that is titled as joint tenants automatically passes to the surviving joint tenant on the death of the first joint tenant to die. In situations where this may not be your intention, or if it conflicts with what your other estate-planning documents provide, it will override them and they become irrelevant where those assets are concerned.

11.1 Action for success

Now's the time to review your property and how it is owned, if you haven't done so already — and not just real estate, as it may refer to bank accounts as well. Take time to look at what you own and how it's owned and determine if you need to restructure some or all of your joint tenancies. If you find that a property is titled as joint tenants that you wanted to go to other heirs, you may need to either re-title it, or reconfigure other aspects of your estate to take care of your original goal for how you wanted to treat your heirs.

12. Failure to Properly Plan for Disability

Just because you have a living trust or a property power of attorney doesn't mean that you are adequately prepared for disability. It is important that your power of attorney document, especially if it is a springing power of attorney, clearly describes a procedure for "springing" the power of attorney into effect. The same thing is true for the activation of a successor trustee in a living trust. If your document doesn't do that, you may have to go to court and incur that expense and time delay. Additionally, if you have a living trust, your property power of attorney and your living trust must be coordinated with each other.

12.1   Actions for success

- First and foremost, make sure you have a power of attorney in place. If you don't, it is essential and should be noted on your calendar as a high priority.

- Review Chapter 6 where powers of attorney are covered at length to determine if yours should be springing or not.

- Make sure that your power of attorneys are designed as you intend, and if you want them to be springing, that you have clearly and specifically delineated what will trigger the springing into effect.

- For those of you with a living trust, or who intend to have a living trust, make sure that your property power of attorney and your living trust are coordinated with each other.

13. Overfunding of the US Marital Deduction Portion

If you have to worry about the US federal estate tax and you are married, overfunding what effectively passes to the surviving spouse could cause you to underutilize your $5,120,000 (in 2012) US estate-tax exemption. Of course, the temporary law of portability, which allows spouses to transfer unused estate-tax exemptions to the surviving spouse, may save the day if that law is made permanent as is expected, although the law of portability has a number of traps for the unwary. One of the biggest traps is what happens in the event that the surviving spouse remarries; this law is somewhat complicated, so your estate-planning attorney can explain it further if need be. We believe that it is strongly advisable for married partners in blended family relationships to each utilize separately their respective estate-tax exemptions.

13.1   Action for success

Make sure you understand fully how to best utilize your respective estate-tax exemptions and work with your advisors to make sure they implement them according to your wishes.

14. Relying on a Beneficiary to Do the "Right Thing"

Believe it or not, there is a good percentage of people who simply wish to leave it up to someone else to determine who gets what out of their estates. For example, they leave their estates to their partners or to one of their children with nonbinding instructions as to how they wish the estate to be divided. Most of the time, these people truly believe that the designated person will do the "right thing" and divide the estate either equally amongst their heirs, or that they will know and do what the person wanted them to do with the property. Sadly, this rarely happens, so the designated person often keeps the entire estate. This type of attitude can be particularly dangerous in blended families since there is less incentive for the designated person, be it a child from a prior relationship or a surviving partner, to share property with their stepfamily.

14.1 Action for success

Our sense is that if this is your preference, you likely have a strong *Innocent* and *Fool* pattern of dealing with overwhelming planning and making significant decisions. We encourage you to review Chapter 2 and become more familiar with the Money Types concept and see how to strengthen your *Warrior* to have a better sense for how you might go about choosing an estate-planning process that will truly yield the results you want. To learn more about Money Types, you can read *Money Magic* by Deborah L. Price. You can also request a personal assessment by going to www.blended-families.com/estateplanning.

CHAPTER 9

Lifetime Estate Planning

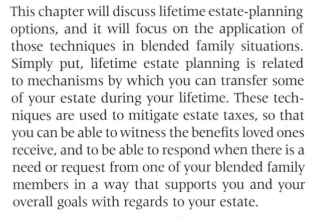

This chapter will discuss lifetime estate-planning options, and it will focus on the application of those techniques in blended family situations. Simply put, lifetime estate planning is related to mechanisms by which you can transfer some of your estate during your lifetime. These techniques are used to mitigate estate taxes, so that you can be able to witness the benefits loved ones receive, and to be able to respond when there is a need or request from one of your blended family members in a way that supports you and your overall goals with regards to your estate.

This chapter will review the potential estate-planning options that are available during one's lifetime. The descriptions are not intended to be an all-encompassing discussion of each particular technique. If you are uncertain about a particular technique, or if you have questions that the discussion doesn't answer, please consult a book on estate-planning techniques. Our discussion of each technique is intended to focus on the use or advised nonuse of that estate-planning technique given the nuances of blended families.

We will break down the discussion by wealth categories for ease of accessing the information most relevant to you. These wealth categories are not set in stone and only represent our opinion. In other words, these categories don't necessarily mean that if you aren't in a particular wealth category, you can't use a particular estate-planning technique. They just mean that, in our opinion, certain techniques work better in certain wealth categories — reasonable minds can and will differ on these wealth categories. It also doesn't mean that if you are in one of these wealth categories, you should use one or more of these techniques. You may have personal circumstances that dictate that you do something else — or even nothing at all. We offer them as guidelines and as a way to help you sort all your options. Your advisor will be able to assist you in determining what makes the most sense for you and your blended family.

Note: There isn't a lot of lifetime estate planning to do in Canada other than to make gifts since there isn't a gift tax. While this chapter covers mostly American options, Canadian readers can discuss similar options with their Canadian advisors.

1. Irrevocable Lifetime Estate Planning

Before we go into the various techniques related to lifetime estate planning, we want to emphasize one aspect that applies to everyone up front: **General admonition against irrevocable lifetime estate planning**.

By *irrevocable* lifetime estate planning, we mean estate planning that, once done, usually can't be undone without a lot of trouble and potential expense. Estate planners often break down lifetime estate-planning considerations to whether or not the client can afford to make lifetime gifts. Estate planners too often attempt to make the determination regarding what the client can afford to do with respect to lifetime gifting, instead of having the *client* make that determination.

Sometimes, the estate planner's advice is couched in terms of what the client cannot afford *not* to do. This is particularly true in the area of *annual exclusion gifting* (i.e., gifts of $13,000 per year in 2012 in the United States to an unlimited number of people) as well as the $5,120,000 per person *gift tax exemption* in the US at least until 2013. Many clients who engage in annual exclusion gifting ultimately cut back on those gifts over time because of fear of running out of money or because of actually running out

or becoming short of money. This can cause stress on family members who have grown accustomed to receiving the gift regularly and planned on it in their budgets. Even with the understanding that it is a gift, it is easy for people to expect it once it happens repeatedly. When the gift stops showing up, often without warning, there can be upset that cannot easily be expressed, as no one wants to seem greedy or entitled. In reality, they just needed to have the change communicated to them so that they could plan accordingly.

We strongly recommend that if you do choose to take advantage of the annual exclusion gifting option, that you do so in a way that ensures the recipients *know* that it is a gift and not to expect it from one year to the next. If you should find that you will not be giving the gift, definitely give your recipients a heads up.

2. Techniques Applicable to All Wealth Categories

The first category of techniques applies to people in all wealth categories, although, again, we're not advocating your use of any technique because we don't know your situation. This is why you need to consult with and listen to an experienced estate planner who knows and understands *your* family's needs.

2.1 Severing joint-tenancy arrangements

One of the most common and effective lifetime estate-tax planning devices involves the severing of joint-tenancy arrangements. A joint tenancy is a form of property ownership in which at least two owners hold title to property as joint tenants with rights of survivorship, meaning that the last surviving joint tenant will become the full owner of the property. People often enter into joint-tenancy arrangements without really thinking or knowing about them. Quite often, someone else, such as a real estate title clerk, decides for them simply by innocently typing the deed to reflect joint tenancy. The good thing about joint tenancy is that it is simple and at least avoids probate in the estate of the first joint tenant to die.

However, joint tenancy can ruin the estate planning of the first joint tenant to die by leaving that property to the surviving joint tenant. This can be crucial to estate planning for a blended family because the property automatically passes to the surviving joint tenant on the death of the first joint tenant. In the context of a blended family, this almost always means that the children and other loved ones of the deceased joint tenant will get nothing with respect to that property. This often conflicts with the intentions of the deceased joint tenant. What is in the deceased joint tenant's will, or, worse yet, what the deceased joint tenant intended is irrelevant.

The US federal estate tax consequences of a joint tenancy differ depending on the identity of the joint tenants. If a husband and wife are the joint tenants, then there will be no federal estate tax for that property on the death of the first joint tenant because of the unlimited marital deduction. However, if anyone but spouses are joint tenants (e.g., a parent and a child or two unmarried partners), the federal estate tax consequences depend on who actually paid for the property. Consider this example: Unmarried partners are joint tenants on property that one of them actually paid for in total. At the death of the one who bought the property, all of the value of the property will be included in the person's estate who purchased the property. Even if spouses are the joint tenants, joint tenancy may cost the estate of the first spouse to die its use of the full estate-tax exemption by overfunding what goes outright to the surviving spouse, which qualifies for the marital deduction.

Paul almost never recommends that couples, particularly those in blended family relationships, own property as joint tenants. An estate planner who represents both partners may have an ethical or a prickly client relation's problem with recommending severance of a joint-tenancy arrangement. This is because joint tenancy may actually work in favor of a younger partner, particularly one who is less wealthy than the other partner, because the younger partner is more likely to survive and get all of that property. This is clearly an area of potential conflict between the partners. Nevertheless, Paul always recommends severance, reasoning that since you never really know who will survive (e.g., Emily's mother was younger and died suddenly at age 44; her father is alive and well at 76), the parties are in the same boat at the time of the severance.

The beauty of severing a joint tenancy is that one partner can do it unilaterally without the other partner having to approve the change or even having to know about it. Again, this is a reason to have separate representation, because a lawyer may be hamstrung by ethical obligations to the other partner and unable to participate in severance without telling the other partner if the lawyer represents both of you (except in the rare circumstance where the lawyer represents each of you separately).

This secrecy might be a signal that your partnership is not as solid as you would like it to be. You may want to ask yourself what it is that has you feeling the need to act in secret. Perhaps it is justified because your partner was asked and is being unreasonable. If that is how you see it, consider for a moment what you would feel if the situation were reversed. If you still believe you should go forward in secret, we strongly recommend you consider the ramifications of your partner finding out that you've gone behind his or her back — especially since he or she could be reading this book as well and considering the same thing.

Emily will often ask her clients who are leaning on the side of being secretive to consider their compelling reason why. She has them articulate what is motivating them and what they hope to accomplish by making that choice. She also has them look at other possible options and scenarios and does what she can to open up new possibilities. Chapter 2 on communication strategies shares some helpful approaches when there's a strong sense of gridlock around a decision such as this.

2.2 Life insurance

Life insurance policies can be owned by the insured or someone who has an "insurable interest" in the insured, such as a spouse, child, or business partner. Strangers can't get insurance on you. Life insurance can be community property or separate property. Life insurance policies can be obtained and owned by a trustee and held in trust for the benefit of beneficiaries who have an insurable interest in you. There are many books about life insurance, so this discussion will be limited to the uses of life insurance in estate planning for blended families.

There are several ways to distinguish between life insurance policy types. However, every type of life insurance is either *whole life* or *term*, or a mix between the two, despite the many different marketing names that insurance companies give life insurance policies, such as *variable life* or *variable universal life*, to name a few.

In a whole life policy, a life insurance policy has a level premium that an insurance company cannot ever increase, no matter how long the insured lives. A term insurance policy has an annual premium that increases every year until the insured's death. Why? Because it is more likely that you will die with each passing year.

Life insurance can be a very valuable and flexible asset for use in the blended family, but it is not without its disadvantages and traps for the unwary. Unlike annuities, which are a bet to live, life insurance is a bet to die. In other words, the sooner that an insured dies, the less expensive the life insurance works out to be. Unfortunately, the flip side also is true: The longer that the insured lives, the more expensive life insurance becomes.

One of the biggest advantages of life insurance is that it provides an immediate benefit on the death of one or two people. Life insurance provides cash, arguably the most flexible asset, at a time when it often is most needed. For example, a father in a blended family could provide an immediate inheritance outright or in trust for the benefit of his children, so that they would not have to wait until their mother's death to receive a significant inheritance. This could dissuade the children of the father from harassing the surviving stepmother for money or for acting as executor or successor trustee. In another example, life insurance could be used to provide a surviving stepfather with an income stream, which would allow a mother to leave an income-producing asset (e.g., a family business) to her children.

Life insurance is not without its disadvantages. Chief among these disadvantages is the cost of maintaining life insurance until the insured's death, particularly where the insured lives well into old age. Many forms of life insurance increase exponentially in price as an insured approaches projected life expectancy age, and increase even more as the insured lives past projected life expectancy. There also is the disadvantage of potentially subjecting the life insurance to estate taxation if the insured either owns or controls the life insurance policy at death, although the insurance could be put into a properly structured life insurance trust and avoid this result, as is discussed in section **3.1**.

There are many different ways to categorize life insurance. However, for our purposes, we will divide life insurance into two types, single-life coverage (i.e., a policy on only one life) and joint-life coverage (i.e., a policy on two lives such as second-to-die or survivorship coverage).

Single-life coverage, whether it is whole life or term insurance, can be helpful in estate planning for blended families in many ways. Perhaps a father has minor children or a special-needs child for whom he needs to provide. Suppose that a partner wants to leave a valuable home to his partner that comprises a large part of his estate, but also wants to leave a significant inheritance to his children by a prior union. Life insurance could be used to provide the children with a significant inheritance while allowing him to give the home to his partner. Life insurance also could be used to create a stream of income for a surviving partner, while passing on other property (e.g., a family business, family homestead, or farm) to the children of the prior union. For blended couples who have their own children together (i.e., "ours"), life insurance could be used to provide for the education and support of joint children, who are younger than the separate children of each partner.

Second-to-die life insurance is typically used to pay for coverage to assist in the payment of US estate taxes where those taxes are deferred until the surviving partner's death through the US federal estate tax marital deduction; although, it is important to note that this marital deduction is only applicable to married partners. In second-to-die life insurance, the partners are not the beneficiaries; the children usually are, or a life insurance trust. In estate planning for blended families, a properly structured second-to-die life insurance policy can assist in the payment of the estate tax not only on the surviving partner's estate, but also on the amount of estate tax that was deferred from the estate of the first partner to die through the marital deduction, at least in estates of married partners. Again, there is no deferred federal estate tax to worry about for unmarried partners since deferral through the marital deduction is not available.

Second-to-die life insurance is also not without its problems, although many of these problems can be substantially reduced by a carefully crafted policy from a solid life insurance company. Second-to-die life insurance is often suggested when only one partner is insurable. However, this often isn't a good idea, because that insurance can be more expensive than a single-life policy on the insurable partner.

Moreover, if the premium on a second-to-die life insurance policy is designed around the US gift tax annual exclusion gifts of both insured partners ($13,000 per donee in 2012), there usually is a problem at the death of the first partner because the deceased partner loses his or her US gift tax annual exclusion gift right at death. This usually means that the surviving partner will have to supply all of the premiums with only one set of annual exclusion gifts to cover them, which requires the surviving partner to use his or her lifetime gift tax exemption, and when that is exhausted, start paying gift taxes. In a blended family situation, a surviving partner who has children of his or her own may balk at essentially giving the children of the deceased partner annual exclusion gifts to pay the annual premiums or, worse yet, paying gift tax for the privilege of making gifts to his or her stepchildren. As you can well imagine, that usually doesn't go over very well and therefore usually doesn't happen.

For example, suppose partners purchase second-to-die life insurance, naming their separate children as the beneficiaries. Suppose further that the life insurance premiums are large enough to require use of both partners' annual exclusions. On the death of the first partner, the life insurance premiums almost always continue until the surviving partner's death, a financial burden usually borne by the surviving partner. Therefore, it might be advisable to create an arrangement with assets set aside to generate enough cash flow to pay the premiums for the remainder of the surviving partner's life. A single-life insurance policy on each partner's life, or a rider on a second-to-die life insurance policy that pays a death benefit at the first death, should be considered.

> **Understand the pros and cons of life insurance before making your decision.**

2.3   Annuities

By annuities we mean contracts sold by life insurance companies. This is to be distinguished from private annuities, which are between individuals (discussed in section **4.1**). This discussion is limited to the use of annuities in estate planning for blended families, as annuities can be quite complex and can have a lot of different features. Annuities are the opposite of life insurance and essentially are a "bet to live" because the issuer of the annuity, a life insurance company, bears the risk of the annuitant living too long. Annuities can provide protection against someone running out of money in old age because most annuities provide lifetime benefits.

In practice, Paul rarely recommends that wealthier people consider annuities because of the severe limitations on the estate planning

that can be done with them. There is also a major US income tax issue with variable annuities in that they essentially trade lower capital gains rates for higher regular income tax rates. However, annuities can play a part in estate planning for blended families. For example, a wealthier partner could buy a lifetime annuity for her husband that could ensure an income stream for him. However, there are other more tax-advantaged alternatives such as private unitrusts, direct gifts, bequests, or lifetime Qualified Terminable Interest Property (QTIP), all of which are discussed later in this book.

2.4   Opportunity shifts

One of the best lifetime estate-planning techniques is called an opportunity shift, which has the benefit of never having the asset in your estate taxed in the first place. Opportunity shifts require either having an idea that will result in a very valuable asset in the future or having an asset that is not worth much now but is expected to significantly appreciate in the future. The technique involves transferring the asset or idea to people or to a trust for the benefit of family members *before* it appreciates in value.

From the standpoint of blended families, opportunity shifts present chances to favor either children of the union, separate children, or both sets of children. This is a technique that should be used by someone who is very confident that the wealth he or she already has will be sufficient for his or her lifetime before he or she passes on an opportunity to increase his or her wealth.

For example, suppose that Mary Ann owns a piece of undeveloped real estate in the country that is worth $1,000 per acre because it was only being used for pasture. However, the property will probably be developable into subdivisions a few years into the future that will be worth $25,000 per acre. Before development reaches her property, Mary Ann could transfer the property into a trust for her grandchildren at the lower value. The trust can then develop the property at the appropriate time and reap the benefits.

2.5 Charitable gift annuities

A charitable gift annuity is simple and is an unsecured promise made by a charity to pay a specified set amount each year to a person, who is called the "annuitant," in exchange for the annuitant contributing property to the charity. The payments to the annuitant depend solely on the age of the annuitant, and the payments are always higher the older an annuitant is when the charitable gift annuity begins. These annuity payments can begin immediately on transfer of the property or they can be deferred to some point in the future.

While any property can be exchanged for a charitable gift annuity, cash is best because contributing appreciated property can create income tax. Since a charitable gift annuity can't be secured by any property of the charity, you should only enter into a charitable gift annuity with a large, financially strong charity. You should only enter into a charitable gift annuity if you have strong charitable intent because the charity will not pay what a life insurance company would pay for a commercial annuity. On the death of the annuitant, the charity keeps the remainder of the property, so that's why charitable intent is so important. There aren't any particular blended family considerations for a charitable gift annuity.

2.6 Below-market loans

At first blush, a loan might not appear to be an estate-planning technique at all. However, if the loan can be made at a favorable interest rate, in other words, a below-market interest rate, this can be a very effective estate-planning

technique, especially if the borrower can invest the loan proceeds to earn more than the interest to be paid on the loan, which would result in a gift-tax-free transfer of wealth. Below-market loans can be a very effective way to transfer wealth free from gift taxes.

3. Strategies for People Who Have Wealth of More Than $1,000,000

In this section, we'll consider some lifetime estate-planning techniques that can be utilized by persons who have more than $1,000,000 in assets.

3.1 Life insurance trusts

A life insurance trust is an irrevocable trust, first and foremost. Once you form a life insurance trust, you usually can't get the policy (or the premiums paid) back from the trust. A life insurance trust involves either the transfer of an existing life insurance policy to a trust or the purchase of a new life insurance policy by a trust.

One primary benefit of a life insurance trust is that, if properly structured, it keeps the insurance proceeds out of your estate for federal estate tax purposes. Ordinarily, when you own or control a life insurance policy, such as having the right to change beneficiaries or borrow against the policy, the proceeds are taxable in your estate for federal estate-tax purposes, which could be catastrophic and a possible waste of the insurance proceeds. However, a life insurance trust can save those proceeds from estate taxation.

A life insurance trust is set up as a regular irrevocable trust. Typically, the life insurance premiums are paid through gifts to the life insurance trust, which are hopefully covered by annual exclusion gifts (see section **3.2**).

A life insurance trust assists in the payment of estate expenses and estate taxes either by loaning funds to your estate or by purchasing assets from your estate. It is imperative that the trustee not be obligated to lend money to your estate or to buy assets from your estate — that's a big no-no as it would cause your policy to be subject to federal estate taxes.

For those who don't have to worry about the US federal estate tax, which is the vast majority of us, a life insurance trust is a wonderful way to preserve life insurance proceeds for beneficiaries and to get independent management of the trust funds. At least until 2013 in the US, the overwhelming majority of families don't have taxable estates courtesy of the $5,120,000 per person exemption. Therefore, the reasons for protecting beneficiaries and providing income to them over time, as opposed to a lump sum, are really far more important than keeping insurance proceeds out of an estate for federal estate-tax purposes.

In blended families, life insurance trusts can be very useful, even for nontaxable estates. For example, a life insurance trust can be arranged to create an income stream for a surviving partner, with the principal going to the insured's children at the surviving partner's death. Likewise, a life insurance trust can be used to leave a significant sum to your children, freeing you to take care of your partner with your other property. It is critical that you select a third party as a trustee of a life insurance trust, especially for blended families.

> **Life insurance trusts are useful tools in blended family estate planning.**

Many blended family clients begin the process believing that they can appoint a child from each of them as co-trustees, but we strongly advise against it unless those two children have worked well together in the past. Usually, a financial institution will decline to serve as trustee of a trust that holds nothing but a life insurance policy (although a financial institution may agree to serve after the insured's death if the policy is large enough to satisfy the bank's minimum requirements), so you'll have to find a suitable third-party trustee. Preferably, this unrelated third party will have no bias against your children or your partner. Again, neither of you, nor your children or even siblings, should serve as trustee of a life insurance trust that holds a life insurance policy on either you or your partner. However, if you insist on having family members or a partner serve as trustee of a life insurance trust, you should work with a competent estate planner to carefully spell out governance provisions, including tiebreaker provisions if you have more than one trustee, and in selecting successor trustees.

Successor trustees are even more important when a partner insists on serving as a trustee, because our desire to serve as trustee (or as executor) often declines when we are attacked for our actions, and when we get older, we may not want to put up with the same hassles as when we were younger and had more energy. In our experience, the likelihood of complaint by a set of beneficiaries about the trustee is much higher in a blended family. This is why it is so important to spend time on this part of the estate-planning process. Your estate plan is only as good as the people that you hire to implement it. In our opinion, the selection of fiduciaries (e.g., trustee, executor, personal representative, conservator) is probably the most important aspect of estate planning, especially for blended families, and woefully too little time is usually spent on this part.

3.2 Annual exclusion gifts

Annual exclusion gifts remain one of the most tax-efficient ways to pass on wealth. In 2012 in the United States, each person may gift up to $13,000 per year to an unlimited number of recipients. For future years, the annual exclusion amount is issued annually by the Internal Revenue Service (IRS) and is based on inflation.

These gifts must be of a "present interest," which, as a practical matter, means that they must either be made directly to the recipient or to a trust that has what is commonly known as a "Crummey" (named after a famous 1968 court decision) clause in it. However, the rules are different and much tighter for annual exclusion gifts to grandchildren in trust. (Paul was fond of saying to clients that "Crummey wasn't crummy"!) A Crummey clause must give a trust beneficiary the unfettered right to withdraw the gift for a stated period of time (e.g., 30 days), meaning that a beneficiary could easily spoil a plan by withdrawing a gift. However, exercise of a Crummey right of withdrawal rarely happens for a whole host of possible reasons, but often because of the veiled but unstated threat to stop making gifts if the beneficiary exercises the withdrawal right.

In blended families, annual exclusion gifts can be used for a variety of reasons. For example, annual exclusion gifts can be used to fund life insurance premiums on the life of a parent or on the lives of the partners. If it is a single-life policy, it can either be owned by a trust for the benefit of the insured partner's children or outright by those children. However, if it is a second-to-die insurance policy insuring the lives of both partners, it should be owned and held by a very carefully crafted trust that is arranged in such a way that the insurance is not included in the estate of either partner. Annual exclusion gifts also may be made to stepchildren.

A lot of annual exclusion gifting is inappropriate and ill-advised. A common example of inappropriate annual exclusion gifting occurs when clients make systematic annual exclusion gifts of income-producing property, such as interests in a family company, yet continue to receive income attributed to the gifted property that is neither reduced nor substantially affected by the gift. This most often happens when clients make gifts of interests in closely held businesses and continue to receive salary or rent or other forms of consideration from those businesses. If a sales opportunity for the business materializes down the road, the senior generation may look adversely at the opportunity, even where the offered price is more than fair (or even generous). This could happen if the senior generation's share of the offer price would be insufficient (due to prior lifetime transfers) to generate the income that the senior generation presently enjoys through the salary and other perks. The junior generation may pass on the sales opportunity, despite the favorable offer, in order to maintain family peace.

There are often unaddressed and unspoken emotional components related to this sort of "gifting" where there is ownership without power or control, and yet there is liability. When the gift is given this way, and the recipient has no say, choice, or buy-in, this can also create resentment and challenges in relating down the road. No one wants to appear ungrateful, so often, your heirs' feelings, thoughts, and concerns go unexpressed and that can cause parents and their children to become less connected and more estranged over time. If this is a strategy you are intending to use as a way to mitigate estate taxes, see what you can do to include your beneficiaries in the decision making, so they know that their input and feelings matter. You'll be much more likely to have buy-in, and when situations arise, there's also a precedent for being able to talk things through together and hear all points of view before making final decisions.

Another fairly common example of inappropriate lifetime giving occurs when life insurance premiums on a second-to-die life insurance policy are tied to annual exclusion gifts from both partners in a union. When one partner dies, that deceased partner may no longer make annual exclusion gifts, yet the policy has not paid off yet because the surviving partner is still alive. The choices are to use part of the survivor's lifetime US gift-tax exemption ($5,120,000 in 2012) to supplement that partner's annual exclusion gifts, or, worse yet, start paying gift tax because the survivor has already exhausted his or her lifetime exemption, or reduce the policy coverage.

There are numerous other examples too, including the gifting of hard-to-value assets that require annual valuations as annual exclusion gifts or where a client isn't likely to have a taxable estate in the first place!

3.3 Unlimited direct payments to qualified educational institutions and qualified health-care providers

Unlimited direct payments to qualified educational institutions and qualified health-care providers is a way to get one of the biggest gift-tax breaks in the US Internal Revenue Code. The provision allows for unlimited direct payments of tuition and other educational expenses to qualified educational institutions and direct payment of health-care expenses, including health-insurance premiums paid to an insurance company, to qualified health-care providers.

In blended families, as in single-union families, this too often forgotten technique can be used to pay educational and health-care expenses for children older than 18 and for

grandchildren. In blended families, this provision can come in handy to assist stepchildren and step-grandchildren too.

3.4 Charitable remainder trusts

Charitable remainder trusts in the US come in two varieties: charitable remainder annuity trust (CRAT) and the charitable remainder unitrust (CRUT). A CRAT is a creature of US tax law, and it is a specially designed trust that can be created during lifetime or at death in a will. In a CRAT, you can retain a right to a set amount (but not less than 5 percent of the initial value of the property put into the CRAT) as an annuity payment, payable at least annually. Conversely, you can create a CRAT for the benefit of others, such as children. A CRAT can be established for lifetime or a term that can't exceed 20 years. One or more qualified charities must be the final principal beneficiary of a CRAT. You can reserve the right to change the identity of the qualified charities that are the final principal beneficiaries.

A CRUT also is a creature of US tax law, and it is a specially designed trust that can be created during lifetime or at death in a will. In a CRUT, one gives or retains a unitrust interest of not less than 5 percent of the value of the CRUT, which must be determined annually, with one or more qualified charities as final principal beneficiaries. The difference between the CRAT and the CRUT is that the payment is fixed at the start in the CRAT, meaning that the payment can neither go up nor go down during the CRAT term. Conversely, the CRUT payment is based solely on the value of the property. Therefore, the CRUT payout can either go up (if the value of the property in the CRUT increases) or down (if the value of the CRUT property declines in value). You can create a CRUT for the benefit of one or both partners or others. A CRUT can be established for lifetime or a term that can't exceed 20 years. One or more qualified charities must be the final principal beneficiary of a CRUT. You can reserve the right to change the identity of the qualified charities that are the final principal beneficiaries.

This example should make clear the difference between a CRAT and a CRUT. Suppose you want to give $100,000 to a charitable remainder trust and retain a lifetime right to 5 percent of the trust per year. Which would you choose between the CRAT and the CRUT? In a CRAT, your annual payment would be set at $5,000 and would last until your death or the CRAT runs out of money, whichever comes first. It would not go up or down. However, in a CRUT, your payment would be tied to the annual value of the CRUT property, meaning that if the property increased in value, your payment would increase. However, if the CRUT property declined in value, your payment would be reduced for that year.

Ordinarily, Paul recommends that younger people use the CRUT so that the value of the payments do not erode over time due to factors such as inflation. Now, this doesn't always mean that older folks should automatically opt for the CRAT. It is just one factor to consider. Another thing you should consider is the type of property that the charitable remainder trust is expected to hold, because if the charitable remainder trust is expected to hold hard-to-value assets, in a CRUT there would have to be an annual appraisal of that property, which could get expensive.

> **Do you know the difference between a CRAT and a CRUT?**

If created during your lifetime, a charitable remainder trust can give you, as the donor, an income tax deduction. The amount of the deduction is a function of the term of the trust, the size of the retained interests of the income beneficiaries, the frequency of the payout and the applicable IRS interest rate in effect at the time of creation of the charitable remainder trust. Generally speaking, the greater the size of the interest of the income beneficiary, the lesser the charitable deduction will be, and vice versa. But whether a charitable remainder trust yields an income tax deduction is a secondary consideration to the requirement that the prospective donor be significantly charitably inclined. Charitable intent is paramount in considering whether to enter into a charitable planning technique because charity will receive a significant gift in any such technique, irrespective of how it is illustrated, which may upset children and other loved ones.

A charitable remainder trust is only appropriate where you are comfortable with a charity ultimately receiving the property because that is what will happen. In a blended family, the beneficiary of the CRAT or CRUT could be a partner with lesser wealth or it could be the children.

3.5 Gift splitting

It is not unusual for one partner to have significantly more wealth than the other partner. Through what is known as *gift splitting*, the wealthier partner could make gifts of the entire amount, but, for gift-tax purposes, it is as if both partners made the gifts. (**Note:** This technique only works if the partners are married.)

Consider the following example: Nancy and Tom have been married for a few years. Nancy has significantly more wealth than Tom and wants to make annual exclusion gifts of $13,000 to each of her three children. Through gift splitting, which requires Tom's cooperation but which costs him nothing, Nancy could give each child $26,000; in other words, twice as much. This also requires the filing of a gift-tax return.

Now, if Nancy wanted to make larger lifetime gifts to her children, Tom could join in and double the amount of the gift. However, in this instance, Tom would have to use part or all of his gift-tax exemption, which he may not want to do, especially if he has heirs of his own. It also may be appropriate to reimburse Tom for the loss of all or a part of his lifetime gift-tax exemption because if his estate is taxable, his heirs will have to pay more tax because of the loss of the lifetime gift-tax exemption.

3.6 Private unitrusts

A private unitrust is a technique where, instead of giving the income beneficiary rights to the trust income, the beneficiary is given a right to a set percentage of the value of the trust, determined annually. The primary benefit of a private unitrust is that it eliminates (or at least minimizes) the potential for bickering between the *income beneficiaries*, who want the assets invested to generate the most income, even at the expense of asset appreciation, and *principal beneficiaries*, who always want the assets invested for growth, even at the expense of immediate trust income. A private unitrust allows the trustee, who is caught in the middle, to invest for growth since it helps both income and principal beneficiaries.

Private unitrusts work very well in blended families, especially where the income beneficiary is one of the partners, and the principal beneficiaries are the children of the other partner. **Caution:** If the partners are married and live in the United States, a private unitrust will not qualify for a marital deduction unless the spouse beneficiary is given the right to the greater of the unitrust percentage or the trust income. However, a marital deduction will not be important in every situation. Your professional advisor can assist you with this consideration.

4. Strategies for Those Who Are Worth More Than $5,000,000

In this section, we consider estate-planning techniques that are available to persons who have more than $5,000,000 in wealth.

4.1 Private annuities

The private annuity is a very simple technique. It is a contract between someone who contributes property, called the "annuitant," to the other, in exchange for an unsecured (and that is very important) promise by the recipient to make lifetime payments to the annuitant. The private annuity comes in two basic varieties: a single-life annuity, in which annuity payments cease on the annuitant's death, and a joint and survivor annuity, in which annuity payments continue until the surviving annuitant's death. The best assets for a private annuity are those that produce income or cash flow and are expected to appreciate in value. Some asset types, like depreciable property such as rental real estate, are disfavored for the private annuity because of the recapture of depreciation and investment tax credits that occur on creation of the private annuity.

For blended families, private annuity transactions are almost always of joint and survivor private annuities. However, caution is advised because of a potentially difficult dynamic that can often arise when the contributing annuitant's children by a prior union are the recipients of private annuity property. Depending on the relationship between your separate children with your surviving partner, a private annuity may not be the optimal plan because the surviving partner will be dependent on their stepchildren for annuity payments and for the prudent management of the property. There can be significant immediate adverse income tax consequences in the creation of a private annuity with certain types of property, so we strongly advise the assistance of a competent estate planner in the creation of a private annuity.

4.2 Qualified Personal Residence Trust (QPRT)

A qualified personal residence trust (QPRT) is purely a creature of US tax law. In a QPRT, a person puts the ownership of his or her home (it must either be a primary residence or a second home) into a specially drafted trust and he or she retains a right to live in the home for a certain period of time (e.g., ten years). At the end of the QPRT term, the donor must vacate the home or start paying fair market value rent to the trust or directly to the former beneficiaries of the trust, usually the children. Many people don't want to pay rent to remain in what they feel is their home. However, the home doesn't belong to them any longer at the end of the term; it belongs to the QPRT.

The benefit of a QPRT is it allows someone to make a discounted gift of his or her residence and thereby help reduce federal estate taxes. That benefit depends on the age of the owner and the number of years that the owner reserves to stay in the home. The fact is the greater the period that someone retains the right to live in the home, the higher the discount of the gift. However, the big downside of a QPRT is that if the donor doesn't survive the retained period of years, the transaction is essentially ignored for federal estate tax purposes, and the value of the home as of the donor's death will be included in the donor's estate for federal estate tax purposes.

In a blended family situation, it is frequently the case that the partners reside in a home that belongs to only one partner. These usually aren't good candidates for a QPRT in that case because the other partner may lack the resources either to find suitable housing if the owner/partner dies during the term of the QPRT, or to pay market rate rent to the owner/partner's children. There may well be no poorer situation than to have to rent from stepchildren, who also could sell the house, not to mention the potential difficulties with determining fair market value rent.

Paul doesn't recall ever advising a blended family couple to use a QPRT because of these potential problems. If the couple owns the home together but only one partner has children, the childless partner may object to leaving his or her share to his or her partner's children. If the couple owns the home together and each has children of a prior union, it may be difficult to leave the home to both sets of children unless there is a third-party trustee (which is unlikely since the only asset that a QPRT can own is a home) because these sets of children may not even know each other or work well together. If only one partner owns the home but wants his or her partner to be able to reside in the property for life rent free, the QPRT will not accomplish this result because fair market value rent will have to be paid after the QPRT term. Again, making a surviving partner a tenant to your children usually is a bad idea. The QPRT might work for the blended couple that has children together, if those children are the sole remainder beneficiaries, as that would be akin to a QPRT for any family.

4.3 Family limited entities

The use of family limited partnerships and family limited liability companies has been going on for a very long time. In a family entity, typically the parents of the children create the family entity and contribute property to the family entity in exchange for interests in it. The principal sought after gift- or estate-tax benefit is the ability to give away discounted interests in the family entity, while retaining control of it. The facts concerning the creation of the family entity are critical to its success. Therefore, we strongly advise that you not form a family entity without competent professional advice.

In blended families, Paul rarely advises his clients to form family entities where there would be a mixing of children from both partners. Unless the children are comfortable being partners with each other, and hopefully have demonstrated some degree of competence in owning and managing something together already, we strongly advise against the use of family entities in such situations.

Some parents with the means to do so will create a family foundation to give *all* the children in their lives (whatever their ages) a chance to work together and build competence. If the parents continue to run the show and wield most of the power and control, then their initial intention is lost and the children do not get the chance to truly see what they can accomplish together (or to determine without a doubt that they cannot work together). Again, it is important to communicate with your children prior to setting up an entity ostensibly to have them work together so that you can get their input and buy-in. Otherwise they may feel put-upon or forced and, while you probably won't hear about it (as they will not want to appear ungrateful), they will have resentment that will likely be played out amongst each other at the time of your death. Where the partners also have children together, likewise, the same admonition applies. An unfortunate occurrence we see all too often in blended families is that in this scenario, the "ours" children frequently are shunned by both sets of separate children, who see their half-siblings as treated differently, and there is perceived favoritism.

5. Strategies for Those Who Are Worth More Than $15,000,000

Finally, in this section, we consider estate-planning techniques that should be considered by persons who possess more than $15,000,000 in wealth.

5.1 Large gifts, including defined value gifts

Where appropriate, making gifts during your lifetime of amounts larger than the available annual exclusions can be the most powerful estate planning that can be done, especially if the donor is able to transfer the wealth through more than one generation (i.e., to grandchildren or beyond). Everyone in the United States has, for at least 2012, a $5,120,000 exemption that can be used during his or her lifetime or at death. Use of that exemption during his or her lifetime gets the future income and appreciation in value of that gifted property out of your estate. Larger gifts tend to be made in trust. It is less expensive to give property away during your lifetime than it is to die with that property due to the way that the gift tax is computed and paid. The recipient does not have to pay the federal gift tax but is responsible for the recipient's share of the federal estate tax.

Consider the following example: Assume that Alice is worth $25,000,000 and that there is a $5,000,000 exemption, and a 35 percent estate- and gift-tax rate. Alice would like to give $10,000,000 to a child and asks whether she should give it away during her lifetime or wait until her death. If Alice gives the $10,000,000 to her child during her lifetime, she'll have to pay $1,750,000 in federal gift tax under our example, but her child gets the whole $10,000,000 because Alice must pay the gift tax out of her remaining $15,000,000.

If, instead, Alice died with a $23,000,000 estate, she would owe $7,000,000 in federal estate tax after using her $5,000,000 exemption ($20,000,000 times 35 percent). The $10,000,000 bequest to her child has to pay for that child's share of federal estate tax. This means that the child would receive a net $6,500,000, since the estate tax on the $10,000,000 is $3,500,000. As you can see, the child comes out much better in the lifetime gift situation as long as the child doesn't need to sell the gifted property right after the gift because the child takes the parent's income tax basis (usually the original cost of the gifted property). If you are interested in this type of situation, discuss it with your tax advisor.

Unfortunately, the costs of lifetime giving are not insignificant. For starters, neither the property nor its future income or appreciation is available to the donor after the gift. It is not unusual for a partner to object to the other partner making such a large gift, and we see this as a much more common objection in blended families.

Secondly, the recipients of a gift of property take the tax basis that you had in the property. For example, suppose you had a piece of real estate that you bought years ago for $100,000 that is now worth $1,000,000. If you gave away that property to your children, you could do so free of federal gift tax. However, if your children sold the property for $1,000,000, they would have $900,000 in taxable gain ($1,000,000 selling price minus $100,000 tax basis).

In blended families, assuming that the other partner is open to the idea even though it means that he or she would be deprived of the continuing use of, or access to income from the property to be gifted, a large gift to the giving partner's children can ensure that certain specific assets such as a family home or a family business stay in the partner's biological family.

A *defined value gift* is one where you can state (usually by formula, but it can be a fixed number) how much is to be given. For example, it may be that you want to make a gift of $5,120,000, which is your 2012 lifetime US gift-tax exemption, and no more. People use defined value gifts in situations in which they are giving property that is hard to value, such as land or interests in a family business. It is extremely important that the lawyer who drafts a defined value gift knows how to draft one. It is also critical that a defined value gift be consistently reported as such on the federal gift-tax return. We strongly advise that you hire a qualified tax professional to prepare a gift-tax return for a defined value gift.

5.2 Equalization of estates

When there is a large disparity in wealth between partners, there can be an estate-planning advantage to having the wealthier partner make a large, tax-free gift to the other partner of an amount that equalizes the partners' estates by value. This was much more common when the federal estate taxable brackets ranged from 37 to 55 percent.

If the federal estate tax is "flat" — in other words, very little spread between the highest and lowest federal estate-tax rates, as has been the case for several years — equalization makes little sense, except in giving the poorer partner enough property to use his or her estate-tax exemption amount. This technique should only be considered by couples who have been together for a long time and who have a solid relationship, because the giving partner can't get his or her wealth back if the couple subsequently splits. Paul rarely ever mentions this technique to blended family couples because of the high incidence of separation among these couples.

For more information about equalization of estates, see Chapter 10.

5.3 Lifetime Qualified Terminable Interest Property (QTIP)

The Lifetime Qualified Terminable Interest Property (QTIP) trust is an irrevocable trust that you create during your lifetime. Irrevocable means exactly that: It's permanent, even if the couple separates, which can be a drawback, particularly in blended family relationships where the incidence of separation exceeds even the high rate of first marriage divorces. (**Note:** The Lifetime QTIP technique is only available to married couples.)

Don't confuse a QPRT and a QTIP.

Paul has worked with couples where one partner didn't have enough wealth to use up the estate-tax exemption if that partner died first, while the other partner had significant wealth and a taxable estate. While the wealthier partner would like to save his or her heirs some estate tax, he or she will usually object to simply giving the other partner significant wealth to equalize the estates. This is much truer in blended family relationships.

There are several requirements for a lifetime QTIP trust. The other partner must be given all of the trust income for that partner's lifetime, even if they divorce. It also requires the filing of a gift-tax return and a special election on that return to be *timely* filed. For these reasons, lifetime QTIP trusts should only be considered by spouses who have a long-term, solid relationship. However, the lifetime QTIP trust can be designed to cause wealth to be taxed in the other partner's estate, thereby using up that other partner's estate-tax exemption, but allowing the wealthier partner to control where that property goes after the other partner's death. This technique could save a significant amount of federal estate tax for the wealthier partner's heirs, while allowing the wealthier partner to direct where the trust assets will go on the death of the other partner. This technique is particularly popular in married blended family relationships.

For more information about QTIP trusts, see Chapter 10.

5.4 Grantor Retained Annuity Trust (GRAT)

The Grantor Retained Annuity Trust (GRAT) is another creature of US tax law. In a GRAT, one creates a specially designed irrevocable trust with property and retains a right to an annuity from the trust for a specified period of time. A GRAT may only be created during one's lifetime. The retained annuity can be a flat annuity or it can increase by as much as 20 percent per year. The benefit of a GRAT is that it allows you to discount the taxable gift by the actuarial value of your retained interest. The longer the GRAT term, the greater will be the amount of the retained interest, and vice versa. The greater the amount of the retained interest, the lesser the amount of the taxable gift, and vice versa. If you survive the term of the GRAT, then your interest ceases, and you can't have any more interest in that property, which passes to the principal beneficiaries tax free. However, if you don't survive the term, the value of the property remaining in the GRAT will be taxed in your estate, which is the significant downside of the GRAT.

The issues with respect to the GRAT for blended families revolve around the identity of the remainder beneficiaries of the GRAT. In the typical blended family GRAT, the children of the contributing partner are almost always the remainder beneficiaries. Blended couples who want to use this tool for both of their children from prior relationships are advised to set up two separate ones, so that the stepsiblings are not joint beneficiaries on one trust. Setting up separate "yours, mine, and ours" GRATs can work well if you communicate with your heirs in advance and they understand the mechanism, the amounts, and what your thinking was in creating your plan this way.

5.5 Charitable lead trusts

Charitable lead trusts received a lot of publicity several years ago when Jacqueline Kennedy Onassis set up one in her will, which, ironically, never came into effect. A charitable lead trust is essentially the flipside of a charitable remainder trust. In a charitable lead trust, one or more charities receive the income interest, with one or more individuals receiving the remaining property at the end of the trust term. Like charitable remainder trusts, there are two basic forms of charitable lead trusts: charitable lead annuity trusts and charitable lead unitrusts. Charitable lead trusts can be formed during your lifetime or at death. Here, we'll focus on charitable lead trusts that can be set up during your lifetime.

There are two types of lifetime charitable lead trusts: a so-called grantor trust and a non-grantor trust. In a *grantor charitable lead trust*, the creator of the trust gets an income and gift-tax charitable contribution deduction but has to pay the income tax on all of the charitable lead trust's income. There are situations when the grantor variety works, such as if you have a really big income year when you don't foresee another one anytime soon. In our experience, most lifetime charitable lead trusts are of the non-grantor variety. The creator of a *non-grantor charitable lead trust* gets a gift tax (but not income tax) charitable contribution deduction. However, the non-grantor charitable lead trust gets an unlimited income tax charitable contribution deduction for all amounts paid to the charitable beneficiaries.

The most important point about any charitable lead trust is that the ultimate recipients must be able to support themselves during the term of the charitable lead trust because they won't receive *anything* from the charitable lead trust until the *end* of the charitable lead trust term, which could go on for many years. Typically, the children (or more remote descendants) of the contributing partner are the remainder beneficiaries of a charitable lead trust. Depending on the terms of the charitable lead trust, the property might be distributed directly to the remainder beneficiaries at the end of the charitable lead trust term or continue to be held in a regular trust. In blended families, if the charitable lead trust will distribute directly to beneficiaries, then children of the partners can be financially separated, which is usually a good thing.

5.6 Sale to an Intentionally Defective Grantor Trust (IDGT)

In a US technique called a sale to an Intentionally Defective Grantor Trust (IDGT), typically a parent sells property to an irrevocable trust in exchange for a promissory note that calls for installment payments. Beneficiaries of the trust are usually the parent's children or more remote descendants. There are several benefits when making a sale to an IDGT. Perhaps the biggest benefit is that a sale of property that is expected to appreciate freezes the value of the seller's estate and passes on the appreciation free from estate or gift tax.

Some estate-planning techniques are on the cutting edge, and there are uncertainties in the law pertaining to these estate-planning techniques, which translates into greater risk. Sales to IDGTs fall into this category since there is some disagreement among estate-planning commentators as to the income tax consequences, if any, of dying with an unpaid installment note after a sale to an IDGT. Nevertheless, there are a lot of reasons to sell assets that are expected to appreciate in the future to an IDGT, usually in exchange for an installment note.

By "intentionally defective," we mean that the irrevocable trust is treated as owned by the creator of the trust for income tax, but not for estate tax purposes. There is nothing defective about the IDGT; it is purposely set up that way. The "intentionally defective" trust part of the technique is very safe from a tax standpoint since the Internal Revenue Code has mandated this result since 1926. Likewise, the ignored sale aspect is also safe as it is the official Internal Revenue Service (IRS) position. The big uncertainty is the tax consequences if the seller dies before the installment note is paid off. It is either a recognized gain or it isn't.

For blended families, sales to Intentionally Defective Grantor Trusts must be very carefully designed, even more so than for other families. The trustee of the purchasing irrevocable trust must be an independent third party because the beneficiaries might be comprised of children from both partners as well as possibly a partner. This is where it will be imperative to coordinate the selection of an executor of the selling partner's estate, which will be a creditor until the note is paid off, with the selection of the trustee of the purchasing irrevocable trust so that there is no friction after the selling partner's death if the note is not paid off by then.

5.7 Guarantees

Like the low-interest loan, the guarantee of certain debts of children and other relatives can be a very effective estate-planning technique if the borrowing children can earn more with the borrowed funds than the cost of the guarantee,

if a guarantee fee is charged. If a guarantee fee is not charged, there is a risk that the extension of the guarantee will be treated as a gift for US gift-tax purposes. However, guarantees can be very dangerous to the financial stability of the guaranteeing partner, especially if the borrowers default on their loans and the guaranteeing partner is called on by the lender to pay off the loans. Paul has seen clients go overboard with guarantees of the debts of children during good times and suffer significant financial reversals in the process. Caution is advised.

In blended families, guarantees must be even more carefully considered than usual because there might be resistance by the one partner to a guaranteeing partner's guaranteeing debts of her children since this could impact his financial security if the loan must be paid off by the guaranteeing partner. Moreover, coordination of selection of executors and successor trustees is critical because, for example, if the other partner is the successor trustee or executor, that partner may not cooperate with the guarantee, possibly resulting in litigation. For example, suppose that Rhett guaranteed a debt for one of his boys, Rex, and then he dies. Rhett named Rex's stepmother, Scarlett, as executrix. Rex is unable to pay the debt, and the creditor calls for Rhett's estate to pay off the guarantee. Scarlett actually objected to Rhett guaranteeing Rex's debt when he did it. If she won't pay off the debt, she will force the creditor (and Rex) to sue Rhett's estate, which will result in legal fees, delays, and probably some hard feelings on the part of Rex.

6. Action Steps

First and foremost, you will need to determine if lifetime estate planning is a viable option for you — given your current needs, your needs going forward that you are aware of, and contingencies you need to plan for (e.g., long-term care and estate taxes). You can work with your accountant or other estate-planning advisors to determine figures that would more than take care of all your concerns, so that you could then know your level of freedom and play beyond those numbers.

If you determine that lifetime estate planning is a good option for you to consider, it's time to spend some quality time reviewing this chapter — make notes about what you could see for your family as a result of using each one. If you don't see one as a good idea, write down your reasons for that too. If it is purely a gut feeling, you may want to consider doing more research before jumping to a conclusion too quickly.

Once you get a sense for which ones seem like the best options, it's time to do more research and determine which will be probable candidates and why; see if you can narrow down your choices even further. As you explore your options, keep a running list of questions to find answers to by researching on the Internet, asking credible sources, and reading relevant books. When you are ready to talk to your attorney and the clock is ticking for billable hours, you will have a clear direction and well-researched questions, which will streamline the whole process and get you the results you want expediently while minimizing costs.

Once you've made your determination about how you would like to implement the lifetime estate-planning options you've chosen, take time to connect with your beneficiaries prior to signing anything to make sure that what you're considering is in alignment with their values, lifestyle choices, and goals. You may learn about concerns that they have that you had not considered that are more pressing than the ones you are addressing. You may learn that there's a great deal of discomfort around being included in a trust with stepsiblings and half-siblings, which may lead to discord and possible litigation down the road if the issues are not attended to. Taking the time to do this part, and doing it in a way that allows for the true hopes and concerns of your intended beneficiaries to come forward, could save everyone a lot of unanticipated grief and upset (and it could save you a lot of money and time by keeping you from preparing documents that you end up not signing).

CHAPTER 10

Testamentary Estate Planning

Chapter 9 dealt with estate planning that you can do during your lifetime that takes effect immediately. This chapter concerns itself with estate planning that goes into effect at death. We address several issues that arise in testamentary planning and how these issues can impact blended family estate planning.

We could also discuss topics such as post-death challenges to marriage contracts or property agreements, but we have opted not to do so since these topics really aren't planning in its truest sense. Nevertheless, such post-death challenges are always on the radar screen and should not be discounted in advance. These issues are covered in more detail in Chapter 8 with respect to why estate plans can fail.

Testamentary estate planning for blended families requires patience and skill. There are a lot of ways to mitigate creating a mess for your loved ones after you are gone. Hopefully, the topics in this chapter will assist you in avoiding many of the obvious and not so obvious traps for the unwary.

1. *In Terrorem* Clauses

An *in terrorem* or "no contest" clause is placed in a will or a trust, and it can effectively prevent heirs or beneficiaries from disputing the terms of the will or trust by taking away whatever they receive in the will or trust if they contest it in court. The purpose of these clauses is to reduce rancor and litigation in estates and trusts. These clauses don't always work, though, as they are very dependent on applicable state or provincial laws and how the courts of each jurisdiction interpret them. Your estate-planning attorney should be able to tell you how these clauses fare in the courts of your state or province.

In terrorem clauses are being used with increasing frequency, particularly in blended families. For example, your children may be at odds with your partner, and you may plan on leaving part of your estate to your children and part to your partner. Maybe the problem is that your children want it all. An *in terrorem* clause could effectively preclude your children from challenging what you are leaving to your partner by forcing your children to surrender their inheritance if they mount a challenge to your estate plan. These clauses send a strong message not to mess with what you want to have happen with your estate.

Communicating your intention before you die and doing what you can to promote peace and reduce rancor will support the purpose of such a clause. If your children were to learn of this clause at the time of your death, without hearing or knowing your concerns, they may find other ways to make your partner's experience less than pleasant — even if they cannot go about it litigiously.

Given the current state of affairs in your blended family, do you see a need for an *in terrorem* clause in your will? If so, take some time to write down your thoughts about what your concerns are and what it is you don't want to see happen that has you choosing to put this into place. Be prepared to share this decision with all your family members preferably while you are alive, so that everyone understands equally what has led you to this decision — and what your hopes are as a result of using it.

2. Disinheriting Family

Of course, some situations call for more drastic action. An *in terrorem* clause won't help in a situation where you wish, for example, to leave nothing to a particular child of yours, because that child has nothing to lose by contesting your estate or trust.

There are many possible reasons why you might disinherit family members such as you may no longer have a relationship with a particular child. The following are scenarios we run across repeatedly in blended families that bring forward a need for this sort of drastic measure:

- When a child vehemently objects to your choice of a partner and, therefore, rejects you as well.

- When a child has been a victim of parental alienation and has been conditioned to not have anything to do with you while being loyal to his or her other biological parent.

- When you have given a particular child significant sums of money or property during your lifetime.

Whatever your reason, we believe that it is important to describe that reason in your will or trust as that allows you to tell your side of the story, because, unfortunately, when you are dead you're unable to speak for yourself. We strongly encourage you to make attempts to communicate with that particular child during your lifetime to at least give him or her a chance to see the consequences of his or her choices while there's still a chance to rectify the breach in your relationship.

At this time, is there anyone in your blended family that you plan on disinheriting? This would mean excluding him or her from any transfer of property, other assets, or monies? This is the time to have an open conversation about how you have come to this conclusion and your particular reasons. Is there anything that individual could say or do that would change your mind in the future? These are important areas to address in writing now, as memories change and so do people over time. If something were to happen to either of you tomorrow, what is it you would want that individual to know about why you've made this choice today, and what you wish you could have seen happen in the future to change your mind.

One powerful exercise to do as you write is to share what you enjoyed most about that person prior to when things went in a different direction. If it is a matter of having already been quite generous towards the person, take time to share what you've enjoyed about giving during your lifetime and witnessing what he or she chose to do as a result of receiving your generosity.

> Communicating your reasons why you've made the choices you have will help to ease the blow and keep your memory focused in a positive direction.

3. Equalization of Estates

We discussed equalization of estates in Chapter 9. Nevertheless, some people are interested in doing this at death rather than during their lifetime. For the reasons that we discussed in Chapter 9, we rarely see partners in blended families wanting to equalize the sizes of their respective estates where one partner is far wealthier than the other partner even if doing so would save estate tax.

If this continues to be a source of conflict for you, there may be an underlying concern that is not getting addressed in other ways in the overall estate-planning process. Chapter 2 provides some useful tools on how to go about attempting to sort out these concerns together. If attempts to communicate do not yield satisfying results, we highly recommend you consider working with a coach, facilitator, or other trained professional who can support you two at getting to the heart of the matter, so that you can both feel good about the final conclusions related to your estate plan.

4. Powers of Appointment

A power of appointment is a tool contained in a trust intended to provide flexibility in estate planning after your death by giving someone a right, called a power of appointment, to shift trust property by *appointing* it between beneficiaries or to remove a beneficiary altogether. A power of appointment can be a dangerous thing because if it is unlimited; the holder of that power could effectively rewrite your estate plan.

Powers of appointment come in two varieties: A *general power of appointment*, where there are no limits on the ability of the power holder to appoint the property, even if appointing the property to or for the benefit of herself or to her estate; and a *limited or special power of appointment*, where the power holder can't appoint the property to himself or to his estate, but rather to or between the persons (or charities) that you name. For example, you may leave your estate equally to your children, but you give someone a power of appointment to be able to shift property only between the children to account for post-death changes in circumstances between the children. Suppose that one of your children has a significant medical need that arises after your death and your other children don't really need the money. In that situation, your power holder could simply shift trust property between your children to increase the share of the sick child.

There is a dark side to powers of appointment. This is why powers of appointment are sometimes referred to as a "power to disappoint." This dark side can rear its ugly head, particularly in blended families. For example, there could be acrimony between your partner and your children after your death. If you leave a significant part of your estate to your children, but you give your partner a *general* power of appointment, your partner could rewrite your estate plan after your death and even shift your property to his or her own children, which is rarely what people want. For this reason, powers of appointment in blended families are almost always carefully crafted *special* or *limited* powers of appointment, particularly where the surviving partner is the one who is given the power of appointment. This is where the "power to disappoint" can "encourage" children to take care of their stepparent after you are gone.

> Before using a power of appointment, consider the potential challenges your heirs will contend with as a result.

Now that you understand what a power of appointment is, you would be wise to discuss as a couple the degree of flexibility you want your estate to have. This is an important decision, especially when you consider the ages of your children now and going forward — as their needs and capacities will shift as they grow. Think about what you want for them and what you hope your estate would provide for them if you were to pass away unexpectedly today. Would you want their access and support to shift based on benchmarks in their lives other than age (e.g., graduation, marriage, birth of first child)? Remember, you get to craft this how you want it. The more you think these things through and capture your thoughts in writing, the easier it will be to address your desires and questions when you work with your attorney to prepare the necessary documents.

Once you determine the degree of flexibility you want, you need to determine who will have that role and how much power you will give to the person. Whomever you choose, make sure you give him or her clear standards to work from, so that he or she knows what is involved in the role. This way he or she can feel guided by your wishes as he or she makes decisions on your behalf for the people you love.

5. Marital Deduction Transfers

This section only applies to married couples in blended family relationships that have to worry about the US federal estate tax. Unfortunately, given the uncertainty in the estate-tax laws that will probably persist for the immediate future, even those who have relatively modest estates may have to worry about the federal estate tax.

There are several ways that a transfer to or for the benefit of a spouse can qualify for the federal estate-tax marital deduction. In the following three scenarios, what is relatively straightforward and an obvious choice for a traditional, nuclear family becomes a bit more challenging for blended family situations. (In the three scenarios, the surviving spouse is effectively the absolute owner or controller of the property.) This is where the "yours, mine, and ours" scenario can cause a lot of concern and conflict, as each spouse tends to want to focus his or her attention and emphasis on the children that are biologically connected to him or her, and there is an underlying fear that the other spouse will likely treat differently, or exclude completely, the non-biological children. With that said, we want to make sure you're aware of the options available to you.

The first type of spousal transfer which is a direct and outright transfer qualifies for the marital deduction of property to a spouse via a will or trust. In a direct bequest, all of the property belongs to the surviving partner, who can do whatever he or she wants with it. In our experience, we don't see direct and outright transfers to a spouse very often in blended family situations because the surviving recipient spouse, especially one who has children of his or her own, will probably not transfer the property at death to the children of the predeceased spouse at his or her death.

The second type of spousal transfer that qualifies is a transfer in trust for the benefit of the surviving spouse, together with giving that spouse a general power of appointment over the property in the trust, meaning that the surviving spouse will be able to give that property to persons of his or her choosing. This doesn't often appeal to people in blended family relationships, particularly where the recipient spouse has his or her own children from prior relationships. The surviving spouse can exercise the general power of appointment to give all of the property to himself or herself, which blended families also usually don't want.

The third type of spousal transfer that qualifies for the federal estate-tax marital deduction is the estate trust, where the recipient spouse has the benefit of all of the trust property during his or her lifetime, and the property passes to persons of the recipient spouse's choosing at his or her death. Again, we don't see this one very often in blended families either because the recipient spouse has the power to direct the trust property to persons of his or her own choosing,

meaning that there is no guarantee that the predeceased transferor spouse's children will receive the amount of the trust property originally desired since the surviving spouse is free to transfer that property at whatever levels to anyone he or she wants. The will or trust can give him or her rights to some principal too though.

So, is it three strikes and you're out? Or is there a way (in the US) to get a marital deduction on a transfer for the benefit of the surviving spouse, yet dictate where the trust property goes when the surviving spouse dies? The answer is yes, and it is called a Qualified Terminable Interest Property (QTIP) trust.

5.1 Qualified Terminable Interest Property (QTIP)

The QTIP trust has several very strict requirements in order to qualify for the federal estate-tax marital deduction. First, there has to be a transfer in trust for the benefit of a spouse, which means the person to whom you are married. Second, the surviving spouse must be a US citizen (there is a way that foreign spouses can receive a marital deduction, which is called a "qualified domestic trust," but the requirements are different and beyond the scope of this book). Third, the trust must provide that during the surviving spouse's lifetime, the only person who can receive any benefits (income or principal) from the trust is the surviving spouse. Fourth, the trust must require that the surviving spouse be given all of the income from the trust at least annually. Finally, the executor of your estate (or the trustee of your living trust, if you've used a living trust instead) must make an election on your federal estate tax return. If you fail *any* of these requirements, you lose all of the marital deduction, which subjects the trust to federal estate tax in the deceased spouse's estate.

What happens when the surviving spouse dies? The cost of making a QTIP election is that the value of the property over which the QTIP election was made, valued as of the date of the surviving spouse's death, is included in the surviving spouse's estate for federal estate-tax purposes as if the surviving spouse owned the property at death. The property is taxed in the surviving spouse's estate even though the surviving spouse has no control over the property and has no say so about who gets that property at the surviving spouse's death. This can have the effect of increasing the amount of estate tax that the surviving spouse's estate will owe, which can be unfair to the recipients of the surviving spouse's estate. This is why there is a provision of the Internal Revenue Code that permits the heirs of the surviving spouse's estate to collect the extra tax from the heirs of the estate of the first spouse to die. The most important thing to know here is that the partners in blended families generally shouldn't waive the right of their estate to pursue the extra tax on their estate caused by the QTIP election in the estate of the predeceased partner from the property of the predeceased partner, since that share hasn't paid any estate tax on it.

5.1a Who should make the QTIP election?

As we discussed in section **5.1**, the QTIP election has to be made by the executor of the deceased spouse's estate or the trustee of the deceased spouse's living trust on the deceased spouse's federal estate-tax return, so the QTIP election is optional. The question becomes: Who should be the executor or trustee for the first spouse to die? Who should decide whether a QTIP election is made, understanding that the surviving spouse's estate could be adversely affected? The answer goes to the question of who should serve as executor or trustee of a partner

in a blended family relationship, since that person will make the call on a QTIP election. For many reasons, we believe it best for a disinterested third party to make the QTIP election.

A surviving spouse can be inclined to make the QTIP election because it puts off estate tax until the surviving spouse dies, thereby preserving the estate for the surviving spouse to live on since the estate tax won't be paid, even if it increases estate tax in the surviving spouse's estate, especially since the property of the first spouse to die will be charged the extra estate tax. Likewise, the children of the first spouse to die might be inclined to not make a QTIP election if it reduces the overall amount of estate tax that they'll have to pay. The problem that children have with the QTIP election is that once the election is made, they'll be liable for an estate tax on that property without any ability to reduce the estate tax through estate planning because the trustee is the owner of the subject property.

We believe that it is best for an independent third party to evaluate a situation and decide whether or not to make a QTIP election in the estate of the first spouse to die. Some of the factors as to whether or not to make a QTIP election include the projection of the size of the surviving spouse's estate, the age differences between the spouses, the health of the surviving spouse, and the expected estate-tax exemption.

5.1b Who should decide what assets fund the QTIP portion?

Again, the executor or trustee makes the decision as to the assets over which the QTIP election is made. The ultimate recipients of the estate of the first spouse to die will want those assets to be invested in high-income and low-appreciation investments (e.g., bonds) because they don't want to increase their estate-tax liability when the stepparent dies. The surviving spouse stepparent will want as much income as he or she can get, but he or she might not care whether the assets experience any growth unless he or she is young at the time of his or her spouse's death. However, his or her children will care a lot because they may have to pay estate tax on the appreciation that arises after their stepparent's death, especially since those children won't receive any of that appreciated property.

5.1c   Should you waive pursuit of estate taxes from the recipients of a QTIP portion?

In single-marriage families where the beneficiaries of the estates are the same, it is common in estate-planning documents for the surviving spouse to waive the pursuit of the estate tax attributable to the QTIP property. However, in blended families, where the ultimate recipients of the spouses' individual estates are usually different people, this type of plan usually will not comport with the desires of most blended family partners. Paul almost always recommends that blended family partners not waive pursuit of federal estate tax.

5.2   Marital deductions and QTIP options

Are there any possible snags you see that need to be considered before making a decision regarding these tax avoidance options? One thing to keep in mind is that most attorneys and accountants who do estate planning are focused on avoiding taxes and looking at "governance" issues (i.e., who will be the decision maker once you are no longer able to make decisions about your possessions and what will be done with them). They will need your guidance to consider other issues that are at stake related to your family's overall structure and differences in need.

6.   Unitrust Option

There is a way to create a win-win for both groups of competing beneficiaries. Where you have a partner as the income beneficiary (e.g., he or she has access to and benefits from the interest that is earned on the assets of the trust) and your children as principal beneficiaries (i.e., your children will receive the assets that remain in the trust at the time of the surviving spouse's death), as in a traditional trust, the age-old conflict is how the trust is to be invested. On the one hand, income beneficiaries want high income, which almost always can be achieved at the cost of growth in the value of the trust's assets. On the other hand, principal beneficiaries want growth, which can generally be achieved only at the cost of income.

In a unitrust, you can give your partner an interest equal to a percentage of the fair market value of the trust annually for life or for a shorter period, which can be payable in monthly or quarterly installments, with your children being the principal beneficiaries. Your partner will benefit from growth in the value of the trust's assets, as will your children as principal beneficiaries. Therefore, the assets can be invested for growth, and both sides will benefit from the growth, which should reduce the tension between traditional trust income and trust beneficiaries.

A client asked Paul to explain a reason why someone would choose not to go this route and use one of the other conventions mentioned. Paul's response was that if you need a QTIP marital deduction, the spousal payout would have to be the greater of the trust's income or the unitrust amount. Additionally, if the trust assets need to be valued annually, it can get expensive to appraise assets such as real estate and closely held business assets.

7. Life Estates

A life estate is a mechanism where an owner of real estate transfers title to another person but retains the sole lifetime right to use the property. On the death of the original owner, who is called a "life tenant," the recipient becomes the full owner of the property. A life estate also can be used to transfer a life estate in your home to your partner and transfer the remainder interest to your children. Life estates can be viewed as a simpler alternative to a trust.

> You can transfer ownership while still retaining use of your property during your lifetime.

For a number of reasons, we don't generally like life estates for blended family estate planning; we prefer trusts instead. For starters, your partner will be liable for real estate taxes and for home repairs, and if he or she lacks the resources to pay these expenses, he or she won't be able to borrow money secured by a mortgage on the home, without the consent of your beneficiaries. In blended families, given that there is a greater likelihood of conflict between your children and your surviving partner, life estates can create more trouble than they are worth. Even if everyone is on good terms right now, we've seen enough instances where underlying resentments and past hurts that were never addressed with the parent who passes away get played out against the surviving partner. Additionally, the property that is subject to the life estate is exposed to the creditors of the surviving partner and your children; however, a properly crafted trust can protect against that.

If you are considering a life estate as a way to have fewer initial expenses than a trust, consider the potential future cost — both emotionally and financially — should family dynamics take a shift for the worse on one of your deaths. What may seem like a money saver now may in the future produce unnecessary suffering and discord that was never intended.

8. Charitable Lead Trusts

Most charitable lead trusts are created to become effective at death. Charitable lead trusts can be set up to "zero out" federal estate tax using a formula. Because heirs won't receive any benefits from a charitable lead trust until it terminates, they should be used only by the very wealthy who have heirs who can afford to wait for their inheritance, possibly for a long time. (See Chapter 9 for more information about charitable lead trusts.)

9. Who Should Serve as Executor and Successor Trustee of a Living Trust?

Having explained what a living trust is and how it is used in Chapter 6, we now want to look at the role of trustee. In our view, a disinterested, third-party professional (which does not necessarily mean a bank or trust company) is the most strongly recommended option to serve as executor and successor trustee of a living trust in the vast majority of blended family situations, in order to reduce rancor between the heirs and to prevent possible shenanigans. We know that this advice will not be taken well either by your partner or your children, both of whom may certainly want the jobs. Unfortunately, the casebooks are littered with family upsets and litigation that wouldn't be there other than for the fact that either children from a prior union or a surviving partner served in one of these fiduciary capacities.

Some of you will wonder if it would work to have your partner serve with a child from a prior union. In our experience, this rarely is successful and often creates more animosity and resentment, translating into higher costs, with the litigation lawyers being the big winners.

Emily knows of one instance where a daughter and a stepmother were coexecutors and had to deal with numerous decisions at the sudden death of the father/husband. The daughter had an MBA, was a successful financial planner, and was well aware of what was required of her to fulfill the role. The stepmother was privy to all of her husband's wishes and had reviewed annually all the estate-planning documents with him as a matter of course. Five years after his death, these two women attended a Women and Wealth Workshop that Emily facilitated, and they discovered that the stepmother never knew that her stepdaughter had not been aware of what the estate-planning documents said prior to her father's death. The two of them were able to share openly about how hard that was for the stepdaughter and what a disadvantage that put her in as an executor. Looking back, while they saw what a remarkable job they did together, they had wished that the father had set it up differently to better prepare his daughter for what was in store.

For those of you who are still attached to having a family member, or multiple family members, fulfill the roles of executor and successor trustee, there's much you can to do prepare them adequately and to allow them to determine if they are truly equipped to meet the requirements of the role and carry out the duties. You would be wise to include communication training and educational support to make sure that they are given every chance of success possible; it's a terrible position to be put in otherwise.

You may ask about a bank or trust company serving as executor, as trustee of trusts set up in a will, or as successor trustee of a living trust. For starters, while the banks and trust companies are professionals and generally do a competent job, there are many situations where they simply will not serve. There are a variety of reasons for this. For starters, the bank or trust company may not like the rules contained in the will or trust document under which it is expected to serve, which is why it is important to have whatever bank or trust company review a draft of the document if you want a particular bank or trust company to serve. Additionally, many banks and trust companies have minimum worth requirements for their service, so the value of the property going into the trust or estate may not be high enough for them to take the job. If you want a particular bank or trust company to serve, you need to inquire as to its investment minimums.

An excellent and typically more affordable alternative to large institutions to select an attorney or a Certified Public Accountant (CPA) you trust and who does this type of work regularly. They are much more likely to have a relationship with you and your family, thereby understanding the specific needs and nuances of your particular blended family scenario, and, your family will less likely be impacted by the ongoing turnover that can often occur in larger institutions. Choosing an individual that does not have a stake or conflict of interest in terms of how the money and assets are invested is also a wise move. The downside to choosing an individual is that he or she takes on all the liability and can be challenged to follow through with the specific wishes of the trust and estate plan. It is essential that you take time to describe your desires in detail so that those in governance roles can rest assured that they are well guided towards making the best fiduciary decisions they can for you, your estate, and the various needs of your different family members, whatever their blood, legal, or love relationship to you.

Despite our strongest recommendations, most people want a family member to serve as executor or trustee. In non-blended-family situations, this can cause problems, particularly if there are hurt feelings or if the wrong family member is chosen. However, in blended families where you intend to leave your estate to both your partner and your children from a prior union, family members often have inherent conflicts of interest that make it ill-advisable for them to serve in either capacity. Sections **10.** and **11.** explain potential conflicts of interest.

10. Why the Surviving Partner May Have Conflicts of Interest

If you are dividing your estate between your partner and your children and you're thinking of naming your partner as executor; trustee of any testamentary trust for the joint benefit of your partner and your children; or as successor trustee of your living trust, you should immediately recognize that your partner, as an interested party, has a conflict of interest. It is merely human instinct to take care of yourself first. There are many judgment calls and elections that need to be made during the course of administering an estate or trust, and these matters can have the effect of favoring one group of heirs or beneficiaries over another, and vice versa. It is human nature to benefit you over the interests of others.

Your partner is probably aware you are doing estate planning, and he or she may express a

strong desire to serve. Your partner may exert pressure on you to allow him or her to serve. It is important to recognize that your partner's desire to serve often is borne out of anxiety and concern over his or her care after you are dead. Your partner is also probably fearful that you'll appoint one of your children who will use the position to disfavor the surviving partner.

There are many drivers to why a partner may express a strong desire to be executor or trustee, all of which are valid and important to figure out together. The more heated the conversation, the more likely there are fears, doubts, and anxiety that definitely need to be addressed in the drafting of your estate plan — especially if you are both clear that neither of you should be in those roles solo, or at all.

After you two have discussed your worries and fears with each other, do your best to honor and acknowledge them as valid and normal. Then, take steps to allay each other's fears by appointing third parties that each of you may not fear as much as one of your children in the role of executor or trustee. Of course, there may be no one that either of you trusts to look after your interests other than yourselves; if that is the case, review all your options and see what steps you could take to allay the fears in other ways. This may be an important juncture at which to look at who you might consult with to learn more about your options.

11. Why the Children of the Deceased Partner May Have Conflicts of Interest

If either of you want to divide your estate between your partner and your children, it is not unusual for your respective children to exert pressure on you to appoint one of them as executor of your estate, trustee of a testamentary trust established in your will, or as successor trustee of your living trust. Like the fears addressed previously of the surviving partner, this pressure could also be borne out of fear of potential differing views and mistreatment by the stepparent. There also may be fear of retaliation if the children have not been particularly kind or generous in their deeds or thoughts towards their stepparent. In some instances, their fear may be attributable to hatred and deep distrust of your partner.

It is important to give your children a chance to express their worries, fears, and distrust and have those feelings acknowledged and understood by you, so that they know you are truly taking their considerations to heart; after all, whatever decision you make will have a lasting impact on their lives and who they will be interacting with after you are no longer there looking out for them. You can then design your documents and statements of your wishes in such a way that they know that their concerns are honored, even as you choose an impartial third party. If you do decide to give a governance role to one of your children, we strongly encourage you to make sure your partner knows and agrees with your decision, and that there is excellent communication between him or her and the child in that role, preferably while you are alive.

When Paul was asked by a client about the possibility of having one of each of their children as co-executors or trustees, Paul had an important perspective to share: "I've seen that situation several times and I don't care for it. Usually the two groups don't know or trust each other, so each gets a separate lawyer, which adds to the expense. Then you've got the whole idea of creating a tiebreaker to clear up deadlocks."

Even larger than the issue of how much estate tax will be owed by the estate is the issue of whose share (i.e., estate-tax apportionment) of the estate will be charged with the estate tax. The next section discusses the unique and potentially dangerous issue of estate-tax apportionment in blended family couples.

> **Understanding both sides of the conflict of interest in blended families is essential as you design your estate plan.**

12. Estate-Tax Apportionment Issues

You can address estate-tax apportionment in your will or living trust. This is often included in the boilerplate legalese in the document, but it might be the most important provision in that document. If you don't address estate-tax apportionment in your will or trust, your jurisdiction provides default estate-tax apportionment rules, and you may or may not like those rules. This means that (in the US) you need to describe your intentions to your estate-planning attorney relative to estate-tax apportionment. You can also provide for whose share is charged with the expenses of administering the estate or trust. (In Canada, taxes on the estate must be paid before beneficiaries receive their inheritances.)

Suppose you decide to equally divide your taxable US estate between your spouse and your own children, which is not uncommon. The problem is that the bequests to your children are taxable, but the bequest to your spouse is totally deductible. This will have the effect of significantly reducing what your children receive by at least 35 percent (the current US federal estate-tax rate) if the estate tax is charged solely to your children's shares, while not affecting the amount that your spouse will receive at all, so your attempt to equalize your estate between your spouse and your children will not be fulfilled as you wanted.

One possible solution is that you could charge your spouse's share with part of the children's estate tax, but that will reduce the marital deduction, which will increase the overall amount of estate tax that your estate will owe. Suppose that a $20,000,000 estate is divided equally between the surviving spouse/stepparent and the decedent's children. The surviving spouse will receive $10,000,000 (less his or her share of the estate's administration expenses); but the children will receive only $8,250,000 because they will have the estate tax deducted from their share plus their share of administrative expenses and assuming other factors were calculated. If the estate tax was partially charged to the share of the surviving spouse, the estate tax would increase and the amount he or she would receive would be reduced, but the share to the children would increase because of being relieved of part of the estate tax.

In blended families, it is not unusual for people to choose higher estate taxes over giving the surviving spouse more and their children less. Many estate-planning attorneys will find this to be somewhat irrational and will have to be convinced that this is what you want, so you need to make sure this decision is well-thought-out and that you've explored all your options — not only will your attorney want to know your reasons, so will your family members. The estate-planning attorney will probably get you to specifically sign off on this to protect the attorney against a malpractice lawsuit by the heirs after you are gone.

If you are able to communicate effectively with your blended family members about your thoughts related to this and why this seems to be the only possible solution, there may be a possibility that you could all decide on something together. When everyone sees the potential financial cost of not getting along, they may discover other alternatives that might have them work together so that the assets can stay together and where all members of the family get to benefit in ways that each of you would ideally like to see. As you contemplate having everyone get together, you will have a sense for the likelihood and possibilities for all concerned.

13. Disclaimers

A disclaimer is a technique where a recipient of a bequest or inheritance simply and unconditionally refuses it timely and in writing, giving notice to the parties and in the way required by the law of your jurisdiction. The important thing in a valid disclaimer is that the person who is disclaiming can't direct where the disclaimed property will go, or the disclaimer will be treated as a gift by the disclaiming person. Disclaimers can be a very powerful and useful tool in estate planning, as they can be used in some circumstances to fix broken estate plans, and they can provide estate-tax benefits.

The importance of disclaimers comes from being able to write your will in a way to anticipate a disclaimer by some of your heirs. For example, suppose one of your children doesn't want his or her share of your estate and he or she would like for you to leave that share to his or her children. However, you still want to leave that share to your child, but you write your will so that if your child disclaims, his or her share goes to his or her children. In traditional, nuclear families, it is not unusual for a spouse to leave his or her entire estate to his or her spouse, with the will written to leave the estate ultimately to the children if the partner disclaims, subject to the spouse's lifetime income rights, which can be very advantageous, estate-tax wise. Talk to your estate planner about this technique.

14. Elections against a Will

You only need to worry about elections against a will if you are legally married. The *elective share* (also known as a "dower") is a share of a spouse's estate that the surviving spouse can claim if the surviving spouse doesn't receive it from his or her spouse. The amount of the elective share and what counts in the deceased spouse's estate vary depending on the jurisdiction in which you live. In most jurisdictions, spouses can waive their rights to the elective share in a marriage contract, which is why you see so many marriage contracts in subsequent marriage situations. In blended family marriages, we see many more elections against a will than in single marriages. The simple way to avoid elections against a will is to either have the spouse waive his or her elective share rights, or leave the surviving spouse enough to forestall a costly, lengthy, and often nasty court battle.

See Chapter 8, section **9.**, for more information about elections against a will.

PART 3

Observations and Suggestions

CHAPTER 11

Working with Estate Planners

This chapter concerns itself with the subject of working with estate planners. Knowing the different advisors and what their particular roles are is empowering, and allows you to be the director of your estate-planning play. Take time to get to know these different characters and roles and what their purpose is so that you know best how to move and direct each of them towards your goals.

1. Who Does Estate Planning?

At this time, many different professions provide various estate-planning and related services. Attorneys (also known as lawyers) are the only ones who can or who should prepare the legal documents that implement an estate plan; this is because if there's a dispute over the documents, the court system will likely be involved. However, here's an extensive, but not exhaustive, list of other professionals who are important to the estate-planning process:

- Accountant, Certified Public Accountant (CPA), and Chartered Accountant (CA)

- Financial planner

- Stockbroker

- Life insurance agent

- Bank trust officer

- Planned giving advisor

- Employee benefits specialist

- Asset protection specialist

- Family business consultant

- Family wealth coach

You would be wise to involve them in rendering estate-planning advice specific to your blended family situation. What you choose to follow can then be included in your estate-planning documents, and these professionals can play key roles in the creation and implementation of an estate plan.

Too often, people think that wills and trusts are the only estate-planning documents. However, this isn't true. Beneficiary designations on life insurance policies, retirement plans, and Individual Retirement Accounts (IRAs) can be much more important traditional estate-planning documents if they transfer more wealth than a will or trust, which is the case for many people.

Additionally, you have to pay attention to how property is titled, especially real estate and bank accounts. As we have discussed several times in this book, property that is titled in joint tenancy or pay-on-death passes to the survivor on the death of the first joint tenant to die irrespective of what your will says, so it really is an estate-planning document. Most people don't realize that they are essentially doing estate planning when they buy a piece of real estate, get a job, buy life insurance, or even go to the bank to open an account.

2. Where Do You Find Estate Planners?

Where to find estate planners is one of the most difficult questions to answer because there are so many different professions that give estate-planning advice. Perhaps the best way to find estate planners is word of mouth. Nothing speaks louder than a satisfied client. However, word of mouth often does not help everyone.

You clearly want estate planners who have significant experience in estate planning; this is not a task for amateurs or people who dabble in estate planning. You want an estate-planning attorney who is competent. Some jurisdictions permit specialization of lawyers in estate planning. Additionally, the American College of Trust and Estate Counsel (ACTEC), which in our opinion is the preeminent trusts and estates attorney organization, maintains a list of its fellows on the public side of its website (www.actec.org). However, there are many qualified estate-planning attorneys who are not fellows in ACTEC. Another helpful attorney organization is WealthCounsel (www.wealthcounsel.com). In Canada, the Society of Trust and Estate Practitioners (www.step.ca) can provide assistance.

In the United States, an organization that can be helpful with finding all sorts of different types of estate planners (i.e., attorneys and non-attorneys) is the National Association of Estate Planners & Councils (www.naepc.org), which has a designation that it gives to qualifying individuals called the Accredited Estate Planner®.

When sorting through all the possibilities you encounter, a good qualifying question to ask up front is whether or not the person has experience with the complexities of blended family estate planning. If the person says that he or she does, ask for specific instances and listen to how he or she goes about describing not only the makeup of a client's family, but also the sorts of ways that he or she approaches handling particular situations that a blended family needs addressed. Ask any questions you have after reading this book that you feel are relevant to your particular family's situation and see how the person responds. Is this something that the person is familiar with? Is it something he or she would recommend? You'll get good information from this initial interview, including how well the person will work with you and allow you to direct the process. You can also ask if he or she has some clients with blended families who would be willing to talk with you so that you can hear about their direct experiences.

3. Who Should Be on Your Estate-Planning Team?

Everyone's situation is different. However, there is a simple answer to this question. You need as many estate-planning team members as it takes to get the job done. Most people will only need an estate-planning attorney, although that attorney should coordinate efforts with the client's other advisors (e.g., accountant, investment advisor, life insurance agent).

Sometimes, there are other estate-planning advisors already in the picture who are working with you. Nevertheless, there will be situations where one of your advisors may recommend bringing in another advisor to assist you. Seriously consider doing that because it is important that you get your estate planning done. This is particularly important in blended families because it is our experience that clients often get stuck in the estate-planning process due to the details and complexity of their particular planning needs.

On the CD you will find the form Estate-Planning Team Contact Information. This form will help you keep track of the important contact information for the members of your estate-planning team.

4. How Do Estate Planners Charge for Their Services?

The fee estate planners charge for their services will vary depending on the type of estate-planning advisor. Most estate-planning attorneys typically charge by the hour, although there will be some attorneys who charge a flat fee for some estate-planning services. The problem with blended family estate planning is that it often depends on the particular family involved.

In our experience, estate plans for blended families often cost more than other estate plans because of the additional complexity that blended families require. Don't let this stop you because this is important to you and your family. We believe that money spent on the front end saves a lot of money in the long run as problems are addressed and minimized or eliminated. An experienced estate-planning attorney should be able to give you a range of expenses to anticipate in your estate-planning legal fees. However, you should understand that if your situation is unusually complex, that range may be wide.

Other estate-planning advisors are compensated in a variety of ways, from hourly to commission-based to a percentage of assets under management. You should always be told in the beginning how the advisor will charge and when he or she will expect payment.

> The more prework you do, the more efficient your advisors' work will be, and the more likely it will yield the results you want.

5. How Do Estate-Planning Attorneys Do Their Work?

There are two ways that an attorney may represent a couple, and this is critical, particularly to the blended family. The first way that an attorney can represent a couple is to represent them *jointly*, which means that he or she *can't* keep secrets from either partner. If one partner asks the attorney to withhold some information from the other partner (e.g., a proposed change to a document), the attorney's only option is to withdraw from representing both of you.

Secrets and differences of opinion and feelings tend to occur more often in blended family situations, so if you know in advance that you want to do something in your estate planning that your partner won't like (e.g., put his or her interests in trust with a third-party trustee or favor your own children), you may want to give serious consideration to being represented by separate estate-planning attorneys.

A note of caution from Emily: When secrets are kept and plans are made that have a direct impact on someone who has no say in the matter, research has shown that 70 percent of those estate plans fail. This is due to a lack of communication and a lack of trust in the family system. Nothing invites litigation more quickly than having something imposed on you from the grave. If you want to know more about this research, read *Preparing Heirs* by Roy Williams and Vic Preisser.

The second way that an attorney can represent a couple is to represent each *separately*. In this situation, the attorney simply treats each partner as a separate client. This may sound strange to you, especially if the two of you are seeing the attorney together. The attorney must be very careful in this situation not to favor one of you over the other. The attorney would have to withdraw from representing both of you if there is an actual conflict between you. However, this would permit the attorney to withhold information and to keep secrets from a partner. This method is not very common, and there is some controversy among attorneys as to the efficacy of this arrangement and the ethics. Nevertheless, many attorneys believe that separate representation is ethically possible (in areas where this is allowed by law).

Paul has never represented a couple separately, but it hasn't come up that often where there was a need to do so. In other words, there are either clear signs that separate representation of only one partner is the necessary route or there are signs that joint representation is possible. Paul does note, however, that he often only represented one partner in a blended family relationship because the partner who hired him wanted it to be that way.

6. The Initial Interview

The formal estate-planning process really begins with the initial client interview by the estate planner. Charts 1 and 2 were designed after having interviewed both clients and estate planners on the initial client interview. These charts contain virtually every thought we've ever heard that can run through the heads of both client and estate planner during the initial client interview. You can use these charts to tap into what resonates with you and what concerns you have. Highlight the ones that jump out at you and your partner. (You can print two copies using the files on the CD so that you can each highlight your concerns separately and go over them together afterwards.)

> **Review Charts 1 and 2 prior to meeting with potential advisors.**

This initial interview is critical. The estate-planning process can come to a screeching halt if the initial interview goes badly. There is no way to predict how an initial client interview will go because each interview is a creative act that can change in an instant and can go from great to terrible with just one comment or look. This is because estate planners are simultaneously trying to obtain the relevant facts and engender or bolster confidence in themselves, while attempting to establish rapport with you too. It's quite the dance for all involved.

It is very important that you feel that the estate planner is truly listening to your goals and concerns and not simply collecting facts in order

Chart 1
Questions a Client May Secretly Have during an Initial Interview with an Estate Planner

- Can this person help me (or us)?
- Will I be able to work with this person?
- Am I physically safe with this person?
- Does this person make me feel uncomfortable?
- Is this person going to be loyal to me?
- Will this person take the time to talk with me, not down to me?
- Can this person explain the issues and considerations to me and my family?
- Is this person going to offend any of my loved ones or hurt anyone's feelings?
- Does this person understand that for me some of these decisions are going to be very trying?
- Will this person be perceptive enough to understand what I do not or cannot express clearly or directly? Will this person even make an effort in this regard?
- Is this person going to take advantage of me either on a fee or work basis?
- What is really in it for this person?
- What is this going to cost me?
- How long will this take?
- Will this person respect my feelings and desires, and not just try to take over to save me taxes?
- Can I call this person whenever I want? If not, when may I call this person?
- May I call this person at home? On weekends? After hours?
- Will this person return my calls in a timely fashion? Are our definitions of "timely" the same?
- Will this person keep my affairs confidential?
- Will this person give me his or her undivided attention during our meetings? Will this person take phone calls or office interruptions while we are meeting?
- Where will I fall into this person's work priorities?
- Will this person meet me at my home or another location, or will he or she meet only at his or her office?
- Will this person be timely and prompt?
- If we eat a meal together, will this person charge me during the time we are eating?
- How will this person handle "soft office costs" (e.g., copies, faxes, long-distance charges)?
- Will I only talk to this person or will I have to deal with other employees in the firm? If so, who else will I have to deal with?
- Does this person have a "gatekeeper," (i.e., someone I have to go through to talk to him or her, such as a personal assistant)?

Chart 1 — Continued

For clients in blended families, the following thoughts are often foremost on their mind:

- Does this person understand the unique situation of my blended family?
- Does this person have experience with blended family scenarios like mine?
- Does this person have judgments or biases when it comes to blended family issues and choices?
- Does this person have personal experience with blended family issues, such as divorce and stepchildren, which may cause him or her to project and not remain objective?
- Can this person effectively help me sort key decisions and understand what I'm up against regarding the conflicting needs of different members of my family?

to plug you into a prefabricated estate plan. Unfortunately, this happens a lot. If you sense that the estate planner is not really listening to you, you need to hire another estate planner.

It doesn't matter how good the estate planner's reputation is. Estate planners are human too, and they have good days and bad ones. They get on well with some people but don't connect with others. A true professional will certainly understand your decision to move on so early in the process.

Note: If you go through more than one estate planner you feel is not a match for you, be careful that you aren't setting yourself up for failure by unconsciously sabotaging the relationship at the outset. Perhaps you aren't ready to delve into estate planning. If both partners in a blended family can't agree on an estate planner, give strong consideration to hiring separate estate planners.

Estate planner "shopping" should only go so far. If it goes too far, it may mean that one or the other partner is simply looking for an estate planner who will agree with him or her, which is an ulterior motive. Or one partner may have unresolved issues related to initiating the estate-planning process. Don't let these strategies keep you from your goal. The very fact that you're reading this book means that

you care about this topic and want to approach it successfully. If your partner is not on board, this is a good indication that some training related to communication strategies may be important to consider and practice, so that you can get to the heart of the matter and move forward together with ease and grace.

In our experience, we have found that estate planners who ask good questions of clients tend to have far better luck getting the necessary information than estate planners who simply ask clients to complete questionnaires or who do all of the talking to demonstrate their estate-planning knowledge and expertise.

At Paul's initial client interviews, he listens to the clients because he figures the clients are there to talk about their situation, and not to hear him pontificate on how smart he is or what, theoretically, could be done without any of their information. After the clients finish talking and providing some information about their goals and concerns, Paul asks questions. Every client is different. Some clients need more prompting than others, while others need help focusing on their pertinent estate-planning issues.

The initial interview in the blended family context presents more opportunities for problems than virtually any other initial client interview. Whether they want to openly admit

Chart 2
What the Estate Planner Is Wondering about the Client during the Initial Interview

- Am I physically safe with this client?
- Does this person make me uncomfortable?
- If meeting with more than one person, either scheduled or unscheduled, is it too many people with which to meet?
- Am I being used as part of this person's agenda other than estate planning?
- Is this client able to pay reasonable fees for me to do the estate-planning work that I feel he or she needs?
- Will this client pay reasonable fees for the work that I perform?
- How likely is it that this client or his or her family will sue me or attempt to drag me into a fight after the client's death or during a divorce on an involuntary, nonpaying basis as a witness?
- Will this client be pleased with my work or with the work of any advisor?
- Can I expand my services with this client into other needs of his or hers, including those of companies owned by the client?
- How likely is it that this client will refer me to other friends or relatives?
- Will I run into a snag or complication that will cause the final cost of my services to be significantly higher than the quoted fee (or fee range)?
- Can I rely on this client's representations of the facts and figures? How much "due diligence" will I have to do?
- Is the client mentally stable? Or at least enough to execute legally valid documents or enter into legally binding agreements?
- Can I fit this client into one of the standard forms or plans that I have developed with minimal "original thought of drafting" (translated, without additional risk-taking or cost)? Will this client understand this reality, or should I go over that now and possibly alarm the client needlessly?
- Will I enjoy working with this client?
- Will I rue the day that I ever agreed to take on this client at the quoted rates?
- What are this client's expectations regarding turnaround time and my personal availability?
- Will this client permit me to allow his or her work, or at least original drafts, to be prepared by the person in my office with the lowest pay scale who is competent to perform the work?
- With whom may I speak in the course of doing this work? With whom should I absolutely not speak?
- What confidentiality issues are present with this client? Should I send mail, faxes, or electronic correspondence to a particular place? Should I call prior to sending? May I leave voicemail messages, to say that I called?
- Will I encounter problems with the client's spouse, children, or significant others? How clear must I be that I do not represent or work for anyone but the client?
- Will this client want me to work with his or her spouse or partner as well, and is this something I will be able to do?

Chart 2 — Continued

- How much "TLC" or hand-holding will this client expect or require? Does this client understand that this can have a bearing on fees or desirability to have him or her as a client?
- Will this client ask or pressure me to do anything that would compromise my personal integrity or even my professional license or designation (e.g., backdating documents, misleading others about effect of documents, forging signatures, not following formal execution procedures, lying or omitting material health information on a life insurance application)?
- How many other advisors has the client gone through before me? Why?
- Will this client present problems that I lack the confidence or competence to handle?
- Would the client allow me to bring in help? Should I discuss this candidly up front, or will this needlessly alert the client that he or she should choose another advisor?
- Will this client work with me in conjunction with the rest of his or her estate-planning team, and give me permission to coordinate with others so that our efforts are all in alignment?

it or not, the blended family couple usually has divergent interests, particularly where at least one of them has children from a prior union. That should come out in the initial interview if people are being candid, but this does not always happen. One partner might want to make sure that his or her children don't get cut out of his or her inheritance, while the other partner may only be worried about what he or she will get from the other (i.e., security).

Paul has seen numerous initial client interviews involving couples in blended family situations end quickly after each party's true intentions were stated. When possible, a referral to someone like Emily was in order to help the couple sort their differences in the best way possible. An initial interview that goes badly can trigger a lot of hurt, misunderstandings, fears, and resentments. Having a place to bring these "emotional land mines" and working with a professional who can help the couple effectively navigate the fallout will make a huge difference in the overall estate-planning process, and more important, in the couple's relationship as a whole.

In instances where a couple is unable to sort out their differences and where their goals continue to be divergent, a valid and viable option available to both partners is to have separate estate planners representing each of their individual interests. We still maintain that having clear communication with each other throughout this process will go a long way towards keeping the family out of courtroom battles after either of your deaths.

6.1 Showing up to the initial interview prepared

During the initial interview, the estate planner will ask you for a lot of information. Checklist 2 contains a list of the things that an estate planner will probably need, although this list can vary from estate planner to estate planner. When in doubt, ask the estate planner why he or she needs particular information. We can assure you that the information listed in Checklist 2 is necessary to do a proper job. (Checklist 2 is also included on the CD.)

Checklist 2
Information the Estate Planner Will Need

The following list includes important information that your estate planner will need for proper estate planning. The list is in no particular order of importance:

- ❑ Copies of all prenuptial, postnuptial, and property agreements with your partner and former partners.
- ❑ Copies of all property settlements and all divorce decrees from former partners.
- ❑ Copies of marriage contracts with current and former spouses.
- ❑ Copies of all life insurance policies and beneficiary designations.
- ❑ Copies of the beneficiary designations for all retirement plans and accounts.
- ❑ Copies of all real estate deeds.
- ❑ Copies of all gift-tax returns filed.
- ❑ Copies of the most recent brokerage and bank statements.
- ❑ Copies of employment-related agreements (e.g., employment contracts, deferred compensation agreements, stock options).
- ❑ Copies of current estate-planning documents (e.g., wills, living trusts, powers of attorney including property and health care, and living wills).
- ❑ Copies of all trusts in which you are a beneficiary or trustee.
- ❑ Copies of all closely held entities (e.g., limited liability company, corporation, partnership), articles of incorporation, bylaws, operating agreements, shareholder agreements, and buy-sell agreements for all businesses in which you have an interest.
- ❑ Names and contact information of all of your children, stepchildren, and any other person to whom you wish to give a share of your estate.
- ❑ Copies of any other estate-planning documents that are presently in place.
- ❑ Names of primary advisors together with request for permission to talk to them.
- ❑ Copies of current financial statement of assets and liabilities.
- ❑ Copies of income tax returns for last two years.
- ❑ Copies of any charitable pledge agreements.
- ❑ Information on all bank and savings accounts (i.e., in whose name each account is titled and method of title as well as joint tenants, tenants-in-common, or pay on death).
- ❑ Information of persons (e.g., children or elderly parents) you are either obligated to support or are supporting.
- ❑ Information on your estate-planning goals.
- ❑ Anything else that is relevant to your particular blended family situation:

_____
_____
_____
_____
_____
_____

Some clients balk at providing so much personal and financial information to an estate planner who, in many cases, will be a total stranger. There are good and valid reasons why the estate planner is asking for that information; many of them should be obvious by reading this book. Your estate-planning advisors need this information in order to provide you with their best efforts and so they do not make mistakes. You should either give them everything that they ask for, or find another estate planner to whom you are willing to entrust such information. It is that vital.

A number of clients purposely exclude very important information because they feel that it is too sensitive or not relevant to estate planning. This happens a lot more when a blended family couple comes in together for estate planning. Some couples haven't developed the trust to give each other all of their information. Sure, there may have been property disclosures if the couple entered into a prenuptial agreement prior to marriage, but this often isn't the entire picture. Lots of significant personal information often gets withheld. Given that only 20 percent of couples who remarry talk about finances prior to the wedding, withholding information is more likely to be the case than not. Understandably, someone entering into a second (or third or fourth) committed relationship is likely to be more wary if his or her first trusted union ended in a contentious divorce. This speaks to the lack of trust the divorced

person may unconsciously have in himself or herself to adequately choose lifelong partnerships that are trusting and lasting.

Paul once had a client who brazenly told him that he wouldn't tell the entire picture to any of his professional advisors, only giving each person what information he felt that each needed. In this way, the client said that he felt safe and more in control of his situation — no one advisor knew everything. This strategy backfired on him when a mistake was made that Paul could have easily caught if he had known all of the facts. In our opinion, this strategy (and we're using the term loosely) is a big mistake and, in Paul's experience, it is probably the number one reason why an estate plan either fails or doesn't get implemented.

There are ways for clients to remain in charge of their estate-planning process without resorting to hiding information. One of the biggest areas of misrepresentations by clients has to do with the value of their estates. In Paul's experience, especially after a certain net worth threshold, people lowball their net worth or leave out a significant part of their property. This is ill-advised to say the very least.

Take a minute and consider the likelihood you will withhold or misrepresent information when sharing with your advisors. We know that many of you will. Paul conducted informal polls at presentations where he asked the audience if they had ever not told the entire story of their financial life to a professional advisor. Almost every time, roughly two-thirds of the audience sheepishly raised their hands.

If you withhold or misrepresent your financial position, you could receive the wrong estate-plan structure — especially if you understate it. The estate planner may have recommended a different estate-planning technique had you accurately stated your financial position. The personal side of the ledger needs to be complete as well.

In blended family initial client interviews, the personal side of the facts often gets swept under a rug of convenient but fragile peace for the sake of the union because the partners know that they won't agree on a particular point, so they simply try to avoid it. These issues often are too raw for the parties to successfully address and work out by themselves. It is not unusual for the parties to have to seek the assistance of a counselor or coach who is trained to work out communication problems in this area. Very few estate planners are trained to help in this way. We encourage you to seek the support you need to move forward openly and respectfully, where you seize this opportunity to strengthen and further deepen your relationship as a couple, and perhaps even with the children in your life (whatever their ages).

If, after attempting to use professional support, you find that you still lack the ability to openly discuss potentially contentious and contradictory concerns, we strongly recommend separate representation of partners. This is because an effective estate plan requires that you have complete candor and honesty with your advisors.

One final note: When working with estate planners, it is important to let them know of your time needs and expectations. Some estate planners are slow; others might move too quickly. You should let them know the speed at which you'd like to proceed. Be aware that they will need and expect you to show up at the pace you set. This book is designed to support you in being as prepared and ready as you can be to efficiently and expediently draft your blended family estate plan.

7. Action Steps

Print a copy of Checklist 2 from the CD. Check the boxes that are relevant so that you have an immediate visual of the task in front of you.

Get two three-ring binders and some clear plastic sleeves that you can store the documents in. You will both want your own binder so that you each have access to all the needed information, especially if you will be working with separate attorneys.

Once you're ready to begin, you'll both need three different highlighters. This is so that you can highlight each item on Checklist 2 as you get them together. One strategy that works well is to use different colors to track your progress. For example, you could highlight in yellow the first one on the list you will address so that it stands out. Starting with an easy one is a great idea, so that you get a sense of accomplishment right away! Put in your calendar when you will put that particular item in the binders. Once you take an action towards getting that documentation in your hands, you will highlight the same one, let's say in orange, so that you know it is in progress. When you have put that particular set of documents or information into the binder, highlight that same line with pink, for example, so that in an instant you can see that is was completed.

Emily recommends doing a little victory acknowledgment of some sort when you've completed one task. People come up with great ideas for this, such as a bite of a favorite chocolate or drinking a nice cup of tea. You'll be much more motivated to keep going if your little wins along the way are acknowledged, even if only by you. You could also show your partner the win, and then look at the list together and see which one you will do next.

Perhaps each of you can take on different tasks which will divvy the work and make it go that much more quickly. You'd then highlight in yellow the next one and start tracking your progress all over again.

Emily's clients often express how this makes the process easier and more enjoyable, as they see the baby steps along the way. The more pleasure you can put into the experience the better! Many clients also report enjoying seeing the checklist become more colorful as they move towards completion. Emily recommends planning to do something special as a couple after the entire checklist is completed and your notebooks are ready to go (e.g., going to dinner or to some other favorite date-night experience you used to enjoy when you first got together). This is not fun work, but it is very important, so it's great to reward yourselves all along the way!

CHAPTER 12

Putting It All Together

In our Introduction, we offered different scenarios we commonly experience in our work with blended family estate planning. What follows are detailed descriptions based on those scenarios to give you a rounded view of how to apply estate-planning strategies as they relate to your specific family's needs. If you find that your family's particular makeup and challenges are not sufficiently addressed in this chapter, contact us at estateplanning@blended-families.com and we will be happy to consult with you about your specific questions.

1. Yours, Mine, and Ours

Harry, age 62, and Marge, age 48, residents of Boston, are looking at updating their estate plan. Harry and Marge have one son together, Tom, age 13, but each has children of prior unions. Harry has two sons, Harry, Jr. age 37, and Steve, age 35, and Marge has a daughter, Anna, age 19, who has a 4.0 in pre-med studies at Stanford University. Harry has been in Anna's life since she was three years old. Harry has two minor grandsons by Harry, Jr., who are the "apples of Harry's eye."

Harry and Marge have been married for 15 years. They have a prenuptial agreement providing for separate property, which they have religiously maintained and kept separate property as separate. In the prenuptial agreement, Marge waived her right to an elective share.

They describe their marriage as stable, but they often disagree on key issues. Other than being a little overweight, Harry is in good health and exercises regularly. Marge has survived both breast cancer and melanoma, and has been cancer free for more than five years. They bring a financial statement, which reflects the following assets:

- Home (held in joint tenancy): $2,000,000 (owned free and clear)

- Vacation condos in Lake Tahoe and in Florida (owned as joint tenants): $1,000,000

- 90 percent interest in Harry's Inc. (Harry's separate property, a C corporation): $15,000,000

- Stock account (Marge's separate property): $1,000,000

- Stocks and bonds (Harry's separate property): $3,000,000

- Stocks and bonds (held as tenants in common): $2,000,000

- 401(k) (Harry's account through Harry's Inc. and Marge is the beneficiary): $1,800,000

- IRA (Marge's daughter, Anna, is the beneficiary): $150,000

- Bank account (held as tenants in common): $1,000,000

- Bank account (Harry's separate property): $1,500,000

- Bank account (Marge's separate property): $500,000

- Miscellaneous personal property (jointly owned): $250,000

- Life insurance: Harry $0; Marge $100,000, which is payable to Anna

- Debts: $0

Harry, Jr. works at Harry's Inc. and is being groomed to be the next CEO. Harry, Jr. is a 10 percent shareholder, and he received that stock as a gift from Harry, which exhausted Harry's $1,000,000 (then) US federal applicable exclusion amount. Harry wants Harry, Jr. to own all of the stock, unless Tom wants to get into the business. Harry's middle son, Steve, is a freelance writer and frustrated actor who earns very little if any money. Marge and Harry support Steve, who also lives with them (which Marge says she really doesn't like supporting or allowing Steve to live with them). However, Anna also lives with them when she's not at school (which Harry likes because he gets along well with Anna, so he gladly pays her tuition and other school expenses, and actually considered adopting her). The income of Harry and Marge consists of the following:

- Harry's salary at Harry's Inc.: $1,200,000

- Harry's interest and dividends: $225,000

- Marge's interest and dividends: $75,000

- Joint interest and dividends: $100,000

Harry prefers to live frugally, but Marge, a former interior designer, does not. Consequently, they require approximately $40,000 per month to live on. Marge has not used any of her US lifetime applicable exclusion amount. The couple says that they're not particularly charitably inclined, although Marge volunteers for the American Cancer Society. However, Harry expressed an interest in giving money to charity instead of to the federal and state governments at death. Harry expresses an interest in "doing something" for his beloved grandchildren and in treating all of his children equally, subject to taking care of Marge for her lifetime, although his sons don't trust Marge and want their shares free of any interest in favor of Marge.

Meanwhile, Marge is steadfast in her belief that the estate plan should favor Tom since he is young and has not yet completed his education, even if it means that Harry's boys get less.

Marge also expresses significant discomfort when Harry exposes his sons' desire to receive their shares at his death, and Marge even said that would hurt her financially, which would be very unfair to her. Marge said that she is giving her entire estate to Anna and Tom, equally, in trust, since Harry has, in her words, "plenty." Harry's Inc. is in a significant growth spurt at present, due in large part to the new ideas of Harry, Jr., in whom Harry has great faith.

Should Harry and Marge be represented by the same estate planners? Given the disparity in both age and wealth levels, Harry and Marge should probably be represented by separate estate planners, even though they have a child together.

Will either Marge or Harry have to worry about a federal estate tax? Under the law as it exists today, if Harry dies first, absent a marital deduction election made in his estate, Harry's estate will owe substantial federal estate tax. At present, Marge's estate is on the cusp of having to worry about the federal estate tax, although if Harry dies first and his executor elects to take a QTIP marital deduction in Harry's estate, then Marge's estate will probably have to worry about significant federal estate tax. Should Harry's executor automatically make a QTIP election if Harry dies first in order to defer the federal estate tax? While it depends on what Harry's will says, Harry's executor should analyze the situation to see if the combined federal estate tax will be higher if the election is made and not simply make a knee-jerk QTIP election.

How should Harry take care of Marge? Harry's biggest concern about taking care of Marge is the disparity between her current opulent lifestyle and the small amount of income that she presently earns on her investments. Harry's problem is that the bulk of his income, his salary from Harry's, Inc., goes away at his death. One thing Harry could do is enter into a salary continuation agreement with Harry's, Inc., which could pay a percentage of his salary to the person of his choosing, presumably Marge if they are still married at his death, for a certain number of years (e.g., ten). Harry's estate also receives installment payments from Harry, Jr. relating to the sale of the stock in Harry's Inc. or even life insurance if Harry buys some life insurance, either owned by him personally or held in a life insurance trust with Marge as an income beneficiary if married to Harry at his death. Harry could give his interests in the real estate (i.e., homes) to Marge if they are married when he dies so she wouldn't have to pay for housing. He could give Marge a lifetime trust income interest in the remainder of his estate in a QTIP trust, with his three sons as principal beneficiaries and successor income beneficiaries. However, Marge may still have to downscale her manner of lifestyle.

If Harry's executor makes a QTIP election, should Marge waive her estate's right of reimbursement of the additional estate tax on her estate that is attributable to the QTIP election made in Harry's estate? While such a waiver is commonplace in single-marriage situations where the heirs of each estate are the same, Marge should definitely not waive her estate's right to reimbursement, although she may carve out from that Tom's share, since both Harry and Marge are Tom's parents.

Should Marge be Harry's executor or trustee? Given the relationship between Harry's older children and Marge, Marge should definitely not be named as Harry's executor or successor trustee if he used a living trust instead. Harry should name an independent third party as executor or as trustee of any trusts that he establishes, save perhaps a separate trust for the benefit of Tom and Marge. If

Marge is named as executor of Harry's estate or of any trust that holds Harry's stock in Harry's, Inc., she could fire Harry, Jr. since the estate is a 90 percent shareholder, which Harry would not want and that would probably not be in the best interests of either Marge or Harry, Jr.

What should they do immediately with their real estate? Given that the marriage might not be as stable as they claim, they should consider severance of the joint tenancies, which would give Marge more net worth if she died before Harry. There is a possible ethical problem for the attorney though; it is that Marge is much more likely to survive Harry given that she is 14 years younger. In fact, given their differences, it may be best for them to be represented by separate counsel. However, given that Marge has survived cancer twice, this might indicate that they are on fairly even footing, since they really don't know who will survive.

It is important to note that in the US, by severing joint tenancies of out-of-state property, you are subjecting those properties to ancillary probate in those states. However, this can be overcome by putting the properties into an LLC. In any event, the ancillary probates might be relatively simple because that tends to be the case in most states.

There is quite a disparity between the net worths of Harry and Marge, so should this be addressed? There is a real issue as to whether the disparity should be addressed at all, given the potential instability of the marriage. However, assuming that they decide to consider techniques, the first possible technique is estate equalization, but this is not a good idea for several reasons. First, the marriage might not be that stable. Second, given that the estate tax is a flat tax now, and probably will remain so in the future, at most, Harry should give Marge enough property to fully exhaust her federal estate tax applicable exclusion amount so it will pass estate-tax free if she dies first. There really is no reason to equalize the estates for estate-tax purposes, especially since Marge would give her share to her children only, to the exclusion of Harry's sons. The problem with that is that we really don't know with any level of certainty what the US estate tax applicable exclusion amount will be when Marge dies, assuming that she predeceases Harry.

If the marriage ends in divorce, Harry will have given Marge property with no recourse to get it back. The second possible technique is the lifetime QTIP, which could put enough property into a trust to exhaust Marge's applicable exclusion amount were she to die first. This is far preferable to estate equalization. For starters, Harry could retain a contingent interest if Marge predeceased him. However, the lifetime QTIP is not without its problems. First, if the marriage fails, Harry cannot divest Marge of her interest, which must be for her lifetime. Second, there is no guarantee that the applicable exclusion amount in effect today will be in effect after 2012.

How can Harry accomplish all of his goals? Harry wants to treat all three of his children equally but he wants Harry, Jr. to get the whole business unless Tom gets involved in the company, in which case he wants the business to be divided between the two boys. At the outset, Harry could consider selling the company during his lifetime, which would probably maximize the value of the company, diversify the "elephant" asset in his estate, facilitate equalization of his estate between the three sons, and create significant liquidity, which would assist in the payment of estate tax. However, this would not meet Harry's expressed goal of passing the family company on to his sons who are involved in the business. In effect, a sale would pull the rug out from under his oldest son, although the son would walk away with considerable wealth.

In order to treat his sons equally, Harry needs to make a catch-up bequest to his two presently uninvolved sons in order to make up for the lifetime gift of stock that he gave to Harry, Jr. Given Steve's lack of ability to handle his economic affairs and Tom's age, these legacies should be held in trust. Harry could accomplish his goals by having Harry, Jr. buy his shares from his estate at death pursuant to a buy-sell agreement. Such a plan could be financed, at least in part, by life insurance on Harry's life since the facts indicate that Harry seems to be reasonably insurable. Of course, life insurance could also be used to "equalize" the shares of each of the other two sons, while passing the company to Harry, Jr. However, the problem with this plan is that it will be several years before Harry knows whether Tom will want to work in the company. Moreover, Harry may not be able to purchase enough insurance to fully equalize the legacies and give the entire company to Harry, Jr. The life insurance could be held in a life insurance trust, which would keep the policy proceeds out of Harry's estate.

How might a charitable lead trust assist in their estate plan? Given the present configuration of their assets, a charitable lead trust will probably not be a useful tool for Marge, whose estate is too small to warrant its use if she dies first and probably not a good fit for Harry's estate plan either. While Harry's estate is certainly large enough to warrant consideration of a charitable lead trust, there are several potential obstacles with the assets in their current configuration. The first such obstacle is that Harry hasn't indicated significant charitable intent, although he would prefer to give money to charity over paying the estate tax. The second obstacle is the excess business holdings rule,

which is a complicated US tax law that makes it hard for a charity to own a large interest in a business for an extended period of time. The third obstacle is that if the charitable lead trust is intended to be a "zero-out estate tax" formula legacy, where is the necessary cash flow going to come from? Under the facts, 75 percent of the couple's income, represented by Harry's salary, goes away when Harry dies. Harry's Inc. is a C corporation that pays little if any dividends at present. This would have to change radically in order for a charitable lead trust to work because it has to make the annual payments to the charity. Would converting Harry's, Inc. to an S corporation help at all? No, because a non-grantor charitable lead trust cannot hold S corporation stock. Therefore, in order for this to work, Harry would have to swap the stock during his lifetime for another asset such as cash or a note, which he could do in an installment sale to Harry, Jr. or to an intentionally defective grantor trust for the benefit of Harry, Jr. and even Tom.

Harry wants to do something for his grandchildren, so what could he do for them? For starters, Harry could pay for their health insurance, health-care expenses, and tuition without triggering a gift tax, so he should do that, which will help Harry, Jr. Secondly, he could make gifts in trust of annual exclusion amounts ($13,000 in 2012) also without triggering the gift tax, although the trust must have a Crummey clause in it. The trust must be drafted to comply with the generation-skipping transfer tax rules, which are narrower than for regular gifts in trust, or Harry would have to file a gift-tax return and allocate some of his $5,120,000 (in 2012) generation-skipping transfer-tax exemption to each such transfer.

If Harry would like to further leverage that gift, the trust could purchase life insurance on his life for the benefit of the grandchildren. In generation-skipping transfer trusts, we usually advise that an independent third party be the trustee instead of the parent because we find a vastly increased incidence of the parent of the grandchildren acting as if the grandchildren's money was really their own. Keeping them out of the role of trustee eliminates this temptation. Sometimes, children actually harbor resentment toward both their parents and their own children for being skipped.

Harry indicated he wants to provide for Anna in his will for her education and to give her money for a wedding and a down payment on a home should he die before then. What could he do? Harry could establish a separate trust in his will for the benefit of Anna for at least $500,000 to cover those expenses. The trust could either terminate when Anna is 35, at which point she'll receive the balance of the trust, or the trust could continue for her benefit with Anna as a co-trustee.

2. Empty Nesters

Bill, age 72, and Marlene, age 72 have been married for five years, each having buried their prior spouses. They do not have a prenuptial agreement and they live in a common-law jurisdiction, (i.e., not a community property jurisdiction). Each has grown children from their prior marriages who don't know each other very well. They live in Marlene's home, which she owns outright as an inheritance from her late husband. They survive on Social Security, rental income from Bill's condo, and Bill's IRA. They have the following assets:

- Home (Marlene): $200,000

- Condo (Bill): $100,000

- IRA (Bill): $750,000

- Personal property (Marlene): $10,000

- Personal property (Bill): $5,000

Bill and Marlene both want to take care of each other for life and to leave what's left to their respective children. Bill started to receive the required minimum distributions from his IRA at age 71.

How should Bill and Marlene deal with their personal property? Bill and Marlene could each leave their respective personal property to their children, to take effect at their respective deaths so that their children receive the family heirlooms and mementoes.

How can Bill provide for both Marlene and his children? Bill's IRA is already being paid out pursuant to his remaining life expectancy. Bill could leave his IRA to a trust for the benefit of Marlene as lifetime income beneficiary and his children as principal beneficiaries.

What should Bill do with the remainder of his estate? Because he is receiving payouts from his IRA, his probate estate is growing by the amount of unspent payout from his IRA, and the IRA is shrinking. Bill should leave the balance of his property to the trust that is receiving the IRA payout.

What can Marlene do with her home? Marlene could leave her home to her children, or subject to Bill's life estate, Marlene could leave her home in trust for the benefit of Bill as income beneficiary and her children as principal beneficiaries, or Marlene could simply give her home to her children if she dies first and Bill could move into his condo.

3. Eat, Drink, and Remarry

John, age 63, marries his fourth wife, Judith, age 35. They've been married for less than three years. John has a son, age 37, and some expensive alimony obligations to his first wife, including a requirement that he maintain life insurance for her.

Judith, who has been divorced twice, has two sons, ages 11 and 8, each with a different father, with whom she splits custody. Judith has substantially more wealth than John, but John has far greater income earning potential as a professional. John and Judith have a separate property prenuptial agreement. They are living in Judith's home and they have the following assets:

- Stocks and bonds (Judith): $5,000,000

- Home (Judith): $500,000

- Personal property and vehicle (Judith): $50,000

- Bank account (Judith): $1,500,000

- Bank account (John): $50,000

- Life insurance (John and Judith is the beneficiary): $250,000 (cash value $0)

- Life insurance (John maintained for ex-wife): $1,000,000 (cash value $0)

- Stocks and bonds (John): $500,000

- Personal property and vehicles (John): $100,000

- Annual income (Judith): $150,000

- Annual income (John): $350,000

Should Judith or John engage in any significant lifetime estate planning in favor of each other? Given that both of them have had multiple partners, we wouldn't recommend any significant lifetime planning in favor of each other. As far as other lifetime planning goes, we wouldn't recommend any lifetime estate planning for John since he doesn't have a taxable estate. Judith has a taxable estate, but her children are still very young, so whatever estate planning for their benefit would have to be in trust. Depending on her individual relationships with her ex-husbands, one or both of

them might make a good trustee for their child, but a non-parent ex-spouse should not be the trustee absent some compelling reasons. Judith could make annual exclusion gifts to the trust for the benefit of her children. Given her age and the current size of her estate, we wouldn't recommend too much significant lifetime estate planning for Judith.

Should John and Judith be represented by the same estate planners? The answer to this question is probably not because of the shortness of the relationship, the number of relationships that each has had, the disparity of wealth between the two, and the fact that they don't share the same circumstances relative to the children (i.e., Judith's children are minors and John's son is older than Judith).

If John survives Judith, what should Judith do for John in her estate plan? Nothing should be done for him unless Judith dies while married to John. She could leave him a lifetime QTIP trust interest in her will or living trust. In that QTIP trust, she could include some of her stocks and bonds as well as her home, although a guardian for her minor children may need the home to raise the children. Given John's ability to earn a living (even though he is 63, which is a factor to consider), Judith may well leave John nothing, although John may be able to make a spousal election, which would entitle John to a significant share of Judith's estate unless he waived his right in the prenuptial agreement.

Who should be the agents under their powers of attorney and/or successor trustees for John and Judith? Given the relatively short history of their relationship, perhaps John and Judith should have different people as their respective agents under their property and health-care powers of attorney. Judith also has the issues of her minor children to deal with. We could see Judith being John's agent under the property power of attorney more than John being Judith's agent under his property power of attorney. Nevertheless, both should at least be included in the consent documents that we discussed in Chapter 6 so that the health-care providers can talk to them about the other's health care even if they aren't each other's agents under the health-care power of attorney.

4. Brady Bunch

Mike, age 40, a widower who has three sons, marries Carol, age 38, a widow who has three daughters. They have no joint children and don't plan to have any children together. The children are all minors who live together. Mike owns his own business, and Carol has a substantial separate estate that she inherited from her late first husband. They have a community property regime, no prenuptial agreement, and they bought their home together, which Mike is paying for with his salary while Carol stays home with the children.

- Business (Mike): $500,000

- Bank account (Mike): $50,000

- Stocks and bonds (Carol): $3,000,000

- Home (Community): $250,000 (subject to $150,000 mortgage)

- Bank account (Community): $100,000

- Life insurance (Mike): $2,000,000 (0 cash value — his late wife is still the beneficiary, with the contingent beneficiary being his estate)

- Life insurance (Carol): $1,000,000 ($50,000 cash value — her children are the named beneficiaries but not in trust)

Should Carol and Mike be represented by the same estate planner? Even though there is a disparity in the relative wealth between the two, it is probably okay for them to be represented by the same estate planners.

Will either Mike's or Carol's estate have a federal estate tax problem? Using the current $5,120,000 federal estate-tax exemption as a barometer, the estates of neither Mike nor Carol will have any federal estate-tax concerns.

Given the young ages of the children and that in both cases the other parent is deceased, shouldn't Carol and Mike consider adopting each other's children? This is an interesting question. Given the disparity in wealth between the two, the answer is probably no, although their relative wealth positions will no doubt change over time, particularly since Mike is young and working while Carol is staying home with the children. Therefore, we see no significant harm in each other adopting the other's children, although the survivor between them could still favor their own blood children in the estate plan.

What should Mike do about his life insurance? Given that Mike's deceased wife is still named as the beneficiary of the policy, Mike should change that immediately. Given the young ages of the children and that Carol will be raising his children, Mike should make Carol a beneficiary of a substantial part, if not all, of the life insurance, although he could leave the insurance in a trust with Carol as the income beneficiary and his children as the principal beneficiaries (which would cover Carol's children too if Mike adopts them).

What should Carol do with her life insurance? Given that her children are minors, Carol definitely should leave the policy proceeds to a trust for their benefit instead of simply letting each child have a substantial amount of money when they turn 18, which would be ill-advised.

What should Mike and Carol do with their respective shares of the family home? Given that they purchased the home together and that the home is community property, each should leave his or her interests in the family home to each other.

What should Carol do with the significant inheritance (which was life insurance proceeds) that she received from her late husband? Given that Mike and Carol have essentially agreed to raise each other's children, who are living together, if one predeceases the other, Carol should probably make Mike the income beneficiary of her estate, with her blood-related children being named the principal beneficiaries. Given that the source of the wealth came from their father, it would not be unreasonable for her blood children to receive more of this property even if she adopts Mike's children, although this could, if not handled with good communication, cause a problem between the blood children and the adopted children. Absent a very compelling reason, we always recommend that blood children and adopted children be treated the same.

5. May-December Relationship

Franklin, age 80, a wealthy widower with three grown children in their 50s, marries Bambi, age 26, an impecunious dance instructor who has a daughter, Dawn, age 7, who she is raising alone. They have a prenuptial agreement, and Bambi waived her right to the spousal election. However, Franklin agreed to leave her, at a minimum, $100,000 for each year of their marriage and a minimum of $3,000,000 if they have a child together. They would like to have a child of their own. Franklin has done a substantial amount of lifetime estate planning and has passed significant wealth on to his children and grandchildren, and he has exhausted his lifetime $5,120,000 gift-tax exemption.

- Stocks and bonds (Franklin): $10,000,000

- Home (Franklin): $1,000,000

- Bank account (Franklin): $4,000,000

- IRA (Franklin): $500,000 (his children are the named beneficiaries)

- Income (Franklin): $750,000

- Debt (Franklin): 0

- Debt (Bambi): $25,000 (credit cards and student loans)

- Income (Bambi): $15,000

- Life insurance (Bambi): $50,000 (Dawn is the beneficiary)

Should Franklin and Bambi be represented by the same estate planners? Would this change if they have a child together? Given the recent marriage, the age disparity, and the wealth disparity between the two, they probably should be represented by separate estate planners, just as they (hopefully) were represented by separate counsel in their prenuptial agreement. If the couple has a child together, caution would still dictate that they be represented by separate estate planners. It may well be, given that Bambi doesn't make much money, Franklin will have to consent to pay for her estate planners, which, if he does that, he should do it without any control or say so over who she hires or how much it costs because if he does, he's opening himself up to a challenge.

How would Franklin go about implementing the prenuptial obligation to Bambi in his will or living trust? Given that the length of the marriage is unknown at present, the only way to do this is to use a formula bequest.

What sort of disability planning should Franklin do? Clearly, Franklin should have a solid property power of attorney and possibly even a living trust in addition to the property power of attorney. His disability planning should limit the agent's ability to rewrite his estate plan or change his IRA beneficiaries to protect both Franklin's children and Bambi. Bambi lacks the financial skills to serve as executor, trustee, or as agent under a property power of attorney. Franklin should name an independent third party as trustee and as agent under his property power of attorney. As far as whether Franklin's children would make a good trustee, it really depends on their relationship with Bambi. We would suggest erring on the side of caution and naming an independent third party as fiduciary.

Who should be Franklin's agent under his health-care power of attorney? We see nothing wrong with naming Bambi as Franklin's agent under his health-care power of attorney. However, there should be coordination between the agents who hold the separate powers of attorney. In any event, Franklin should give his grown children access to his health-care providers through his consent form as discussed in Chapter 6.

6. Nontraditional Blended Family

Marie, age 46, and Angela, age 37, became a couple recently, although they don't yet have a property agreement. As a single parent, Marie adopted a child, who is now 18. Angela, who has been divorced once, has a child, age 10, whom she is raising alone. Marie stands to inherit a lot of money from her parents, but that could be in doubt due to her recent lifestyle choices.

Angela has the greater income between the two, and she owns the home in which they live, although both are contributing to payment of the mortgage. Angela also has a potentially valuable piece of real estate that is situated on an exit corner of a proposed thoroughfare.

- Home (Angela): $250,000 (subject to $200,000 mortgage)
- Potential inheritance (Marie): $5,000,000
- Parcel of real estate (Angela): $50,000 (potentially worth about $1,000,000)
- 401(k) (Marie): $150,000
- 401(k) (Angela): $50,000
- Income (Angela): $100,000
- Income (Marie): $70,000
- Stocks and bonds (Marie): $100,000
- Stocks and bonds (Angela): $25,000
- Life insurance (Angela): $100,000 (her child is the beneficiary)
- Life insurance (Marie): $50,000 (her child is the beneficiary)

Should Marie and Angela be represented by the same estate planners? Even though there are some differences between the two women's situations, we don't see any major impediment to using the same estate planners. However, if they enter into a property agreement, they should be represented separately for that.

Should Angela and Marie have a property agreement? Given the separate nature of their respective estates and separate heirs, even though Marie is helping Angela with the mortgage on her home, the two probably should have a property agreement that could, among other things, describe the reimbursement method for the mortgage payments that Angela will owe Marie if they separate.

What should Marie do about her potential inheritance? Even though Marie may not ever see any inheritance from her parents, she should have a talk with them about what they may have planned because it could impact what she does in her estate plan and how she does it. She doesn't have to (or get to) tell them what to do for her. However, she could give them valuable input on what she has planned for her child and how they might structure an inheritance for her child if she was to either predecease her parents or disclaim some or all of her share of the inheritance.

What should Angela do about that potentially valuable piece of real estate? Given that Angela's estate will likely not be subject to the federal estate tax, she should definitely hold on to it unless someone is willing to pay close to what it might be worth one day if the thoroughfare comes into fruition. If her estate is taxable in the future, and if the real estate's value hasn't increased much, she could transfer the opportunity to a trust for the benefit of her child.

CHAPTER 13

Last Words of Advice

A long time ago, a client of Paul's had an unusual and refreshing spin on this inquiry, and she really caused him to think and feel. That client asked for the last advice Paul would impart to her, meaning if *he* were on *his* deathbed. She said that in constructing her estate plan, they would start with that most important advice, and then work from there. In other words, she was asking Paul for the nuggets of advice that he would consider so important that he would expend his final breaths on that advice — his "last, best" advice. He had to think about that carefully.

He wouldn't really have the luxury of time in which to give final advice (he'd be dying after all). He'd only have about 2,000 or so words to spare here.

1. First, Involve Your Family

Involve your family directly in your estate-planning decisions. Your estate- and financial-planning decisions have ramifications and impacts on your family and loved ones (including key employees in your company). These impacts can be financial and personal, and your decisions can and will affect their social relationships, jobs, and even health.

Consider the words of Seneca (a first century CE Roman philosopher), who said: "What madness is it for a man to starve himself to enrich his heir, and so turn a friend into an enemy! For his joy at your death will be proportioned to what you leave him."

Marcus Aurelius (Emperor of the Roman Empire in the second century CE) said: "A great estate is a great disadvantage to those who do not know how to use it, for nothing is more common than to see wealthy persons living scandalously and miserably; riches do them no service in order to virtue and happiness; it is precept and principle, not an estate, that makes a man good for something."

Niccolò Machiavelli (a 15th and 16th century Italian politician and author), in the famous work, *The Prince*: "A son can bear with equanimity the death of his father, but the loss of his inheritance will drive him to despair."

I could go on with quotes from others at all times of history and in different cultures. The message remains the same: People will be impacted by their ancestors' estate planning in ways other than just financially.

Since your family and loved ones are going to be changed by the results of your estate plan, why not involve them in its formulation? Even if someone is not going to get what he or she wants (or feels that he or she deserves), it is usually better for the other survivors to have everyone know your plans while you are still alive. Otherwise, a complainer might deny that this was your real intention. Or the person might accuse the survivors who fared better of plotting against him or her. The prospects for challenge or acrimony increase dramatically when bad news is sprung on people who then feel trapped and without options other than to attack.

One of the biggest problems in estate fights is that the star of the show has already departed the great world's stage. The job of the litigants and the court is to ferret out, often with only indirect evidence, which is usually colored by the position or feelings of the giver of that evidence, what you really intended and whether you were of sound mind and free from undue influence when you did it.

2. Shouldn't Privacy Take Precedence?

Some clients are taken aback by my suggestion that they discuss their estate planning with their family and loved ones, believing that their privacy was supposed to be the most important aspects of their estate planning. Quite often, the clients' parents didn't involve them in their own estate-planning process.

This oversight on their parents' part is not justification for the client to repeat the mistake. I'm not suggesting that you give your loved ones a vote in your estate-planning decisions. Estate planning doesn't have to be a democracy. However, their input and understanding of your intent could be vital to the success or effectiveness of your estate plan as well as in the relationships of your surviving loved ones. This is especially true in family businesses.

3. Different Tools and Techniques Have Different Effects

Estate-planning techniques have differing impacts on your loved ones. There are many different types of estate-planning techniques, and there are many variations and options within each technique. Each technique (and variation thereon) has differing potential results on relationships and finances of your loved ones. Be cognizant of the differences when you are evaluating these for your family.

4. Understanding Taxes

Be wary of some types of techniques that some estate planners want you to implement just because they save taxes. In my opinion, too many estate planners pass up the opportunity to facilitate a family's healing or staying together by simply uniting them against a straw man enemy (in the US known as the IRS).

Now here's a real secret: It's much harder (and more important) to create an estate plan that focuses on not negatively altering relationships than it is to, say, beat Uncle Sam out of estate taxes!

5. Be Careful about Buying into Panaceas

We have seen popularity waves of various estate-planning techniques. Currently in vogue is the family partnership or LLC, which has always been — and continues to be — a fine estate-planning technique. The family partnership/LLC has taken on increased usage and popularity, particularly in the last five to ten years, often because of its attractiveness as an estate tax-planning technique.

However, family partnerships/LLCs are not for every family, even if they save estate taxes. Many spouses make fine business partners, but not all. Silent, dutiful, or cooperative children usually make fine partners, typically while at least one parent is alive. However, some children are not as silent, dutiful, and cooperative. This can be especially problematic when the parents ignore the partnership/LLC once established, which has tax and nontax risks. Some children aren't suited to be, or don't know how to be, partners with parents or siblings. Some aren't suitable partners, period! The worst case here is a free-for-all by people who have been consigned together. The costs of untangling the financial and relationship matters (if it can be done) often are close to any tax savings achieved. Additionally, the IRS is more aggressively going after family entities, particularly those formed close

to the time of death and funded with almost all of the decedent's property.

I am not intending to be critical of the family partnership/LLC as an estate-planning technique. I have assisted many in the formation of family partnerships/LLCs. However, it may well be that some estate planners have been heavy-handed in their "prescriptions" of family partnerships/LLCs without discussing the side effects or doing any real analysis of the profile of the persons likely to be involved.

Maslow's admonition applies here: "He who is good with a hammer begins to believe that everything is a nail."

6. Take Control, Get Involved, and Stay in Control

You must be in control of your estate-planning process. Even though most estate plans are built to ensure control by a client, the sad fact is that most clients were not, will not be, or are not in control of the estate-planning process. You may not have been in real control of selecting your estate-planning advisors. Even if you were, you probably have had little say so about the makeup of the aspects of your estate plan.

Given all of the complexities involved in the techniques of estate planning, you cannot be expected to know as much about the technical ins and outs of estate planning as your estate-planning advisors. That is why you hired them. However, don't you know more about yourself, your family, and your property than that advisor does? Of course you do. Your knowledge and input are key ingredients in your estate plan. I firmly believe that if people felt like they could be in control of their estate planning, more people would do the estate planning that they know they should do.

My experience has been that the quality and strength of a client's estate plan is directly proportional to the client's control of and true involvement in the estate-planning process. Yet this seems to happen too seldom. Why? For starters if you are like most people, you don't have a real idea of what you can truly accomplish, or indeed what you want to accomplish, in your estate planning. Your notion of your estate planning may vary significantly from what it could be. There may be psychological reasons you will not tend to your estate planning. Maybe you feel that the grim reaper will not come for you for a long time. Or perhaps you are superstitious and believe that once your plan is done that you will die.

7. Avoid Planning Paralysis

I offer the following as another possible explanation for the avoidance of doing estate planning — *planning paralysis*. Planning paralysis is a feeling of helplessness or a fear of feeling helpless about the estate-planning process. It is also a feeling which arises when people are dazed by the staggering number of estate-planning options and decisions. We all like to be our own persons. We each want to control our own destiny.

Maybe you had (or heard about) a bad experience with an estate-planning advisor. Maybe you are uncomfortable revealing personal or financial information to an estate-planning advisor or to anyone else. Maybe you just do not trust advisors, or you feel intimidated by them. You might be concerned about cost or about not hurting someone's feelings. Or perhaps you just don't want to deal with uncomfortable thoughts.

I suspect the real reason that most people are slow to begin or follow through on estate planning is a fear of loss of control. Individuals fear the unknown, the "ride" the advisor will put you on once you get started with estate planning. I believe that people's fear of loss of control manifests itself in procrastination. Some may feel that they lack the requisite knowledge of the "bricks" of estate planning to intelligently debate, discern, and decide.

There is no question that your estate plan should be much more important to you than to your estate-planning advisors. Advisors can and should only push a client so far. However, an advisor should at least assist a client with drawing a clear picture as to why the client has not made progress with an estate plan. Once a client understands the real reason he or she has not progressed, the client should be able to begin the process of dealing with his or her obstacles.

This is where the Money Types that Emily describes in Chapter 2 on communication come in. Once you understand your key Money Types, you can work closely with your advisor and your partner to shift those patterns and get moving towards successful completion. You will be more empowered with your advisors as you understand how to best work when, say, your *Innocent* is caught in planning paralysis, or when your *Tyrant* is afraid of losing control, or when your *Fool* is ready to make a decision before having all the data.

Most of all, don't delay, because time *is* of the essence — and no one knows if their time may be up soon.